THE DIARIES OF FRANZ KAFKA
1910–1913

THE DIARIES OF
FRANZ KAFKA

1910-1913

EDITED BY Max Brod

SCHOCKEN BOOKS · NEW YORK

TRANSLATED BY JOSEPH KRESH

First SCHOCKEN PAPERBACK edition 1965

FOURTH PRINTING, 1974

CONTENTS *

* Only longer compositions, or those of a finished nature, are listed here.

THE DIARIES OF FRANZ KAFKA
1910–1913

Die Zuschauer erstarren, wenn der Zug vorbeifährt.

Wenn er mich immer fragt" das ä losgelöst vom Satz flog dahin wie ein Ball auf der Wiese.

Sein Ernst bringt mich um; den Kopf im Kragen, die Haar unbeweglich um den Schädel geordnet, die Muskeln unten an den Wangen an ihrem Platz gespannt

Ist der Wald noch immer da? Der Wald war noch ziemlich da. Kaum aber war mein Blick zehn Schritte weit, ließ ich ab wieder eingefangen vom langweiligen Gespräch. Im dunklen Wald im durchweichten Boden fand ich mich nur durch das Weiß seines Kragens zurecht. Ich bat im Traum die Tänzerin Eduardowa sie möchte doch den Czardas noch einmal tanzen Sie hatte einen breiten Streifen Schatten oder Licht mitten

Initial Page of the Manuscript of the *Diaries*

The onlookers go rigid when the train goes past. ✳

"If he should forever ahsk me." The *ah*, released from the sentence, flew off like a ball on the meadow.

His gravity is the death of me. His head in its collar, his hair arranged immovably on his skull, the muscles of his jowls below, tensed in their places——

Are the woods still there? The woods were still almost there. But hardly had my glance gone ten steps farther when I left off, again caught up in the tedious conversation.

In the dark woods, on the sodden ground, I found my way only by the whiteness of his collar.

✳ In a dream I asked the dancer Eduardova [1] to dance the Czardas just one time more. She had a broad streak of shadow or light across the middle of her face between the lower part of her forehead and the cleft of her chin. Just then someone with the loathsome gestures of an unconscious intriguer approached to tell her the train was leaving immediately. The manner in which she listened to this announcement made it terribly clear to me that she would not dance again. "I am a wicked, evil woman, am I not?" she said. "Oh no," I said, "not that," and turned away aimlessly.

Before that I had questioned her about the many flowers

that were stuck into her girdle. "They are from all the princes of Europe," said she. I pondered as to what this might mean—that all those fresh flowers stuck in her girdle had been presented to the dancer Eduardova by all the princes of Europe.

The dancer Eduardova, a lover of music, travels in the trolley, as everywhere else, in the company of two vigorous violinists whom she has play often. For there is no known reason why one should not play in the trolley if the playing is good, pleasing to the fellow passengers, and costs nothing; i.e., if the hat is not passed around afterward. Of course, at first it is a little surprising and for a short while everybody finds it improper. But at full speed, in a strong breeze and on a silent street, it sounds quite nice.

The dancer Eduardova is not as pretty in the open air as on the stage. Her faded color, her cheekbones which draw her skin so taut that there is scarcely a trace of motion in her face and a real face is no longer possible, the large nose, which rises as though out of a cavity, with which one can take no liberties—such as testing the hardness of the point or taking it gently by the bridge and pulling it back and forth while one says, "But now you come along." The large figure with the high waist in skirts with too many pleats—whom can that please?—she looks like one of my aunts, an elderly lady; many elderly aunts of many people look like that. In the open air Eduardova really has nothing to compensate for these disadvantages, moreover, aside from her very good feet; there is actually nothing that would give occasion for enthusiasm, astonishment or even for respect. And so I have actually seen Eduardova very often treated with a degree of indifference that even gentlemen, who were otherwise very adroit, very correct, could not conceal, although they naturally made every effort to do so in the presence of so famous a dancer as Eduardova still was.

The auricle of my ear felt fresh, rough, cool, succulent as a leaf, to the touch.

I write this very decidedly out of despair over my body and over a future with this body.

When despair shows itself so definitely, is so tied to its object, so pent up, as in a soldier who covers a retreat and thus lets himself be torn to pieces, then it is not true despair. True despair overreaches its goal immediately and always, (at this comma it became clear that only the first sentence was correct).

Do you despair?

Yes? You despair?

You run away? You want to hide?

I passed by the brothel as though past the house of a beloved.

Writers speak a stench.

The seamstresses in the downpour of rain.[2]

Finally, after five months of my life during which I could write nothing that would have satisfied me, and for which no power will compensate me, though all were under obligation to do so, it occurs to me to talk to myself again. Whenever I really questioned myself, there was always a response forthcoming, there was always something in me to catch fire, in this heap of straw that I have been for five months and whose fate, it seems, is to be set afire during the summer and consumed more swiftly than the onlooker can blink his eyes. If only that would happen to me! And tenfold ought that to happen to me, for I do not even regret this unhappy time. My condition is not unhappiness, but it is also not happiness, not indifference, not weakness, not fatigue, not another interest—so what is it then? That I do not know this is probably connected with my inability to write. And without knowing the reason for it, I believe I understand the latter. All those things, that is to say, those things which occur to me, occur to me not from the root up but rather only from somewhere about their middle. Let someone then attempt to seize them, let someone attempt to seize a blade of grass and hold fast to it when it begins to grow only from the middle.

There are some people who can do this, probably, Japanese jugglers, for example, who scramble up a ladder that does not rest on the ground but on the raised soles of someone half lying on the ground, and which does not lean against a wall but just goes up into the air. I cannot do this—aside from the fact that my ladder does not even have those soles at its disposal. This, naturally, isn't all, and it isn't such a question that prompts me to speak. But every day at least one line should be trained on me, as they now train telescopes on comets. And if then I should appear before that sentence once, lured by that sentence, just as, for instance, I was last Christmas, when I was so far gone that I was barely able to control myself and when I seemed really on the last rung of my ladder, which, however, rested quietly on the ground and against a wall. But what ground, what a wall! And yet that ladder did not fall, so strongly did my feet press it against the ground, so strongly did my feet raise it against the wall.

Today, for instance, I acted three pieces of insolence, toward a conductor, toward someone introduced to me—well, there were only two, but they hurt like a stomach-ache. On the part of anyone they would have been insolent, how much the more so on my part. Therefore I went outside myself, fought in the air amid the mist, and, worst of all, no one noticed that I was even insolent to my companions, a piece of insolence as such, and had to be, and had to assume the proper manner for it and the responsibility; but the worst was when one of my acquaintances took this insolence not even as the indication of a personality but rather as the personality itself, called my attention to my insolence and admired it. Why don't I stay within myself? To be sure, I now say to myself: Look, the world submits to your blows, the conductor and the person introduced to you remained undisturbed; as you left, the latter even said goodbye. But that means nothing. You can achieve nothing if you forsake yourself; but what do you miss, aside from this, in your circle? To this appeal I answer only: I too would rather submit to blows within the circle than myself deal the blows outside it—but where the devil is this circle? For a time, indeed, I did see it lying on the earth, as if sprayed in lime, but now it just sort of hovers about me, indeed, does not even hover.

Night of comets, May 17–18.

Together with Blei, his wife and child, from time to time listened to myself outside of myself, it sounded like the whimpering of a young cat.

How many days have again gone silently by; today is May 28. Have I not even the resolution to take this pen-holder, this piece of wood, in my hand every day? I really think I do not. I row, ride, swim, lie in the sun. Therefore my calves are good, my thighs not bad, my belly will pass muster, but my chest is very shabby and if my head set low between my shoulders——

Sunday, July 19, slept, awoke, slept, awoke, miserable life.

When I think about it, I must say that my education has done me great harm in some respects. I was not, as a matter of fact, educated in any out-of-the-way place, in a ruin, say, in the mountains—something against which in fact I could not have brought myself to say a word of reproach. In spite of the risk of having the entire roster of my former teachers not understand this, I should prefer most of all to have been such a little dweller in the ruins, burnt by the sun which would have shone for me there on the tepid ivy between the remains on every side; even though I might have been weak at first under the pressure of my good qualities, which would have grown tall in me with the might of weeds.

When I think about it, I must say that my education has done me great harm in some respects. This reproach applies to a multitude of people—that is to say, my parents, several relatives, individual visitors to our house, various writers, a certain particular cook who took me to school for a year, a crowd of teachers (whom I must press tightly together in my memory, otherwise one would drop out here and there—but since I have pressed them together so, the whole mass crumbles away bit by bit anyhow), a school inspector, slowly walking passers-by; in short, this reproach twists through society like a dagger. And no one, I repeat, unfortunately no one, can be sure as to whether the point of the dagger won't suddenly appear sometime in front, in back, or from the side. I do not want to hear this reproach contradicted; since I have already heard too many contradictions, and since most of the contradictions, moreover, have refuted me, I include these contradictions in my reproach and now declare that my education and this refutation have done me great harm in many respects.

Often I think it over and then I always have to say that my education has done me great harm in some ways. This reproach is directed against a multitude of people; indeed, they stand here together and, as in old group photographs, they do not know what to do about each other, it simply does not occur to them to lower their eyes, and out of anticipation they do not dare smile. Among them are my parents, several relatives, several teachers, a certain particular cook, several girls at dancing school, several visitors to our house in earlier times, several writers, a swimming teacher, a ticket-seller, a school inspector, then some people that I met only once on the street, and others that I just cannot recall and those whom I shall never again recall, and those, finally, whose instruction, being somehow distracted at the time, I did not notice at all; in short, there are so many that one must take care not to name anyone twice. And I address my reproach to them all, introduce them to one another in this way, but tolerate no contradiction. For honestly I have borne enough contradictions already, and since most of them have refuted me, all I can do is include these refutations, too, in my reproach, and say that aside from my education these refutations have also done me great harm in some respects.

Does one suspect, perhaps, that I was educated in some

out-of-the-way place? No, I was educated in the middle of the city, in the middle of the city. Not, for example, in a ruin in the mountains or beside the lake. My reproach had until now covered my parents and their retinue and made them gray; but now they easily push it aside and smile, because I have drawn my hands away from them to my forehead and am thinking: I should have been that little dweller in the ruins, hearkening to the cries of the crows, soared over by their shadows, cooling under the moon, burnt by the sun which would have shone for me from all sides on my bed of ivy, even though I might have been a little weak at first under the pressure of my good qualities, which would have had to grow in me with the might of weeds.

Often I think it over and give my thoughts free rein, without interfering, and always, no matter how I turn or twist it, I come to the conclusion that in some respects my education has done me terrible harm. There inheres in the recognition of this a reproach directed against a multitude of people. There are my parents and my relatives, a certain particular cook, my teachers, several writers—the love with which they harmed me makes their guilt even greater, for how much [good] they could have [done] me with their love—several families friendly with my family, a swimming teacher, natives of summer resorts, several ladies in the city park of whom this would not at all have been expected, a hairdresser, a beggarwoman, a helmsman, the family doctor, and many more besides; and there would be still more if I could and wanted to name them all; in short, there are so many that one must be careful not to name anyone in the lot twice.

Now one might think that these great numbers would make a reproach lose its firmness, that it would simply have to lose its firmness, because a reproach is not an army general, it just goes straight ahead and does not know how to distribute its forces. Especially in this case, when it is directed against persons in the past. Forgotten energy may hold these persons fast in memory, but they would hardly have any ground left under them and even their legs would have already turned to smoke. And how expect it to be of any use to throw up to people in such a condition the mistakes they once made in earlier times in educating a boy who is as incomprehensible to them now as they to us. But indeed one cannot even do as much as make them remember those times, no person can compel them to do so; obviously one cannot mention compulsion at all, they can remember nothing, and if you press them, they push you dumbly aside, for most probably they do not even hear the words. Like tired dogs they stand there, because they use up all their strength in remaining upright in one's memory.

But if you actually did make them hear and speak, then your ears would only hum with counterreproaches, for people take the conviction of the venerability of the dead along with them into the beyond and uphold it ten times as much from there. And if perhaps this opinion is not correct and the dead do stand in especially great awe of the living, then they would side with their own living past all the more—after all, it's closest to them—and again our ears would hum. And if this opinion, too, is not correct and the dead are after all very impartial, even then they could never sanction their being disturbed by unverifiable reproaches. For such reproaches are unverifiable even as between one person and another. The existence of past mistakes in education cannot be proved, so how much the less the original responsibility for them. And now let me see a reproach that in such a situation would not be transformed into a sigh.

That is the reproach that I have to make. It has a sound core, theory supports it. That which really has been spoiled in me, however, I forget for the moment or excuse, and don't as yet make any fuss about it. On the other hand, I can prove at any time that my education tried to make another person out of me than the one I became. It is for the harm, therefore, that my educators could have done me in accordance with their intentions that I reproach them; I demand from their hands the person I now am, and since they cannot give him to me, I make of my reproach and laughter a drumbeat sounding into the world beyond. But all this only serves a different purpose. The reproach for having after all spoiled a part of me—for having spoiled a good, beautiful part (in my dreams sometimes it appears to me the way a dead bride appears to others)—this reproach that is forever on the point of becoming a sigh, this reproach should before all else reach there undamaged as an honest reproach, which is what it is, too. Thus it happens that the great reproach, to which nothing can happen, takes the small one by the hand; if the great one walks, the small one hops, but when once the small one gets there, it distinguishes itself—which is what we have always expected —and sounds the trumpet for the drummer.

Often I think it over and give my thoughts free rein, without interfering, but I always come to the conclusion that my education has spoiled me more than I can understand. Externally I am a man like others, for my physical education kept as close to the ordinary as my body itself was ordinary, and even if I am pretty short and a little stout, I still please many, even girls. There is nothing to be said about that. Only recently one of them said something very intelligent: "Ah, if I could only see you naked once, then you ought to be really pretty and kissable." But if I lacked an upper lip here, there an ear, here a rib, there a finger, if I had hairless spots on my head and pockmarks on my face, this would still be no adequate counterpart to my inner imperfection. This imperfection is not congenital and therefore so much the more painful to bear. For like everyone, I too have my center of gravity inside me from birth, and this not even the most foolish education could displace. This good center of gravity I still have, but to a certain extent I no longer have the corresponding body. And a center of gravity that has no work to do becomes lead, and sticks in the body like a musket ball. But this imperfection is not earned either, I have suffered its emergence through no fault of my own. This is why I can find nowhere within myself any repentance, much as I may seek it. For repentance would be good for me, it cries itself out all by itself, it takes the pain to one side and settles everything alone like an affair of honor; we remain upright because it relieves us.

My imperfection is, as I said, not congenital, not earned, nevertheless I bear it better than others, by means of great labor of the imagination and sought-out expedients, bear much smaller misfortunes—a horrible wife, for instance, poverty, a miserable profession—and am at the same time not at all black in the face with despair, but rather white and red.

I would not be so, if my education had penetrated into me as deeply as it wanted to. Perhaps my youth was too short for that, in which case, now in my forties,[3] I still rejoice over its shortness with all my heart. That alone made it possible for me to have enough strength left to become conscious of the deprivations of my youth; further, to suffer through these deprivations; further, to reproach the past in all respects; and, finally, to have left a remnant of strength for myself. But all these strengths are, again, only a remnant of those I possessed as a child, which exposed me more than others to the corruptors of youth, yes, a good racing chariot is the first to be pursued and overtaken by dust and wind, and its wheels fly over obstacles so that one might almost believe in love.

What I still am now is revealed most clearly to me by the strength with which the reproaches urge their way out of me. There were times when I had nothing else inside me except reproaches driven by rage, so that, although physically well, I would hold on to strangers in the street because the reproaches inside me tossed from side to side like water in a basin that was being carried rapidly.

Those times are past. The reproaches lie around inside me like strange tools that I hardly have the courage to seize and lift any longer. At the same time the corruption left by my old education seems to begin to affect me again more and more; the passion to remember, perhaps a general characteristic of bachelors of my age, opens my heart again to those people who should be the objects of my reproaches, and an event like that of yesterday, formerly as frequent as eating, is now so rare that I make a note of it.

But even above and beyond that, I myself, I who have just now put down my pen in order to open the window, am perhaps the best aid of my assailants. For I underestimate myself, and that in itself means an overestimation of others; but even aside from that I overestimate them. And aside from that I also do harm to myself directly. If I am overcome by the desire to make reproaches, I look out of the window. Who could deny that the fishermen sit there in their boats like pupils who have been taken out to the river from school; good, their immobility is often incomprehensible, like that of flies on windowpanes. And over the bridge go the trolleys, naturally as always with a roaring rude as the wind's, and they sound like spoiled clocks; and the policeman, no doubt, black from head to foot, with the yellow light of the badge on his chest, reminds one of nothing else but hell when now, with thoughts similar to mine, he contemplates a fisherman who suddenly—is he crying, has he seen an apparition or is his float bobbing?—bends down to the side of his boat. All this is all right, but in its own time; now only my reproaches are right.

They are directed against a multitude of people; this is really frightening and not only I at the open window but everyone else as well would rather look at the river. There are my parents and relatives. That they have done me harm out of love makes their guilt all the greater, for how much good they could have done me out of love; then friendly families with the evil eye, out of their sense of guilt they make themselves heavy and refuse to rise up into memory; then a crowd of nurses, teachers and writers and among them a certain particular cook; then, their punishment being that they fade into one another, a family doctor, a hairdresser, a helmsman, a beggarwoman, a newspaper vendor, a park watchman, a swimming teacher, then strange ladies in the city park of whom one would not have expected it at all, natives of summer resorts, an insult to the innocence of nature, and many others; but there were still more, if I could and wanted to name them all; in short, there are so many that one must take care not to name any one of them twice.

I often think it over and give my thoughts free rein without interfering, but I always come to the same conclusion: that my education has spoiled me more than all the people I know and more than I can conceive. Yet only once in a long while can I say this, for if I am asked immediately after, "Really? Is that possible? Are you supposed to believe that?" out of nervous fear I immediately try to restrict it.

Externally I look like everybody else; have legs, body and head, trousers, coat and hat; they put me through a thorough course of gymnastics and if I have nevertheless remained rather short and weak, that just could not be helped. Besides, I am agreeable to many people, even young girls, and those to whom I am not agreeable still find me bearable.

It is reported, and we are inclined to believe it, that when men are in danger they have no consideration even for beautiful strange women; they shove them against walls, shove them with head and hands, knees and elbows, if these women happen only to be in the way of their flight from the burning theater. At this point our chattering women fall silent, their endless talking reaches a verb and period, their eyebrows rise out of their resting places, the rhythmic movement of their thighs and hips is interrupted; into their mouths, only loosely closed by fear, more air than usual enters and their cheeks seem a little puffed out.[4]

"You," I said, and gave him a little shove with my knee (at this sudden utterance some saliva flew from my mouth as an evil omen), "don't fall asleep!"

"I'm not falling asleep," he answered, and shook his head while opening his eyes. "If I were to fall asleep, how could I guard you then? And don't I have to do that? Isn't that why you grabbed hold of me then in front of the church? Yes, it was a long time ago, we know it, just leave your watch in your pocket."

"It's really very late," I said. I had to smile a little and in order to conceal it I looked intently into the house.

"Does it really please you so much? So you would like to go up, very much like to? Then just say so, after all, I won't bite you. Look, if you think that it will be better for you up there than down here, then just go up there at once without thinking of me. It's my opinion—therefore the opinion of a casual passer-by—that you will soon come down again and that it would then be very good if somehow someone should be standing here whose face you won't even look at, but who'll take you under the arm, strengthen you with wine in a nearby tavern and then lead you to his room which, miserable as it is, still has a few panes of glass between itself and the night; for the time being you don't have to give a damn about this opinion. True it is, and I can repeat that in front of anyone you like, that it goes badly with us here below; yes, it's even a dog's life, but there's no help for me now; whether I lie here in the gutter and stow away the rain water or drink champagne with the same lips up there under the chandelier makes no difference to me. Besides, I don't even have so much as a choice between the two things; indeed, anything that attracts people's attention never happens to me, and how could it happen within the framework of the ceremonies that are necessary for me, within which indeed I can only crawl on, no better than some sort of vermin. You, to be sure, who know all that may be hidden in yourself, you have courage, at least you think you have. Try it anyhow, what do you have to lose, after all—often you can already recognize yourself, if you pay attention, in the face of the servant at the door."

"If I just knew definitely that you were being sincere with me. I should have been up there long ago. But how could I even tell whether you were sincere with me? You're looking at me now as though I were a little child, that doesn't help me at all, that indeed makes it even worse. But perhaps you want to make it worse. At the same time I can no longer stand the air in the street, so I already belong with the company up there. When I pay attention there's a scratching in my throat, there you have it. Besides, I cough. And have you any idea how I'll get along up there? The foot with which I step into the hall will already be transformed before I can draw the other one after it."

"You are right, I am not sincere with you."

"I want to leave, want to mount the steps, if necessary, by turning somersaults. From that company I promise myself everything that I lack, the organization of my strength, above all, for which the sort of intensification that is the only possibility for this bachelor on the street is insufficient. The latter would be satisfied just to maintain his—really—shabby physique, protect his few meals, avoid the influence of other people, in short, to preserve only as much as is possible in the disintegrating world. But if he loses anything, he seeks to get it back by force, though it be transformed, weakened, yes, even though it be his former property only in seeming (which it is for the most part). His nature is suicidal, therefore, it has teeth only for his own flesh and flesh only for his own teeth. For without a center, without a profession, a love, a family, an income; i.e., without holding one's own against the world in the big things —only tentatively, of course—without, therefore, making to a certain extent an imposing impression on it by a great complex of possessions, one cannot protect oneself from losses that momentarily destroy one. This bachelor with his thin clothes, his art of prayer, his enduring legs, his lodgings that he is afraid of, with his otherwise patched-up existence now brought out again after a long period—this bachelor holds all this together with his two arms and can never pick up any unimportant chance object without losing two others of his own. The truth, naturally, lies in this, the truth that is nowhere so clearly to be seen. For whoever appears as a complete citizen, that is, travels over the sea in a ship with foam before him and wake behind, that is, with much effect round about, quite different from the man in the waves on a few planks of wood that even bump against and submerge each other—he, this gentleman and citizen, is in no lesser danger. For he and his property are not one, but two, and whoever destroys the connection destroys him at the same time. In this respect we and our acquaintances are indeed unknowable, for we are entirely concealed; I, for instance, am now concealed by my profession, by my imagined or actual sufferings, by literary inclinations, etc., etc. But it is just I who feel my depth much too often and much too strongly to be able to be even only halfway satisfied. And this depth I need but feel uninterruptedly for a quarter of an hour and the poisonous world flows into my mouth like water into that of a drowning man.

"There is at the moment scarcely any difference between me and the bachelor, only that I can still think of my youth in the village and perhaps, if I want to, perhaps even if my situation alone demands it, can throw myself back there. The bachelor, however, has nothing before him and therefore nothing behind him. At the moment there is no difference, but the bachelor has only the moment. He went astray at that time—which no one can know today, for nothing can be so annihilated as that time—he went astray at that time when he felt his depth lastingly, the way one suddenly notices an ulcer on one's body that until this moment was the least thing on one's body—yes, not even the least, for it appeared not yet to exist and now is more than everything else that we had bodily owned since our birth. If until now our whole person had been oriented upon the work of our hands, upon that which was seen by our eyes, heard by our ears, upon the steps made by our feet, now we suddenly turn ourselves entirely in the opposite direction, like a weather vane in the mountains.

"Now, instead of having run away at that moment, even in this latter direction, for only running away could have kept him on the tips of his toes and only the tips of his toes could have kept him on the earth, instead of that he lay down, as children now and then lie down in the snow in winter in order to freeze to death. He and these children, they know of course that it is their fault for having lain down or yielded in some other way, they know that they should not have done it at any cost, but they cannot know that after the transformation that is taking place in them on the fields or in the cities they will forget every former fault and every compulsion and that they will move about in the new element as if it were their first. But forgetting is not the right word here. The memory of this man has suffered as little as his imagination. But they just cannot move mountains; the man stands once and for all outside our people, outside our humanity, he is continually starved, he has only the moment, the everlasting moment of torment which is followed by no glimpse of a moment of recovery, he has only one thing always: his pain; in all the circumference of the world no second thing that could serve as a medicine, he has only as much ground as his two feet take up, only as much of a hold as his two hands encompass, so much the less, therefore, than the trapeze artist in a variety show, who still has a safety net hung up for him below.

"We others, we, indeed, are held in our past and future. We pass almost all our leisure and how much of our work in letting them bob up and down in the balance. Whatever advantage the future has in size, the past compensates for in weight, and at their end the two are indeed no longer distinguishable, earliest youth later becomes distinct, as the future is, and the end of the future is really already experienced in all our sighs, and thus becomes the past. So this circle along whose rim we move almost closes. Well, this circle indeed belongs to us, but belongs to us only so long as we keep to it, if we move to the side just once, in any chance forgetting of self, in some distraction, some fright, some astonishment, some fatigue, we have already lost it into space, until now we had our noses stuck into the tide of the times, now we step back, former swimmers, present walkers, and are lost. We are outside the law, no one knows it and yet everyone treats us accordingly."

"You mustn't think of me now. And how can you want to compare yourself with me? I have been here in the city for more than twenty years already. Can you even imagine what that means? I have spent each season here twenty times."—Here he shook his slack fist over our heads.—"The trees have been growing here for twenty years, how small should a person become under them. And all these nights, you know, in all the houses. Now you lie against this, now against that wall, so that the window keeps moving around you. And these mornings, you look out of the window, move the chair away from the bed and sit down to coffee. And these evenings, you prop up your arm and hold your ear in your hand. Yes, if only that weren't all! If only you at least acquired a few new habits such as you can see here in the streets every day.—Now it perhaps seems to you as though I wanted to complain about it? But no, why complain about it, after all neither the one nor the other is permitted me. I must just take my walks and that must be sufficient, but in compensation there is no place in all the world where I could not take my walks. But now it looks again as though I were being vain of it."

"I have it easy, then. I shouldn't have stopped here in front of the house."

"Therefore don't compare yourself in that with me and don't let me make you doubtful. You are after all a grown man, are besides, as it seems, fairly forsaken here in the city."

I am indeed close to being so. Already, what protected me seemed to dissolve here in the city. I was beautiful in the early days, for this dissolution takes place as an apotheosis, in which everything that holds us to life flies away, but even in flying away illumines us for the last time with its human light. So I stand before my bachelor and most probably he loves me for it, but without himself really knowing why. Occasionally his words seem to indicate that he knows himself thoroughly, that he knows whom he has before him and that he may therefore allow himself anything. No, it is not so, however. He would rather meet everyone this same way, for he can live only as a hermit or a parasite. He is a hermit only by compulsion, once this compulsion is overcome by forces unknown to him, at once he is a parasite who behaves insolently whenever he possibly can. Of course, nothing in the world can save him any longer and so his conduct can make one think of the corpse of a drowned man which, borne to the surface by some current, bumps against a tired swimmer, lays its hands upon him and would like to hold on. The corpse does not come alive, indeed is not even saved, but it can pull the man down.

"You," I said, and gave him a little shove with my knee (at this sudden utterance some saliva flew from my mouth as an evil omen), "now you're falling asleep."

"I haven't forgotten you," he said, and shook his head while he was still opening his eyes.

"I wasn't afraid of it either," I said. I ignored his smile and looked down on the sidewalk. "I just wanted to tell you that now, come what may, I am going up. For, as you know, I have been invited up there, it is already late and the company is waiting for me. Perhaps some arrangements have been put off until I come. I don't insist it is so, but it is always possible. You will now ask me whether I could not perhaps forgo the company altogether."

"I won't, for in the first place you are burning to tell me, and in the second place it doesn't interest me at all, down here and up there are all the same to me. Whether I lie here in the gutter and stow away the rain water or drink champagne up there with the same lips makes no difference to me, not even in the taste, for which, besides, I easily console myself, for neither the one nor the other is permitted me and therefore it is not right for me to compare myself to you. And you! How long really have you been in the city? How long have you been in the city, I ask?"

"Five months. But still, I know it well enough already. You, I have given myself no rest. When I look back like this I don't know at all whether there have been any nights, everything looks to me, can you imagine, like one day without any mornings, afternoons and evenings, even without any differences in light."

November 6. Lecture by a Madame Ch. on Musset. Jewish women's habit of lip-smacking. Understand French through all the preliminaries and complications of the anecdote, until, right before the last word, which should live on in the heart on the ruins of the whole anecdote, the French disappears before our eyes, perhaps we have strained ourselves too much up to that point, the people who understand French leave before the end, they have already heard enough, the others haven't yet heard nearly enough, acoustics of the hall which favor the coughing in the boxes more than the words of the lecturer. Supper at Rachel's, she is reading Racine's *Phèdre* with Musset, the book lies between them on the table upon which in addition there is everything else imaginable lying.

Consul Claudel,[5] brilliance in his eyes, which his broad face picks up and reflects, he keeps wanting to say goodbye, he succeeds in part too, but not entirely, for when he says goodbye to one, another is standing there who is joined again by the one to whom goodbye has already been said. Over the lecture platform is a balcony for the orchestra. All possible sorts of noise disturb. Waiters from the corridor, guests in their rooms, a piano, a distant string orchestra, hammering, finally a squabble that is irritating because of the difficulty of telling where it is taking place. In a box a lady with diamonds in her earrings that sparkle almost uninterruptedly. At the box office young, black-clothed people of a French Circle. One of them makes a sharp bow in greeting that causes his eyes to sweep across the floor. At the same time he smiles broadly. But he does this only before girls, immediately after he looks the men straight in the face with his mouth solemnly pursed, by which he at the same time declares the former greeting to be perhaps a ridiculous but in any case unavoidable ceremony.

November 7. Lecture by Wiegler [6] on Hebbel. Sits on the stage against a set representing a modern room as if his beloved will bound in through a door to begin the play at last. No, he lectures. Hunger of Hebbel. Complicated relationship with Elisa Lensing. In school he has an old maid for a teacher who smokes, takes snuff, thrashes, and gives the good ones raisins. He travels everywhere (Heidelberg, Munich, Paris) with no real apparent purpose. Is at first a servant of a parish bailiff, sleeps in the same bed with the coachman under the steps.

Julius Schnorr von Carolsfeld—drawing by Friedrich Olivier, he is sketching on a slope, how pretty and earnest he is there (a high hat like a flattened clown's cap with a stiff, narrow brim extends over his face, curly, long hair, eyes only for his picture, quiet hands, the board on his knees, one foot has slipped down a little on the slope). But no, that is Friedrich Olivier, drawn by Schnorr.

10 o'clock, November 15. I will not let myself become tired. I'll jump into my story even though it should cut my face to pieces.

12 o'clock, November 16. I'm reading *Iphigenie auf Tauris*. Here, aside from some isolated, plainly faulty passages, the dried-up German language in the mouth of a pure boy is really to be regarded with absolute amazement. The verse, at the moment of reading, lifts every word up to the heights where it stands in perhaps a thin but penetrating light.

November 27. Bernhard Kellermann read aloud. "Some unpublished things from my pen," he began. Apparently a kind person, an almost gray brush of hair, painstakingly close-shaven, a sharp nose, the flesh over his cheekbones often ebbs and flows like a wave. He is a mediocre writer with good passages (a man goes out into the corridor, coughs and looks around to see if anyone is there), also an honest man who wants to read what he promised, but the audience wouldn't let him; because of the fright caused by the first story about a hospital for mental disorders, because of the boring manner of the reading, the people, despite the story's cheap suspense, kept leaving one by one with as much zeal as if someone were reading next door. When, after the first third of the story, he drank a little mineral water, a whole crowd of people left. He was frightened. "It is almost finished," he lied outright. When he was finished everyone stood up, there was some applause that sounded as though there were one person in the midst of all the people standing up who had remained seated and was clapping by himself. But Kellermann still wanted to read on, another story, perhaps even several. But all he could do against the departing tide was to open his mouth. Finally, after he had taken counsel, he said, "I should still like very much to read a little tale that will take only fifteen minutes. I will pause for five minutes." Several still remained, whereupon he read a tale containing passages that were justification for anyone to run out from the farthest point of the hall right through the middle of and over the whole audience.

December 15. I simply do not believe the conclusions I have drawn from my present condition, which has already lasted almost a year, my condition is too serious for that. Indeed, I do not even know whether I can say that it is not a new condition. My real opinion, however, is that this condition is new—I have had similar ones, but never one like this. It is as if I were made of stone, as if I were my own tombstone, there is no loophole for doubt or for faith, for love or repugnance, for courage or anxiety, in particular or in general, only a vague hope lives on, but no better than the inscriptions on tombstones. Almost every word I write jars against the next, I hear the consonants rub leadenly against each other and the vowels sing an accompaniment like Negroes in a minstrel show. My doubts stand in a circle around every word, I see them before I see the word, but what then! I do not see the word at all, I invent it. Of course, that wouldn't be the greatest misfortune, only I ought to be able to invent words capable of blowing the odor of corpses in a direction other than straight into mine and the reader's face. When I sit down at the desk I feel no better than someone who falls and breaks both legs in the middle of the traffic of the Place de l'Opéra. All the carriages, despite their noise, press silently from all directions in all directions, but that man's pain keeps better order than the police, it closes his eyes and empties the Place and the streets without the carriages having to turn about. The great commotion hurts him, for he is really an obstruction to traffic, but the emptiness is no less sad, for it unshackles his real pain.

December 16. I won't give up the diary again. I must hold on here, it is the only place I can.

I would gladly explain the feeling of happiness which, like now, I have within me from time to time. It is really something effervescent that fills me completely with a light, pleasant quiver and that persuades me of the existence of abilities of whose nonexistence I can convince myself with complete certainty at any moment, even now.

Hebbel praises Justinus Kerner's *Reiseschatten*. "And a book like this hardly exists, no one knows it."

Die Strasse der Verlassenheit by W. Fred. How do such books get written? A man who on a small scale produces something fairly good here blows up his talent to the size of a novel in so pitiful a manner that one becomes ill even if one does not forget to admire the energy with which he misuses his own talent.

This pursuit of the secondary characters I read about in novels, plays, etc. This sense of belonging together which I then have! In the *Jungfern vom Bischofsberg* (is that the title?), there is mention made of two seamstresses who sew the linen for the play's one bride. What happens to these two girls? Where do they live? What have they done that they may not be part of the play but stand, as it were, outside in front of Noah's ark, drowning in the downpour of rain, and may only press their faces one last time against a cabin window, so that the audience in the orchestra sees something dark there for a moment?

December 17. Zeno, pressed as to whether anything is at rest, replied: Yes, the flying arrow rests.

If the French were German in their essence, then how the Germans would admire them!

That I have put aside and crossed out so much, indeed almost everything I wrote this year, that hinders me a great deal in writing. It is indeed a mountain, it is five times as much as I have in general ever written, and by its mass alone it draws everything that I write away from under my pen to itself.

December 18. If it were not absolutely certain that the reason why I permit letters (even those that may be foreseen to have insignificant contents, like this present one) to lie unopened for a time is only weakness and cowardice, which hesitate as much to open a letter as they would hesitate to open the door of a room in which someone, already impatient, perhaps, is waiting for me, then one could explain this allowing of letters to lie even better as thoroughness. That is to say, assuming that I am a thorough person, then I must attempt to protract everything pertaining to the letter to the greatest possible extent, I must open it slowly, read it, slowly and often, consider it for a long time, prepare a clean copy after many drafts, and finally delay even the mailing. All this lies within my power, only the sudden receipt of the letter cannot be avoided. Well, I slow even that down in an artificial manner, I do not open it for a long time, it lies on the table before me, it continuously offers itself to me, continuously I receive it, but do not accept it.

11:30 P.M. That I, so long as I am not freed of my office, am simply lost, that is clearer to me than anything else, it is just a matter, as long as it is possible, of holding my head so high that I do not drown. How difficult that will be, what strength it will necessarily drain me of, can be seen already in the fact that today I did not adhere to my new time schedule, to be at my desk from 8 to 11 P.M., that at present I even consider this as not so very great a disaster, that I have only hastily written down these few lines in order to get into bed.

December 19. Started to work in the office. Afternoon at Max's.

Read a little in Goethe's diaries. Distance already holds this life firm in tranquillity, these diaries set fire to it. The clarity of all the events makes it mysterious, just as a park fence rests the eye when looking at broad tracts of turf, and yet inspires inadequate respect in us.

Just now my married sister [7] is coming to visit us for the first time.

December 20. How do I excuse yesterday's remark about Goethe (which is almost as untrue as the feeling it describes, for the true feeling was driven away by my sister)? In no way. How do I excuse my not yet having written anything today? In no way. Especially as my disposition is not so bad. I have continually an invocation in my ear: "Were you to come, invisible judgment!"

In order that these false passages which refuse to leave the story at any price may at last give me peace, I write down two here:

"His breathing was loud like sighs in a dream, where unhappiness is more easily borne than in our world so that simple breathing can serve as sighs."

"Now I look him over as aloofly as one looks over a small puzzle about which one says to oneself: What does it matter if I cannot get the pellets into their holes, it all belongs to me, after all, the glass, the case, the pellets, and whatever else there is; I can simply stick the whole affair into my pocket."

December 21. Curiosities from *Taten des grossen Alexander* by Michail Kusmin:

"Child whose upper half dead, lower alive, child's corpse with moving little red legs."

"The foul kings Gog and Magog, who were nourished on worms and flies, he drove into riven cliffs and sealed them in until the end of the world with the seal of Solomon."

"Rivers of stone, where in place of water stones rolled with a great din past the brooks of sand that flow for three days to the south and for three days to the north."

"Amazons, women with their right breasts burned away, short hair, male footgear."

"Crocodiles who with their urine burned down trees."

Was at Baum's,[8] so heard nice things. I, frail as before and always. To have the feeling of being bound and at the same time the other, that if one were unbound it would be even worse.

December 22. Today I do not even dare to reproach myself. Shouted into this empty day, it would have a disgusting echo.

December 24. I have now examined my desk more closely and have seen that nothing good can be done on it. There is so much lying about, it forms a disorder without proportion and without that compatibility of disordered things which otherwise makes every disorder bearable. Let disorder prevail on the green baize as it will, the same is true of the orchestras of old theaters. But that (December 25) wads of old newspapers, catalogues, picture postcards, letters, all partly torn, partly open, should stick out from the standing-room—the open pigeonhole under the center-piece—in the shape of a staircase, this unseemly state of affairs spoils everything. Individual, relatively huge things in the orchestra appear in the greatest possible activity, as though it were permissible for the merchant to audit his books in the theater, the carpenter to hammer, the officer to brandish his saber, the cleric to speak to the heart, the scholar to the reason, the politician to the sense of citizenship, the lovers not to restrain themselves, etc. Only the shaving mirror stands erect on my table, in the way it is used for shaving, the clothesbrush lies with its bristles on the cloth, the wallet lies open in case I want to make a payment, from the key ring a key sticks out in readiness and the tie still twines itself partly around the collar I have taken off. The next higher open pigeonhole, already hemmed in by the small closed drawers, is nothing but a lumber room, as though the first balcony of the auditorium, really the most visible part of the theater, were reserved for the most vulgar people, for old men-about-town in whom the dirt gradually moves from the inside to the outside, rude fellows who let their feet hang down over the balcony railing. Families with so many children that one merely glances at them without being able to count them here set up the filth of poor nurseries (indeed, it is already running into the orchestra), in the dark background sit the incurably sick, fortunately one sees them only when one shines a light in there, etc. In this pigeonhole lie old papers that I should long ago have thrown away if I had a waste-paper basket, pencils with broken points, an empty match-box, a paperweight from Karlsbad, a ruler with an edge the unevenness of which would be awful even for a country road, a lot of collar buttons, used razor blades (for these there is no place in the world), tie clips and still another heavy iron paperweight. In the pigeonhole above——

Wretched, wretched, and yet with good intentions. It

is midnight, but since I have slept very well, that is an excuse only to the extent that by day I would have written nothing. The burning electric light, the silent house, the darkness outside, the last waking moments, they give me the right to write even if it be only the most miserable stuff. And this right I use hurriedly. That's the person I am.

December 26. Two and a half days I was, though not completely, alone, and already I am, if not transformed, at any rate on the way. Being alone has a power over me that never fails. My interior dissolves (for the time being only superficially) and is ready to release what lies deeper. A slight ordering of my interior begins to take place and I need nothing more, for disorder is the worst thing in small talents.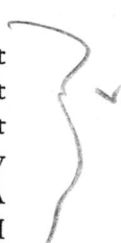

December 27. My strength no longer suffices for another sentence. Yes, if it were a question of words, if it were sufficient to set down one word and one could turn away in the calm consciousness of having entirely filled this word with oneself.

I slept part of the afternoon away, while I was awake I lay on the sofa, thought about several love experiences of my youth, lingered in a pique over a neglected opportunity (at the time I was lying in bed with a slight cold and my governess read me *The Kreutzer Sonata*, which enabled her to enjoy my agitation), imagined my vegetarian supper, was satisfied with my digestion and worried whether my eyesight would last all my life.

December 28. When I have acted like a human being for a few hours, as I did today with Max and later at Baum's, I am already full of conceit before I go to sleep.

January 3. "You," I said, and then gave him a little shove with my knee, "I want to say goodbye." At this sudden utterance some saliva flew from my mouth as an evil omen.

"But you've been considering that for a long time," he said, stepped away from the wall and stretched.

"No, I haven't been considering it at all."

"Then what have you been thinking about?"

"For the last time I have been preparing myself a little more for the company. Try as you may, you won't understand that. I, an average man from the country, whom at any moment one could exchange for one of those who wait together by the hundreds in railroad stations for particular trains."

January 4. *Glaube und Heimat* by Schönherr.

The wet fingers of the balconyites beneath me who wipe their eyes.

January 6. "You," I said, aimed, and gave him a little shove with my knee, "but now I'm going. If you want to see it too, open your eyes."

"Really, then?" he asked, at the same time looking at me from wide-open eyes with a direct glance that nevertheless was so weak that I could have fended it off with a wave of my arm. "You're really going, then? What shall I do? I cannot keep you. And if I could, I still wouldn't want to. By which I simply want to make clear to you your feeling that you could still be held back by me." And immediately he assumed that inferior servants' face by means of which they are permitted within an otherwise regulated state to make the children of their masters obedient or afraid.

January 7. N.'s sister who is so in love with her fiancé that she maneuvers to speak with each visitor individually, since one can better express and repeat one's love to a single person.

As though by magic, since neither external nor internal circumstances—which are now more friendly than they have been for a year—prevented me, I was kept from writing the entire holiday, it is a Sunday.—Several new perceptions of the unfortunate creature that I am have dawned upon me consolingly.

January 12. I haven't written down a great deal about myself during these days, partly because of laziness (I now sleep so much and so soundly during the day, I have greater weight while I sleep), but also partly because of the fear of betraying my self-perception. This fear is justified, for one should permit a self-perception to be established definitively in writing only when it can be done with the greatest completeness, with all the incidental consequences, as well as with entire truthfulness. For if this does not happen—and in any event I am not capable of it—then what is written down will, in accordance with its own purpose and with the superior power of the established, replace what has been felt only vaguely in such a way that the real feeling will disappear while the worthlessness of what has been noted down will be recognized too late.

A few days ago Leonie Frippon, cabaret girl, Stadt Wien. Hair dressed in a bound-up mass of curls. Bad girdle, very old dress, but very pretty with tragic gestures, flutterings of the eyelids, thrusts of the long legs, skilful stretching of the arms along the body, significance of the rigid throat during ambiguous passages. Sang: Button Collection in the Louvre.

Schiller, as drawn by Schadow in 1804 in Berlin, where he had been greatly honored. One cannot grasp a face more firmly than by this nose. The partition of the nose is a little pulled down as a result of the habit of pulling on his nose while working. A friendly, somewhat hollow-cheeked person whom the shaven face has probably made senile.

January 14. Novel, *Eheleute*, by Beradt. A lot of bad Jewishness. A sudden, monotonous, coy appearance of the author; for instance: All were gay, but one was present who was not gay. Or: Here comes a Mr. Stern (whom we already know to the marrow of his novelistic bones). In Hamsun too there is something like this, but there it is as natural as the knots in wood, here, however, it drips into the plot like a fashionable medicine onto sugar. Odd turns of expression are clung to interminably, for instance: He was busy about her hair, busy and again busy. Individual characters, without being shown in a new light, are brought out well, so well that even faults here and there do not matter. Minor characters mostly wretched.

January 17. Max read me the first act of *Abschied von der Jugend*. How can I, as I am today, come up to this; I should have to look for a year before I found a true emotion in me, and am supposed, in the face of so great a work, in some way to have a right to remain seated in my chair in the coffeehouse late in the evening, plagued by the passing flatulence of a digestion which is bad in spite of everything.

January 19. Every day, since I seem to be completely

finished—during the last year I did not wake up for more than five minutes at a time—I shall either have to wish myself off the earth or else, without my being able to see even the most moderate hope in it, I shall have to start afresh like a baby. Externally, this will be easier for me than before. For in those days I still strove with hardly a suspicion after a description in which every word would be linked to my life, which I would draw to my heart, and which would transport me out of myself. With what misery (of course, not to be compared with the present) I began! What a chill pursued me all day long out of what I had written! How great the danger was and how uninterruptedly it worked, that I did not feel that chill at all, which indeed on the whole did not lessen my misfortune very much.

Once I projected a novel in which two brothers fought each other, one of whom went to America while the other remained in a European prison. I only now and then began to write a few lines, for it tired me at once. So once I wrote down something about my prison on a Sunday afternoon when we were visiting my grandparents and had eaten an especially soft kind of bread, spread with butter, that was customary there. It is of course possible that I did it mostly out of vanity, and by shifting the paper about on the tablecloth, tapping with my pencil, looking around under the lamp, wanted to tempt someone to take what I had written from me, look at it and admire me. It was chiefly the corridor of the prison that was described in the few lines, above all its silence and coldness; a sympathetic word was also said about the brother who was left behind, because he was the good brother. Perhaps I had a momentary feeling of the worthlessness of my description, but before that afternoon I never paid much attention to such feelings when among relatives to whom I was accustomed (my timidity was so great that the accustomed was enough to make me halfway happy), I sat at the round table in the familiar room and could not forget that I was young and called to great things out of this present tranquillity. An uncle who liked to make fun of people finally took the page that I was holding only weakly, looked at it briefly, handed it back to me, even without laughing, and only said to the others who were following him with their eyes, "The usual stuff," to me he said nothing. To be sure, I remained seated and bent as before over the now useless page of mine, but with one thrust I had in fact been banished from society, the judgment of my uncle repeated itself in me with what amounted almost to real significance and even within the feeling of belonging to a family I got an insight into the cold space of our world which I had to warm with a fire that first I wanted to seek out.

February 19. When I wanted to get out of bed this morning I simply folded up. This has a very simple cause, I am completely overworked. Not by the office but my other work. The office has an innocent share in it only to the extent that, if I did not have to go there, I could live calmly for my own work and should not have to waste these six hours a day which have tormented me to a degree that you cannot imagine, especially on Friday and Saturday, because I was full of my own things. In the final analysis, I know, that is just talk, the fault is mine and the office has a right to make the most definite and justified demands on me. But for me in particular it is a horrible double life from which there is probably no escape but insanity. I write this in the good light of the morning and would certainly not write it if it were not so true and if I did not love you like a son.

For the rest, I shall certainly be myself again by tomorrow and come to the office where the first thing I hear will be that you want to have me out of your department.

The special nature of my inspiration in which I, the most fortunate and unfortunate of men, now go to sleep at 2 A.M. (perhaps, if I can only bear the thought of it, it will remain, for it is loftier than all before), is such that I can do everything, and not only what is directed to a definite piece of work. When I arbitrarily write a single sentence, for instance, "He looked out of the window," it already has perfection.

"Will you stay here for a long time?" I asked. At my sudden utterance some saliva flew from my mouth as an evil omen.

"Does it disturb you? If it disturbs you or perhaps keeps you from going up, I will go away at once, but otherwise I should still like to remain, because I'm tired."

But finally he had every right to be satisfied too, and to become continually more satisfied the better I knew him. For he continually knew me even better, apparently, and could certainly stick me, with all my perceptions, in his pocket. For how otherwise could it be explained that I still remained on the street as though no house but rather a fire were before me. When one is invited into society, one simply steps into the house, climbs the stairs and scarcely notices it, so engrossed is one in thought. Only so does one act correctly toward oneself and toward society.[9]

February 20. Mella Mars in the Cabaret Lucerna. A witty tragedienne who so to speak appears on a stage turned wrong side out in the way tragediennes sometimes show themselves behind the scenes. When she makes her appearance she has a tired, indeed even flat, empty, old face, which constitutes for all famous actors a natural beginning. She speaks very sharply, her movements are sharp too, beginning with the thumb bent backward, which instead of bone seems to be made of stiff fiber. Unusual changeability of her nose through the shifting highlights and hollows of the playing muscles around it. Despite the eternal flashing of her movements and words she makes her points delicately.

Small cities also have small places to stroll about in.

The young, clean, well-dressed youths near me on the promenade reminded me of my youth and therefore made an unappetizing impression on me.

Kleist's early letters, twenty-two years old. Gives up soldiering. They ask him at home: Well, how are you going to earn a living, for that was something they considered a matter of course. You have a choice of jurisprudence or political economy. But then do you have connections at court? "I denied it at first in some embarrassment, but then declared so much the more proudly that I, even if I had connections, should be ashamed, with my present ideas, to count on them. They smiled, I felt that I had been too hasty. One must be wary of expressing such truths."

February 21. My life here is just as if I were quite certain of a second life, in the same way, for example, I got over the pain of my unsuccessful visit to Paris with the thought that I would try to go there again very soon. With this, the sight of the sharply divided lights and shadows on the pavement of the street.[10]

For the length of a moment I felt myself clad in steel.

How far from me are—for example—my arm muscles.

Marc Henry—Delvard. The tragic feeling bred in the audience by the empty hall increases the effect of the serious songs, detracts from that of the merry ones. Henry does the prologue, while Delvard, behind a curtain that she doesn't know is translucent, fixes her hair. At poorly attended performances, W., the producer, seems to wear his Assyrian beard—which is otherwise deep black—streaked with gray. Good to have oneself blown upon by such a temperament, it lasts for twenty-four hours, no, not so long. Much display of costumes, Breton costumes, the undermost petticoat is the longest, so that one can count the wealth from a distance.—Because they want to save an accompanist, Delvard does the accompaniment first, in a very low-cut green dress, and freezes.—Parisian street cries. Newsboys are omitted.—Someone speaks to me; before I draw a breath I have been dismissed.—Delvard is ridiculous, she has the smile of an old maid, an old maid of the German cabaret. With a red shawl that she fetches from behind the curtain, she plays revolution. Poems by Dauthendey in the same tough, unbreakable voice. She was charming only at the start, when she sat in a feminine way at the piano. At the song "à Batignolles" I felt Paris in my throat. Batignolles is supposed to live on its annuities, even its Apaches. Bruant wrote a song for every section of the city.

THE URBAN WORLD

Oscar M., an older student—if one looked at him closely one was frightened by his eyes—stopped short in the middle of a snowstorm on an empty square one winter afternoon, in his winter clothes with his winter coat, over it a shawl around his neck and a fur cap on his head. His eyes blinked reflectively. He was so lost in thought that once he took off his cap and stroked his face with its curly fur. Finally he seemed to have come to a conclusion and turned with a dancing movement onto his homeward path.

When he opened the door to his parental living room he saw his father, a smooth-shaven man with a heavy, fleshy face, seated at an empty table facing the door.

"At last," said the latter, when Oscar had barely set foot in the room. "Please stay by the door, I am so furious with you that I don't know what I might do."

"But Father," said Oscar, and became aware only when he spoke how he had been running.

"Silence," shouted the father and stood up, blocking a window. "Silence, I say. And keep your 'buts' to yourself, do you understand?" At the same time he took the table in both hands and carried it a step nearer to Oscar. "I simply won't put up with your good-for-nothing existence any longer. I'm an old man. I hoped you would be the comfort of my old age, instead you are worse than all my illnesses. Shame on such a son, who through laziness, extravagance, wickedness and—why shouldn't I say so to your face—stupidity, drives his old father to his grave!" Here the father fell silent, but moved his face as though he were still speaking.

"Dear Father," said Oscar, and cautiously approached the table, "calm yourself, everything will be all right. Today I have had an idea that will make an industrious person out of me, beyond all your expectations."

"How is that?" the father asked, and gazed toward a corner of the room.

"Just trust me, I'll explain everything to you at supper. Inwardly I was always a good son, but the fact that I could not show it outwardly embittered me so, that I preferred to vex you if I couldn't make you happy. But now let me go for another short walk so that my thoughts may unfold more clearly."

The father, who, becoming attentive at first, had sat down on the edge of the table, stood up. "I do not believe that what you just said makes much sense, I consider it only idle talk. But after all you are my son. Come back early, we will have supper at home and you can tell me all about this matter then."

"This small confidence is enough for me, I am grateful to you from my heart for it. But isn't it evident in my very appearance that I am completely occupied with a serious matter?"

"At the moment, no, I can't see a thing," said the father. "But that could be my fault too, for I have got out of the habit of looking at you at all." With this, as was his custom, he called attention to the passage of time by regularly tapping on the surface of the table. "The chief thing, however, is that I no longer have any confidence at all in you, Oscar. If I sometimes yell at you—when you came in I really did yell at you, didn't I?—then I do it not in the hope that it will improve you, I do it only for the sake of your poor, good mother who perhaps doesn't yet feel any immediate sorrow on your account, but is already slowly going to pieces under the strain of keeping off such sorrow, for she thinks she can help you in some way by this. But after all, these are really things which you know very well, and out of consideration for myself alone I should not have mentioned them again if you had not provoked me into it by your promises."

During these last words the maid entered to look after

the fire in the stove. She had barely left the room when Oscar cried out, "But Father! I would never have expected that. If in the past I had had only one little idea, an idea for my dissertation, let's say, which has been lying in my trunk now for ten years and needs ideas like salt, then it is possible, even if not probable, that, as happened today, I would have come running from my walk and said: 'Father, by good fortune I have such-and-such an idea.' If with your venerable voice you had then thrown into my face the reproaches you did, my idea would simply have been blown away and I should have had to march off at once with some sort of apology or without one. Now just the contrary! Everything you say against me helps my ideas, they do not stop; becoming stronger, they fill my head. I'll go, because only when I am alone can I bring them into order." He gulped his breath in the warm room.

"It may be only a piece of rascality that you have in your head," said the father with his eyes opened wide in surprise. "In that case I am ready to believe that it has got hold of you. But if something good has lost its way into you, it will make its escape overnight. I know you."

Oscar turned his head as though someone had him by the throat. "Leave me alone now. You are worrying me more than is necessary. The bare possibility that you can correctly predict my end should really not induce you to disturb me in my reflections. Perhaps my past gives you the right to do so, but you should not make use of it."

"There you see best how great your uncertainty must be when it forces you to speak to me so."

"Nothing forces me," said Oscar, and his neck twitched. He also stepped up very close to the table so that one could no longer tell to whom it belonged. "What I said, I said with respect and even out of love for you, as you will see later, too, for consideration for you and Mama plays the greatest part in my decisions."

"Then I must thank you right now," the father said, "as it is indeed very improbable that your mother and I will still be capable of it when the time comes."

"Please, Father, just let tomorrow sleep on as it deserves. If you awaken it before its time, then you will have a sleepy today. But that your son must say this to you! Besides, I really didn't intend to convince you yet, but only to break the news to you. And in that, at least, as you yourself must admit, I have succeeded."

"Now, Oscar, there is only one thing more that really makes me wonder: why haven't you been coming to me often with something like this business of today. It corresponds so well with your character up to now. No, really, I am being serious."

"Yes, wouldn't you have thrashed me, then, instead of listening to me? I ran home, God knows, in a hurry to give you a little pleasure. But I can't tell you a thing as long as my plan is not complete. Then why do you punish me for my good intentions and demand explanations from me that at this time might still injure the execution of my plan?"

"Keep quiet, I don't want to know a thing. But I have to answer you very quickly because you are retreating toward the door and apparently have something very urgent in hand: You have calmed my first anger with your trick, but now I am even sadder in spirit than before and therefore I beg you—if you insist, I can even fold my hands—at least say nothing to your mother of your ideas. Be satisfied with me."

"This can't be my father speaking to me," cried Oscar, who already had his arm on the door latch. "Something has happened to you since noon, or I'm meeting a stranger now

for the first time in my father's room. My real father"—
Oscar was silent for a moment with his mouth open—"he
would certainly have had to embrace me, he would have
called my mother. What is wrong with you, Father?"

"Then you ought to have supper with your real father, I
think. It would be more fun."

"He will come, you can be sure of that. In the end he
can't stay away. And my mother must be there. And Franz,
whom I am now going to fetch. All." Thereupon Oscar
pressed his shoulder against the door—it opened easily—as
though he were trying to break it down.

Having arrived in Franz's home, he bowed to the little
landlady and said, "The Herr Engineer is asleep, I know,
it doesn't matter." And without bothering about the woman, who because she was displeased by the visit walked aimlessly up and down in the anteroom, he opened the glass
door—it quivered under his hand as though it had been
touched in a sensitive spot—and called, paying no heed to
the interior of the room into which he could scarcely see,
"Franz, get up. I need your expert advice. But I can't stand
it here in the room, we must go for a little walk, you must
also have supper with us. Quick, then."

"Gladly," said the engineer from his leather sofa, "but
which first? Get up, have supper, go for a walk, give advice? And some of it I probably haven't caught."

"Most important, Franz, don't joke. That's the most important thing, I forgot that."

"I'll do you that favor at once. But to get up! I would
rather have supper for you twice than get up once."

"Get up now! No arguments." Oscar grabbed the weak
man by the front of his coat and sat him up.

"You're mad, you know. With all due respect. Have I

ever pulled you off a sofa like that?" He wiped his closed eyes with his two little fingers.

"But Franz," said Oscar with a grimace. "Get dressed now. After all, I'm not a fool, to have waked you without a reason."

"Just as I wasn't sleeping without a reason, either. Yesterday I worked the night shift, after that I'm done out of my afternoon nap, also because of you."

"Why?"

"Oh, well, it annoys me how little consideration you have for me. It isn't the first time. Naturally, you are a free student and can do whatever you want. Not everyone is so fortunate. So you really must have some consideration, damn it! Of course, I'm your friend, but they haven't taken my profession away yet because of that." This he indicated by shaking his hands up and down, palm to palm.

"But to judge by your present jabbering don't I have to believe that you've had more than your fill of sleep?" said Oscar, who had drawn himself up against a bedpost whence he looked at the engineer as though he now had somewhat more time than before.

"Well, what is it you really want of me? Or rather, why did you wake me?" the engineer asked, and rubbed his neck hard under his goatee in that more intimate relationship which one has to one's body after sleep.

"What I want of you," said Oscar softly, and gave the bed a kick with the heel of his foot. "Very little. I already told you what I want while I was still in the anteroom: that you get dressed."

"If you want to point out by that, Oscar, that your news interests me very little, then you are quite right."

"All the better. Then the interest my news will kindle in you will burn entirely on its own account, without our friendship adding to it. The information will be clearer too. I need clear information, keep that in mind. But if you are perhaps looking for your collar and tie, they are lying there on the chair."

"Thanks," said the engineer, and started to fasten his collar and tie. "A person can really depend on you after all."

March 26. Theosophic lectures by Dr. Rudolf Steiner, Berlin. Rhetorical effect: Comfortable discussion of the objections of opponents, the listener is astonished at this strong opposition, further development and praise of these objections, the listener becomes worried, complete immersion in these objections as though there were nothing else, the listener now considers any refutation as completely impossible and is more than satisfied with a cursory description of the possibility of a defense.

Continual looking at the palm of the extended hand.— Omission of the period. In general, the spoken sentence starts off from the speaker with its initial capital letter, curves in its course, as far as it can, out to the audience, and returns with the period to the speaker. But if the period is omitted then the sentence, no longer held in check, falls upon the listener immediately with full force.

Before that, lecture by Loos and Kraus.

In Western European stories, as soon as they even begin to include any groups of Jews, we are now almost used immediately to hunting for and finding under or over the plot the solution to the Jewish question too. In the *Jüdinnen*, however, no such solution is indicated, indeed not even conjectured, for just those characters who busy themselves with such questions stand farthest from the center of the story at a point where events are already revolving more rapidly, so that we can, to be sure, still observe them closely, but no longer have an opportunity to get from them a calm report of their efforts. Offhand, we recognize in this a fault in the story, and feel ourselves all the more entitled to such a criticism because today, since Zionism came into being, the possibilities for a solution stand so clearly marshaled about the Jewish problem that the writer would have had to take only a few last steps in order to find the possibility of a solution suitable to his story.

This fault, however, has still another origin. The *Jüdinnen* lacks non-Jewish observers, the respectable contrasting persons who in other stories draw out the Jewishness so that it advances toward them in amazement, doubt, envy, fear, and finally, finally is transformed into self-confidence, but in any event can draw itself up to its full height only before them. That is just what we demand, no other principle for the organization of this Jewish material seems justified to us. Nor do we appeal to this feeling in this case alone, it is universal in at least one respect. In the same way, too, the convulsive starting up of a lizard under our feet on a footpath in Italy delights us greatly, again and again we are moved to bow down, but if we see them at a dealer's by hundreds crawling over one another in confusion in the large bottles in which otherwise pickles are usually packed, then we don't know what to do.

Both faults unite into a third. The *Jüdinnen* can do without that most prominent youth who usually, within his story, attracts the best to himself and leads it nicely along a radius to the borders of the Jewish circle. It is just this that we will not accept, that the story can do without this youth, here we sense a fault rather than see it.

March 28. P. Karlin the artist, his wife, two large, wide

upper front teeth that gave a tapering shape to the large, rather flat face, Frau Hofrat B., mother of the composer, in whom old age so brings out her heavy skeleton that she looks like a man, at least when she is seated.

Dr. Steiner is so very much taken up with his absent disciples. At the lecture the dead press so about him. Hunger for knowledge? But do they really need it? Apparently, though.—Sleeps two hours. Ever since someone once cut off his electric light he has always had a candle with him.— He stood very close to Christ.—He produced his play in Munich (you can study it all year there and won't understand it), he designed the costumes, composed the music.— He instructed a chemist. Löwy Simon, soap dealer on Quai Moncey, Paris, got the best business advice from him. He translated his works into French. The wife of the Hofrat therefore has in her notebook, "How Does One Achieve Knowledge of the Higher Worlds? [11] At S. Löwy's in Paris."

In the Vienna lodge there is a theosophist, sixty-five years old, strong as a giant, a great drinker formerly, and a blockhead, who constantly believes and constantly has doubts. It is supposed to have been very funny when once, during a congress in Budapest, at a dinner on the Blocksberg one moonlit evening, Dr. Steiner unexpectedly joined the company; in fear he hid behind a beer barrel with his beer mug (although Dr. Steiner would not have been angered by it).

He is, perhaps, not the greatest contemporary psychic scholar, but he alone has been assigned the task of uniting theosophy and science. And that is why he knows everything too. Once a botanist came to his native village, a great master of the occult. He enlightened him.

That I would look up Dr. Steiner was interpreted to me by the lady as the beginning of recollection. The lady's doctor, when the first signs of influenza appeared in her, asked Dr. Steiner for a remedy, prescribed this for the lady and restored her to health with it immediately. A French woman said goodbye to him with "Au revoir." Behind her back he shook his head. In two months she died. A similar case in Munich. A Munich doctor cures people with colors decided upon by Dr. Steiner. He also sends invalids to the picture gallery with instructions to concentrate for half an hour or longer before a certain painting.

End of the Atlantic world, lemuroid destruction, and now through egoism. We live in a period of decision. The efforts of Dr. Steiner will succeed if only the Ahrimanian forces do not get the upper hand.

He eats two liters of emulsion of almonds and fruits that grow in the air.

He communicates with his absent disciples by means of thought-forms which he transmits to them without bothering further about them after they are generated. But they soon wear out and he must replace them.

Mrs. F.: "I have a poor memory." Dr. St.: "Eat no eggs."

MY VISIT TO DR. STEINER

A WOMAN is already waiting (upstairs on the third floor of the Victoria Hotel on Jungmannstrasse), but urges me to go in before her. We wait. The secretary arrives and gives us hope. I catch a glimpse of him down the hall. Immediately thereafter he comes toward us with arms half spread. The woman explains that I was there first. So I walk behind him as he leads me into his room. His black Prince Albert which on those evenings when he lectures looks polished (not polished but just shining because of its clean blackness) is now in the light of day (3 P.M.) dusty and even spotted, especially on the back and elbows.

In his room I try to show my humility, which I cannot feel, by seeking out a ridiculous place for my hat, I lay it down on a small wooden stand for lacing boots. Table in the middle, I sit facing the window, he on the left side of the table. On the table papers with a few drawings which recall those of the lectures dealing with occult physiology. An issue of the *Annalen für Naturphilosophie* topped a small pile of the books which seemed to be lying about in other places as well. However, you cannot look around because he keeps trying to hold you with his glance. But if for a moment he does not, then you must watch for the return of his glance. He begins with a few disconnected sentences: So you are Dr. Kafka? Have you been interested in theosophy long?

But I push on with my prepared address: I feel that a great part of my being is striving toward theosophy, but at the same time I have the greatest fear of it. That is to say, I am afraid it will result in a new confusion which would be very bad for me, because even my present unhappiness consists only of confusion. This confusion is as follows: My happiness, my abilities and every possibility of being useful in any way have always been in the literary field. And here I have, to be sure, experienced states (not many) which in my opinion correspond very closely to the clairvoyant states described by you, Herr Doktor, in which I completely dwelt in every idea, but also filled every idea, and in which I not only felt myself at my boundary, but at the boundary of the human in general. Only the calm of enthusiasm, which is probably characteristic of the clairvoyant, was still lacking in those states, even if not completely. I conclude this from the fact that I did not write the best of my works in those states. I cannot now devote myself completely to this literary field, as would be necessary and indeed for various reasons. Aside from my family relationships, I could not live by literature if only, to begin with, because of the slow maturing of my work and its special character; besides, I am prevented also by my health and my character from devoting myself to what is, in the most favorable case, an uncertain life. I have therefore become an official in a social insurance agency. Now these two professions can never be reconciled with one another and admit a common fortune. The smallest good fortune in one becomes a great misfortune in the other. If I have written something good one evening, I am afire the next day in the office and can bring nothing to completion. This back and forth continually becomes worse. Outwardly, I fulfil my duties satisfactorily in the office, not my inner duties, however, and every unfulfilled inner duty becomes a misfortune that never leaves. And to these two never-to-be-reconciled endeavors shall I now add theosophy as a third? Will it not disturb both the others and itself be disturbed by both? Will I, at present already so unhappy a person, be able to carry the three to completion? This is what I have come to ask you, Herr Doktor, for I have a presentiment that if you consider me capable of this, then I can really take it upon myself.

He listened very attentively without apparently looking at me at all, entirely devoted to my words. He nodded from time to time, which he seems to consider an aid to strict concentration. At first a quiet head cold disturbed him, his nose ran, he kept working his handkerchief deep into his nose, one finger at each nostril.

Since in contemporary Western European stories about Jews the reader has become used immediately to hunting for and finding under or over the story the solution to the Jewish question too, and since in the *Jüdinnen* no such solution is indicated or even conjectured, therefore it is possible that offhand the reader will recognize in this a fault of the *Jüdinnen*, and will look on only unwillingly if Jews go about in the light of day without political encouragement from the past or the future. He must tell himself in regard to this that, especially since the rise of Zionism, the possibilities for a solution stand marshaled so clearly about the Jewish problem that in the end all the writer has to do is turn his body in order to find a definite solution, suitable to the part of the problem under discussion.

May 27. Today is your birthday, but I'm not even sending you the usual book, for it would be only pretense; at bottom I am after all not even in a position to give you a book. I am writing only because it is so necessary for me today to be near you for a moment, even though it be only by means of this card, and I have begun with the complaint only so that you may recognize me at once.

August 15. The time which has just gone by and in which I haven't written a word has been so important for me because I have stopped being ashamed of my body in the swimming schools in Prague, Königssaal and Czernoschitz. How late I make up for my education now, at the age of twenty-eight, a delayed start they would call it at the race track. And the harm of such a misfortune consists, perhaps, not in the fact that one does not win; this is indeed only the still visible, clear, healthy kernel of the misfortune, progressively dissolving and losing its boundaries, that drives one into the interior of the circle, when after all the circle should be run around. Aside from that I have also observed a great many other things in myself during this period which was to some small extent also happy, and will try to write it down in the next few days.

August 20. I have the unhappy belief that I haven't the time for the least bit of good work, for I really don't have time for a story, time to expand myself in every direction in the world, as I should have to do. But then I once more believe that my trip will turn out better, that I shall comprehend better if I am relaxed by a little writing, and so I try it again.

From his appearance I had a suspicion of the exertions which he had taken upon himself for my sake and which now, perhaps only because he was tired, gave him this certainty. A little more effort might have sufficed and the deception would have succeeded, it succeeded perhaps even now. Did I defend myself, then? Indeed, I stood stiff-necked here in front of the house, but—just as stiff-necked —I hesitated to go up. Was I waiting until the guests came to fetch me with a song? [12]

I have been reading about Dickens. Is it so difficult and can an outsider understand that you experience a story within yourself from its beginning, from the distant point up to the approaching locomotives of steel, coal and steam, and you don't abandon it even now, but want to be pursued by it and have time for it, therefore are pursued by it and of your own volition run before it wherever it may thrust and wherever you may lure it.

I can't understand it and can't believe it. I live only here and there in a small word in whose vowel ("thrust" above, for instance) I lose my useless head for a moment. The first and last letters are the beginning and end of my fishlike emotion.

August 24. Sitting with acquaintances at a coffeehouse table in the open air and looking at a woman at the next table who has just arrived, breathing heavily beneath her heavy breasts, and who, with a heated, brownish, shining face, sits down. She leans her head back, a heavy down becomes visible, she turns her eyes up, almost in the way in which she perhaps sometimes looks at her husband, who is now reading an illustrated paper beside her. If one could only persuade her that one may read at most a newspaper but never a magazine beside one's wife in a coffeehouse. After a moment she becomes aware of the fulness of her body and moves back from the table a little.

August 26. Tomorrow I am supposed to leave for Italy. Father has been unable to fall asleep these evenings because of excitement, since he has been completely caught up in his worries about the business and in his illness, which they have aggravated. A wet cloth on his heart, vomiting, suffocation, walking back and forth to the accompaniment of sighs. My mother in her anxiety finds new solace. He was always after all so energetic, he got over everything, and now... I say that all the misery over the business could after all last only another three months, then everything will have to be all right. He walks up and down, sighing and shaking his head. It is clear that from his point of view his worries will not be taken from his shoulders and will not even be made lighter by us, but even from our point of view they will not, even in our best intentions there is still something of the sad conviction that he must provide for his family.—By his frequent yawning or his poking into his nose (on the whole not disgusting) Father engenders a slight reassurance as to his condition, which scarcely enters his consciousness, despite the fact that when he is well he usually does not do this. Ottla confirmed this for me.—Poor Mother will go to the landlord tomorrow to beg.[13]

It had already become a custom for the four friends, Robert, Samuel, Max and Franz, to spend their short vacations every summer or fall on a trip together. During the rest of the year their friendship consisted mostly of the fact that they all four liked to come together one evening every week, usually at Samuel's, who, as the most well-to-do, had a rather large room, to tell each other various things and to accompany it by drinking a moderate amount of beer. They were never finished with the telling of things when they separated at midnight; since Robert was secretary of an association, Samuel an employee in a business office, Max a civil service official and Franz an employee in a bank, almost everything that anyone had experienced in his work during the week was not only unknown to the other three and had to be told to them quickly, but it was also incomprehensible without rather lengthy explanations. But more than anything else the consequence of the difference of these professions was that each was compelled to describe his profession to the others again and again, since the descriptions (they were all only weak people, after all) were not thoroughly enough understood, and for that very reason and also out of friendship were demanded again and again.

Talk about women, on the other hand, was seldom engaged in, for even if Samuel for his part would have found it to his liking he was still careful not to demand that the conversation adapt itself to his requirements, in this regard the old maid who brought up the beer often appeared to him as an admonition. But they laughed so much during these evenings that Max said on the way home that this eternal laughing is really to be regretted, because of it one forgets all the serious concerns of which everyone, after all, really has enough. While one laughs one thinks there is still time enough for seriousness. That isn't correct, however, for seriousness naturally makes greater demands on a person, and after all it is clear that one is also able to satisfy greater demands in the society of friends than alone. One should laugh in the office because there is nothing better to be accomplished there. This opinion was aimed at Robert, who worked hard in the art association he was putting new life into and at the same time observed in the old the most comical things with which he entertained his friends.

As soon as he began, the friends left their places, stood around him or sat down on the table, and laughed so self-obliviously, especially Max and Franz, that Samuel carried all the glasses over to a side table. If they tired of talking Max sat down at the piano with suddenly renewed strength and played, while Robert and Samuel sat beside him on the bench; Franz, on the other hand, who understood nothing of music, stood alone at the table and looked through Samuel's collection of picture postcards or read the paper. When the evenings became warmer and the window could be left open, all four would perhaps come to the window and with their hands behind their backs look down into the street without letting themselves be diverted from their conversation by the light traffic outside. Now and then one returned to the table to take a swallow of beer, or pointed to the curls of two girls who sat downstairs in front of their wineshop, or to the moon that quietly surprised them, until finally Franz said it was getting cool, they ought to close the window.

In summer they sometimes met in a public garden, sat at a table off to one side where it was darker, drank to one another and, their heads together in conversation, hardly noticed the distant brass band. Arm in arm and in step, they then walked home through the park. The two on the outside twirled their canes or struck at the shrubs, Robert called on them to sing, but then he sang alone, well enough for four, the other one in the middle felt himself made especially comfortable by this.

On one such evening, Franz, drawing his two neighbors more closely to him, said it was really so beautiful to be together that he couldn't understand why they met only once a week when they could certainly arrange without difficulty to see each other, if not often, then at least twice a week. They all were in favor of it, even the fourth one on the end, who had heard Franz's soft words only indistinctly. A pleasure of this sort would certainly be worth the slight effort which it would now and then cost one of them. It seemed to Franz as though he had a hollow voice as punishment for speaking uninvited for all of them. But he did not stop. And if sometimes one of them couldn't come, that's his loss and he can be consoled for it the next time, but do the others then have to give each other up, aren't three enough for each other, even two, if it comes to that? Naturally, naturally, they all said. Samuel disengaged himself from the end of the line and stood close in front of the three others, because in this way they were closer to each other. But then it didn't seem so, and he preferred to link up with the others again.

Robert made a proposal. "Let's meet every week and study Italian. We are determined to learn Italian, last year already we saw in the little part of Italy where we were that our Italian was only sufficient to ask the way when we got lost, remember, among the vineyard walls of the Campagna. And even then it managed to do only thanks to the greatest efforts on the part of those we asked. We'll have to study it if we want to go to Italy again this year. We simply have to. And so isn't it best to study together?"

"No," said Max, "we shall learn nothing together. I am as certain of that as you, Samuel, are certain that we ought to study together."

"Am I!" Samuel said. "We shall certainly learn very well together, I always regret that we weren't together even at school. Do you realize that we've known each other only two years?" He bent forward to look at all three. They had slowed down their steps and let go their arms.

"But we haven't studied anything together yet," said Franz. "I like it very well that way, too. I don't want to learn a thing. But if we have to learn Italian, then it is better for each one to learn it by himself."

"I don't understand that," Samuel said. "First you want us to meet every week, then you don't want it."

"Come now," Max said. "Franz and I, after all, just don't want our being together to be disturbed by studying, or our studying by being together, nothing else."

"Yes," said Franz.

"And indeed there isn't much time," said Max. "It is June now and in September we want to leave."

"That's the very reason why I want us to study together," Robert said, and stared in surprise at the two who opposed him. His neck became especially flexible when someone contradicted him.[14]

One thinks that one describes him correctly, but it is only approximate and is corrected by the diary.

It probably lies in the essence of friendship and follows it like a shadow—one will welcome it, the second regret it, the third not notice it at all——

September 26. The artist Kubin recommends Regulin as a laxative, a powdered seaweed that swells up in the bowels, shakes them up, is thus effective mechanically in contrast to the unhealthy chemical effect of other laxatives which just tear through the excrement and leave it hanging on the walls of the bowels.

He met Hamsun at Langen. He (Hamsun) grins mockingly for no reason. During the conversation, without interrupting it, he put one foot on his knee, took a large pair of paper shears from the table and trimmed the frayed edges of his trousers. Shabbily dressed, with one or so rather expensive details, his tie, for example.

Stories about an artist's pension in Munich where painters and veterinaries lived (the latters' school was in the neighborhood) and where they acted in such a debauched way that the windows of the house across the way, from which a good view could be had, were rented out. In order to satisfy these spectators, one of the residents in the pension would sometimes jump up on the window sill in the posture of a monkey and spoon his soup out of the pot.

A manufacturer of fraudulent antiques who got the worn effect by means of buckshot and who said of a table: Now we must drink coffee on it three more times, then it can be shipped off to the Innsbruck Museum.

Kubin himself: very strong, but somewhat monotonous facial expression, he describes the most varied things with the same movement of muscles. Looks different in age, size and strength according to whether he is sitting, standing, wearing just a suit, or an overcoat.

September 27. Yesterday on the Wenzelsplatz met two girls, kept my eye too long on one while it was just the other, as it proved too late, who wore a plain, soft, brown, wrinkled, ample coat, open a little in front, had a delicate throat and delicate nose, her hair was beautiful in a way already forgotten.—Old man with loosely hanging trousers on the Belvedere. He whistles; when I look at him he stops; if I look away he begins again; finally he whistles even when I look at him.—The beautiful large button, beautifully set low on the sleeve of a girl's dress. The dress worn beautifully too, hovering over American boots. How seldom I succeed in creating something beautiful, and this unnoticed button and its ignorant seamstress succeeded.—The woman talking on the way to the Belvedere, whose lively eyes, independent of the words of the moment, contentedly surveyed her story to its end.—The powerful half-turn of the neck of a strong girl.

September 29. Goethe's diaries. A person who keeps none is in a false position in the face of a diary. When for example he reads in Goethe's diaries: "1/11/1797. All day at home busy with various affairs," then it seems to him that he himself had never done so little in one day.

Goethe's observations on his travels different from today's because made from a mail-coach, and with the slow changes of the region develop more simply and can be followed much more easily even by one who does not know those parts of the country. A calm, so-to-speak pastoral form of thinking sets in. Since the country offers itself unscathed in its indigenous character to the passengers in a wagon, and since highways too divide the country much more naturally than the railway lines to which they perhaps stand in the same relationship as do rivers to canals, so too the observer need do no violence to the landscape and he can see systematically without great effort. Therefore there are few observations of the moment, mostly only indoors, where certain people suddenly and hugely bubble up before one's eyes; for instance, Austrian officers in Heidelberg, on the other hand the passage about the men in Wiesenheim is closer to the landscape, "They wear blue coats and white vests ornamented with woven flowers" (quoted from memory). Much written down about the falls of the Rhine at Schaffhausen, in the middle in larger letters: "Excited ideas."

Cabaret Lucerna. Lucie König showing photographs with old hair-styles. Threadbare face. Sometimes, with her turned-up nose, with her arm held aloft and a turn of all her fingers, she succeeds in something. A milksop face.—Longen [15] (the painter Pittermann), mimic jokes. A production that is obviously without joy and yet cannot be considered so, for if it were, then it couldn't be performed every evening, particularly since it was so unhappy a thing even at the moment it was created that no satisfactory pattern has resulted which would dispense with frequent appearances of the whole person. Pretty jump of a clown over a chair into the emptiness of the wings. The whole thing reminds one of a private production where, because of social necessity, one vigorously applauds a wretched, insignificant performance in order to get something smooth and rounded from the minus of the production by means of the plus of the applause.

The singer Vaschata. So bad that one loses oneself in his appearance. But because he is a powerful person he holds the attention of the audience with an animal force of which certainly I am consciously aware.

Grünbaum is effective with what is apparently only the seeming inconsolability of his existence.

Odys, dancer. Stiff hips. Real fleshlessness. Red knees only suit the "Moods of Spring" dance.

September 30. The girl in the adjoining room yesterday. I lay on the sofa and, on the point of dozing off, heard her voice. She seemed to me in my mind to be overdressed not only because of the clothes she wore, but also because of the entire room; only her shapely, naked, round, strong, dark shoulders which I had seen in the bath prevailed against her clothes. For a moment she seemed to me to be steaming and to be filling the whole room with her vapors. Then she stood up in her ash-gray-colored bodice that stood off from her body so far at the bottom that one could sit down on it and after a fashion ride along.

More on Kubin: The habit always of repeating in an approving tone someone else's last words, even if it appears from his own words added on that he by no means agrees with the other person. Provoking.—When you listen to his many stories it is easy to forget his importance. Suddenly you are reminded of this and become frightened. Someone said that a place we wanted to go to was dangerous; he said he wouldn't go there, then; I asked him whether he was afraid to, and he answered (moreover, his arm was passed through mine): Naturally, I am young and have a lot in front of me yet.

All evening he spoke often and—in my opinion—entirely

seriously about my constipation and his. Toward midnight, however, when I let my hand hang over the edge of the table, he saw part of my arm and cried: But you are really sick. Treated me from then on even more indulgently and later also kept off the others who wanted to talk me into going to the brothel with them. When we had already said goodbye he called to me again from the distance: "Reg-ulin!"

Tucholsky and Szafranski. The aspirated Berlin dialect in which the voice makes use of intervals consisting of "nich." The former, an entirely consistent person of twenty-one. From the controlled and powerful swing of his walking stick that gives a youthful lift to his shoulders to the deliberate delight in and contempt for his own literary works. Wants to be a defense lawyer, sees only a few obstacles and at the same time how they may be overcome: his clear voice that after the manly sound of the first half hour of talk pretends to become revealingly girlish—doubt of his own capacity to pose, which, however, he hopes to get with more experience of the world—fear, finally, of changing into a melancholic, as he has seen happen in older Berlin Jews of his type, in any event for the time being he sees no sign of this. He will marry soon.

Szafranski, a disciple of Bernhardt's, grimaces while he observes and draws in a way that resembles what is drawn. Reminds me that I too have a pronounced talent for meta-morphosing myself, which no one notices. How often I must have imitated Max. Yesterday evening, on the way home, if I had observed myself from the outside I should have taken myself for Tucholsky. The alien being must be in me, then, as distinctly and invisibly as the hidden object in a picture-puzzle, where, too, one would never find anything if one did not know that it is there. When these metamorphoses take place, I should especially like to believe in a dimming of my own eyes.

October 1. The Altneu Synagogue yesterday. Kol Nidre.[16] Suppressed murmur of the stock market. In the entry, boxes with the inscription: "Merciful gifts secretly left assuage the wrath of the bereft." Churchly inside. Three pious, apparently Eastern Jews. In socks. Bowed over their prayer books, their prayer shawls drawn over their heads, become as small as they possibly can. Two are crying, moved only by the holy day. One of them may only have sore eyes, perhaps, to which he fleetingly applies his still folded handkerchief, at once to lower his face to the text again. The words are not really, or chiefly, sung, but behind them arabesque-like melodies are heard that spin out the words as fine as hairs. The little boy without the slightest conception of it all and without any possibility of understanding, who, with the clamor in his ears, pushes himself among the thronging people and is pushed. The clerk (apparently) who shakes himself rapidly while he prays, which is to be understood only as an attempt at putting the strongest possible—even if possibly incomprehensible—emphasis on each word, by means of which the voice, which in any case could not attain a large, clear emphasis in the clamor, is spared. The family of a brothel owner. I was stirred immeasurably more deeply by Judaism in the Pinkas Synagogue.

The day before the day before yesterday. The one, a Jewish girl with a narrow face—better, that tapers down to a narrow chin, but is loosened by a broad, wavy hair-do.

The three small doors that lead from the inside of the building into the salon. The guests as though in a police station on the stage, drinks on the table are scarcely touched.

Several girls here dressed like the marionettes for children's theaters that are sold in the Christmas market, i.e., with ruching and gold stuck on and loosely sewn so that one can rip them with one pull and they then fall apart in one's fingers. The landlady with the pale blond hair drawn tight over doubtless disgusting pads, with the sharply slanting nose the direction of which stands in some sort of geometric relation to the sagging breasts and the stiffly held belly, complains of headaches which are caused by the fact that today, Saturday, there is so great an uproar and there is nothing in it.

More on Kubin: The story about Hamsun is suspect. One could tell such stories as one's own experiences by the thousand from his works.

More on Goethe: "Excited ideas" are only the ideas which the Rhine falls excite. One sees this from a letter to Schiller.—The isolated momentary observation, "Castanet rhythms of the children in wooden shoes," made such an impression, is so universally accepted, that it is unthinkable that anyone, even if he had never read this remark, could feel this observation as an original idea.

October 2. Sleepless night. The third in a row. I fall asleep soundly, but after an hour I wake up, as though I had laid my head in the wrong hole. I am completely awake, have the feeling that I have not slept at all or only under a thin skin, have before me anew the labor of falling asleep and feel myself rejected by sleep. And for the rest of the night, until about five, thus it remains, so that indeed I sleep but at the same time vivid dreams keep me awake. I sleep alongside myself, so to speak, while I myself must struggle with dreams. About five the last trace of sleep is exhausted, I just dream, which is more exhausting than wakefulness. In short, I spend the whole night in that state in which a healthy person finds himself for a short time before really falling asleep. When I awaken, all the dreams are gathered about me, but I am careful not to reflect on them. Toward morning I sigh into the pillow, because for this night all hope is gone. I think of those nights at the end of which I was raised out of deep sleep and awoke as though I had been folded in a nut.

The horrible apparition last night of a blind child, apparently the daughter of my aunt in Leitmeritz who, however, has no daughter but only sons, one of whom once broke his leg. On the other hand there were resemblances between this child and Dr. M.'s daughter who, as I have recently seen, is in the process of changing from a pretty child into a stout, stiffly dressed little girl. This blind or weak-sighted child had both eyes covered by a pair of eyeglasses, the left, under a lens held at a certain distance from the eye, was milky-gray and bulbous, the other receded and was covered by a lens lying close against it. In order that this eyeglass might be set in place with optical correctness it was necessary, instead of the usual support going back of the ears, to make use of a lever, the head of which could be attached no place but to the cheekbone, so that from this lens a little rod descended to the cheek, there disappeared into the pierced flesh and ended on the bone, while another small wire rod came out and went back over the ear.

I believe this sleeplessness comes only because I write. For no matter how little and how badly I write, I am still made sensitive by these minor shocks, feel, especially toward evening and even more in the morning, the approaching, the imminent possibility of great moments which would tear me open, which could make me capable of anything, and in the general uproar that is within me and which I have no time to command, find no rest. In the end this uproar is only a suppressed, restrained harmony, which, left free, would fill me completely, which could even widen me and yet still fill me. But now such a moment arouses only feeble hopes and does me harm, for my being does not have sufficient strength or the capacity to hold the present mixture, during the day the visible world helps me, during the night it cuts me to pieces unhindered. I always think in this connection of Paris, where at the time of the siege and later, until the Commune, the population of the northern and eastern suburbs, up to that time strangers to the Parisians, for a period of months moved through the connecting streets into the center of Paris, dawdling like the hands of a clock.

My consolation is—and with it I now go to bed—that I have not written for so long, that therefore this writing could find no right place within my present circumstances, that nevertheless, with a little fortitude, I'll succeed, at least temporarily.

I was so weak today that I even told my chief the story of the child. I remembered that the eyeglasses in the dream derive from my mother, who in the evening sits next to me and while playing cards looks across at me not very pleasantly under her eyeglasses. Her eyeglasses even have, which I do not remember having noticed before, the right lens nearer the eye than the left.

October 3. The same sort of night, but fell asleep with even more difficulty. While falling asleep a vertically moving pain in my head over the bridge of the nose, as though from a wrinkle too sharply pressed into my forehead. To make myself as heavy as possible, which I consider good for falling asleep, I had crossed my arms and laid my hands on my shoulders, so that I lay there like a soldier with his pack. Again it was the power of my dreams, shining forth into wakefulness even before I fall asleep, which did not let me sleep. In the evening and the morning my consciousness of the creative abilities in me is more than I can encompass. I feel shaken to the core of my being and can get out of myself whatever I desire. Calling forth such powers, which are then not permitted to function, reminds me of my relationship with B. Here too there are effusions which are not released but must instead spend themselves in being repulsed, but here—this is the difference—it is a matter of more mysterious powers which are of an ultimate significance to me.

On the Josefsplatz a large touring car with a family sitting crowded together drove by me. In the wake of the automobile, with the smell of gas, a breath of Paris blew across my face.

While dictating a rather long report to the district Chief of Police, toward the end, where a climax was intended, I got stuck and could do nothing but look at K., the typist, who, in her usual way, became especially lively, moved her chair about, coughed, tapped on the table and so called the attention of the whole room to my misfortune. The sought-for idea now has the additional value that it will make her be quiet, and the more valuable it becomes the more difficult it becomes to find it. Finally I have the word "stigmatize" and the appropriate sentence, but still hold it all in my mouth with disgust and a sense of shame as though it were raw meat, cut out of me (such effort has it cost me). Finally I say it, but retain the great fear that everything within me is ready for a poetic work and such a work would be a heavenly enlightenment and a real coming-alive for me, while here, in the office, because of so wretched an official document, I must rob a body capable of such happiness of a piece of its flesh.

October 4. I feel restless and vicious. Yesterday, before falling asleep, I had a flickering, cool little flame up in the left side of my head. The tension over my left eye has already settled down and made itself at home. When I think about it, it seems to me that I couldn't hold out in the office even if they told me that in one month I'd be free. And most of the time in the office I do what I am supposed to, am quite calm when I can be sure that my boss is satisfied, and do not feel that my condition is dreadful. By the way, last night I purposely made myself dull, went for a walk, read Dickens, then felt a little better and had lost the strength for sorrow. I still regarded the sorrow as justified but it seemed to have withdrawn somewhat, I looked at it from a distance and therefore hoped for better sleep. It was a little deeper too, but not enough, and often interrupted. I told myself, as consolation, that I had indeed once more repressed the great agitation in me but that I did not wish to succumb at once, as I had always done in the past after such occasions; rather, I wished to remain entirely conscious of the final flutterings of that agitation, which I had never done before. Perhaps in this way I would find hidden steadfastness in myself.

Toward evening, in the dark of my room on the sofa. Why does one take a rather long time to recognize a color, but then, after the understanding has reached the decisive turning point, quickly become all the more convinced of the color. If the light from the anteroom and the kitchen shines on the glass door simultaneously from the outside, then greenish—or rather, not to detract from the definiteness of the impression—green light pours down almost the length of the panes. If the light in the anteroom is turned off and only the kitchen light remains, then the pane nearer the kitchen becomes deep blue, the other whitish blue, so whitish that all the drawings on the frosted glass (stylized poppies, tendrils, various rectangles and leaves) dissolve.

The lights and shadows thrown on the walls and the ceiling by the electric lights in the street and the bridge down below are distorted, partly spoiled, overlapping and hard to follow. When they installed the electric arc lamps down below and when they furnished this room, there was simply no housewifely consideration given to how my room would look from the sofa at this hour without any lights of its own.

The glare thrown on the ceiling by the trolley passing down below moves whitely, wraithlike and with mechanical pauses along the one wall and ceiling, broken in the corner. The globe stands on the linen chest in the first, fresh, full reflection of the street lights, a greenishly clean light on top, has a highlight on its roundness and gives the impression that the glare is really too strong for it, although the light passes over its smoothness and goes off leaving it rather brownish like a leather apple. The light from the anteroom throws a large patch of glare on the wall over the bed. This patch is bounded by a curved line beginning at the head of the bed, gives the illusion that the bed is pressed down, widens the dark bedposts, raises the ceiling over the bed.

October 5. Restlessness again for the first time in several days, even now that I am writing. Rage at my sister who comes into the room and sits down at the table with a book. Waiting for the next trifling occasion to let this rage explode. Finally she takes a visiting card from the tray and fiddles around with it between her teeth. With departing rage, of which only a stinging vapor remains behind in my head, and dawning relief and confidence, I begin to work.

Last night Café Savoy. Yiddish troupe.[17] Mrs. K., "male impersonator." In a caftan, short black trousers, white stockings, from the black vest a thin white woolen shirt emerges that is held in front at the throat by a knot and then flares into a wide, loose, long, spreading collar. On her head, confining her woman's hair but necessary anyhow and worn by her husband as well, a dark, brimless skull cap, over it a large, soft black hat with a turned-up brim.

I really don't know what sort of person it is that she and her husband represent. If I wanted to explain them to someone to whom I didn't want to confess my ignorance, I should find that I consider them sextons, employees of the temple, notorious lazybones with whom the community has come to terms, privileged shnorrers for some religious reason, people who, precisely as a result of their being set apart, are very close to the center of the community's life, know many songs as a result of their useless wandering about and spying, see clearly to the core the relationship of all the members of the community, but as a result of their lack of relatedness to the workaday world don't know what to do with this knowledge, people who are Jews in an especially pure form because they live only in the religion, but live in it without effort, understanding or distress. They seem to make a fool of everyone, laugh immediately after the murder of a noble Jew, sell themselves to an apostate, dance with their hands on their earlocks in delight when the unmasked murderer poisons himself and calls upon God, and yet all this only because they are as light as a feather, sink to the ground under the slightest pressure, are sensitive, cry easily with dry faces (they cry themselves out in grimaces), but as soon as the pressure is removed haven't the slightest specific gravity but must bounce right back up in the air.

They must have caused a lot of difficulty in a serious play, such as *Der Meshumed* [18] by Lateiner is, for they are forever—large as life and often on tiptoe or with both feet in the air—at the front of the stage and do not unravel but rather cut apart the suspense of the play. The seriousness of the play spins itself out, however, in words so compact, carefully considered even where possibly improvised, so full of the tension of a unified emotion, that even when the plot is going along only at the rear of the stage, it always keeps its meaning. Rather, the two in caftans are suppressed now and then, which befits their nature, and despite their extended arms and snapping fingers one sees behind them only the murderer, who, the poison in him, his hand at his really too large collar, is staggering to the door.

The melodies are long, one's body is glad to confide itself to them. As a result of their long-drawn-out forward movement, the melodies are best expressed by a swaying of the hips, by raising and lowering extended arms in a calm rhythm, by bringing the palms close to the temples and taking care not to touch them. Suggests the *šlapák*.[19]

Some songs, the expression "yiddische kinderlach," some of this woman's acting (who, on the stage, because she is a Jew, draws us listeners to her because we are Jews, without any longing for or curiosity about Christians) made my cheeks tremble. The representative of the government, with the exception of a waiter and two maids standing to the left of the stage, perhaps the only Christian in the hall, is a wretched person, afflicted with a facial tic that—especially on the left side of his face, but spreading also far onto the right—contracts and passes from his face with the almost merciful quickness, I mean the haste but also the regularity, of a second hand. When it reaches the left eye it almost obliterates it. For this contraction new, small, fresh muscles have developed in the otherwise quite wasted face.

The talmudic melody of minute questions, adjurations or explanations: The air moves into a pipe and takes the pipe along, and a great screw, proud in its entirety, humble in its turns, twists from small, distant beginnings in the direction of the one who is questioned.

October 6. The two old men up front at the long table near the stage. One leans both his arms on the table and has only his face (whose false, bloated redness with an irregular, square, matted beard beneath it sadly conceals his old age) turned up to the right toward the stage, while the other, directly opposite the stage, holds his face, which old age has made quite dry, back away from the table on which he leans only with his left arm, holding his right arm bent in the air in order better to enjoy the melody that his fingertips follow and to which the short pipe in his right hand weakly yields. "Tateleben, come on and sing," cries the woman now to one, now to the other, at the same time stooping a little and stretching her arms forward encouragingly.

The melodies are made to catch hold of every person who jumps up and they can, without breaking down, encompass all his excitement even if one won't believe they have inspired it. The two in caftans are particularly in a hurry to meet the singing, as though it were stretching their body according to its most essential needs, and the clapping of the hands during the singing is an obvious sign of the good health of the man in the actor. The children of the landlord, in a corner of the stage, remain children in their relationship to Mrs. K. and sing along, their mouths, between their pursed lips, full of the melody.

The play: Twenty years ago Seidemann, a rich Jew, obviously having marshaled all his criminal instincts toward that end, had himself baptized, poisoning his wife at the same time, since she would not let herself be forced into baptism. Since then he has made every effort to forget the jargon that unintentionally echoes in his speech, especially at first so that the audience can notice it and because the approaching events still leave time for it, and continually expresses great disgust for everything Jewish. He has promised his daughter to the officer, Dragomirow, while she, who is in love with her cousin, young Edelmann, in a big scene, drawing herself up in an unusual stony position, broken only at the waist, declares to her father that she holds fast to Judaism and ends a whole act with contemptuous laughter for the violence done her. (The Christians in the play are: an honest Polish servant of Seidemann's who later contributes to his unmasking, honest chiefly because Seidemann must be ranged round with contrasts; the officer with whom the play—aside from portraying his guilt—concerns itself little, because as a distinguished Christian he interests no one, just the same as a presiding judge who appears later; and finally a court attendant whose malice does not exceed the requirements of his position and the mirth of the two in caftans, although Max calls him a pogromist.) Dragomirow, however, for some reason or other can marry only if his notes, which old Edelmann holds, are taken up, but which the latter, although he is about to leave for Palestine and although Seidemann wants to pay them in cash, will not hand over. The daughter acts haughtily toward the enamored officer and boasts of her Judaism although she has been baptized, the officer does not know what to do, and, his arms slack, his hands loosely clasped at the ends of them, looks beseechingly at the father. The daughter runs away to Edelmann, she wants to be married to her beloved, even if for the time being in secret, since according to civil law a Jew cannot marry a Christian woman and she obviously cannot convert to Judaism without the consent of her father. The father arrives, sees that without some stratagem all is lost, and outwardly gives his blessing to this marriage. They all forgive him, yes, begin to love him as though they had been in the wrong, even old Edelmann, and especially he, although he knows that Seidemann had poisoned his sister. (These inconsistencies arose perhaps through cutting, but perhaps also because the play is passed on orally most of the time, from one troupe of actors to another.) Through his reconciliation Seidemann gets hold, first of all, of Dragomirow's notes— "You know," he says, "I don't want this Dragomirow to speak badly of the Jews"—and Edelmann gives them to him for nothing, then Seidemann calls him to the portière in the background, ostensibly to show him something, and from behind gives him a fatal thrust with a knife through his dressing gown into his back. (Between the reconciliation and the murder Seidemann was removed from the stage for a time to think out the plan and buy the knife.) In this way he intends to bring young Edelmann to the gallows, for it is he whom suspicion must fall upon, and his daughter will become free for Dragomirow. He runs away, Edelmann lies behind the portière. The daughter, wearing her bridal veil, enters on the arm of young Edelmann, who has put on his prayer shawl. The father, they see, unfortunately is not yet there. Seidemann enters and seems happy at the sight of the bridal couple.

October 8. Then a man appears, perhaps Dragomirow himself, perhaps only an actor, but actually a detective unknown to us, and explains that he has to search the house since "your life isn't safe in this house." Seidemann: "Children, don't worry, this is of course an obvious mistake. Everything will be straightened out." Edelmann's body is found, young Edelmann torn from his beloved and arrested. For a whole act Seidemann, with great patience and very well-stressed little asides (Yes, yes, very good. No, that's wrong. Yes, now that's better. Of course, of course), instructs the two in caftans how they are to testify in court concerning the alleged enmity that has existed between old and young Edelmann for years. They get going with difficulty, there are many misunderstandings (they come forward at an improvised rehearsal of the court scene and declare that Seidemann had commissioned them to represent the affair in the following way), until finally they immerse themselves in that enmity so thoroughly that even Seidemann can no longer restrain them—they now know how the murder itself took place and the man stabs the woman to death with a French bread. This of course is again more than will be required of them. But Seidemann is satisfied enough with the two and hopes with their help for a favorable outcome to the trial. Here, for the spectator who is religious, without its having been expressed because it is self-evident, God himself reaches into the play in place of the author and strikes the villain blind.

In the last act the presiding judge is again the eternal

Ich schreibe das ganz bestimmt. aus Verzweiflung über meinen Körper und über die Zukunft mit diesem Körper

Wenn sich die Verzweiflung so bestimmt gibt so an ihren Gegenstand gebunden ist, so zurückgehalten wie von einem Soldaten, der den Rückzug deckt und sich dafür zerreißen läßt, dann ist es nicht die richtige Verzweiflung. Die richtige Verzweiflung hat ihr Ziel gleich und immer überholt (Bei diesem Beistrich zeigte es sich, daß nur der erste Satz richtig war)

A Manuscript Page of the *Diaries*

(SEE PAGE 11)

Dragomirow actor (in this, too, contempt is revealed for the Christian, one Jewish actor can play three Christian roles well, and if he plays them badly, it doesn't matter either) and beside him, as defense attorney, with great display of hair and mustache, recognized at once, Seidemann's daughter. Of course, you recognize her easily, but in view of Dragomirow you assume for a long time that she is playing a second part until, toward the middle of the act, you realize that she has disguised herself to save her beloved. The two in caftans are each supposed to testify individually, but that is very difficult for them as they have rehearsed it together. Also, they don't understand the judge's High German, although it is true that the defense attorney helps him out when he gets too involved, as he has to prompt him in other respects as well. Then comes Seidemann, who had already tried to direct the two in caftans by tugging at their clothes, and by his fluent, decisive speech, by his reasonable bearing, by correctly addressing the presiding judge in contrast to the former witnesses, makes a good impression which is in terrible contrast to what we know of him. His testimony is pretty much without content, unfortunately he knows very little about the whole case. But the last witness, the servant, is, though not entirely aware of it, Seidemann's real accuser. He had seen Seidemann buy the knife, he knows that at the crucial time Seidemann was at Edelmann's, he knows, finally, that Seidemann hates the Jews and especially Edelmann and wanted his notes. The two in caftans jump up and are happy to be able to confirm all this. Seidemann defends himself as a somewhat confused man of honor. Then the discussion turns to his daughter. Where is she? At home, naturally, and she'll bear him out. No, that she won't do, insists the defense attorney, and he will prove it, turns to the wall, takes off the wig and turns toward the horrified Seidemann in the person of his daughter. The clean whiteness of her upper lip looks threatening when she takes off the mustache. Seidemann has taken poison in order to escape the justice of this world, confesses his misdeeds, but hardly any longer to the people, rather to the Jewish God whom he now professes. Meanwhile the piano player has struck up a tune, the two in caftans feel moved by it and must start dancing. In the background stands the reunited bridal pair, they sing the melody, especially the serious bridegroom, in the customary old way.

First appearance of the two in caftans. They enter Seidemann's empty room with collection boxes for the temple, look around, feel ill at ease, look at each other. Feel along the doorposts with their hand, don't find a *mezuzah*.[20] None on the other doors, either. They don't want to believe it and jump up beside doors as if they were catching flies, jumping up and falling back, slapping the very tops of the doorposts again and again. Unfortunately all in vain. Up to now they haven't spoken a word.

Resemblance between Mrs. K. and last year's Mrs. W. Mrs. K. has a personality perhaps a trifle weaker and more monotonous, to make up for it she is prettier and more respectable. Mrs. W.'s standing joke was to bump her fellow players with her large behind. Besides, she had a worse singer with her and was quite new to us.

"Male impersonator" is really a false title. By virtue of the fact that she is stuck into a caftan, her body is entirely forgotten. She only reminds one of her body by shrugging her shoulder and twisting her back as though she were being bitten by fleas. The sleeves, though short, have to be pulled up a little every minute; this the spectator enjoys and even watches for it to happen, anticipating the great relief it will be for this woman who has so much to sing and to explain in the talmudic manner.

Would like to see a large Yiddish theater as the production may after all suffer because of the small cast and inadequate rehearsal. Also, would like to know Yiddish literature, which is obviously characterized by an uninterrupted tradition of national struggle that determines every work. A tradition, therefore, that pervades no other literature, not even that of the most oppressed people. It may be that other peoples in times of war make a success out of a pugnacious national literature, and that other works, standing at a greater remove, acquire from the enthusiasm of the audience a national character too, as is the case with *The Bartered Bride*, but here there appear to be only works of the first type, and indeed always.

The appearance of the simple stage that awaits the actors as silently as we. Since, with its three walls, the chair and the table, it will have to suffice for all the scenes, we expect nothing from it, rather with all our energy await the actors and are therefore unresistingly attracted by the singing from behind the blank walls that introduces the performance.

October 9. If I reach my fortieth year, then I'll probably marry an old maid with protruding upper teeth left a little exposed by the upper lip. The upper front teeth of Miss K., who was in Paris and London, slant toward each other a little like legs which are quickly crossed at the knees. I'll hardly reach my fortieth birthday, however; the frequent tension over the left half of my skull, for example, speaks against it—it feels like an inner leprosy which, when I only observe it and disregard its unpleasantness makes the same impression on me as the skull cross-sections in textbooks, or as an almost painless dissection of the living body where the knife—a little coolingly, carefully, often stopping and going back, sometimes lying still—splits still thinner the paper-thin integument close to the functioning parts of the brain.

Last night's dream which in the morning I myself didn't even consider beautiful except for a small comic scene consisting of two counterremarks which resulted in that tremendous dream satisfaction but which I have forgotten.

I walked—whether Max was there right at the start I don't know—through a long row of houses at the level of the first or second floor, just as one walks through a tunnel from one carriage to another. I walked very quickly, perhaps also because the house was so rickety that for that reason alone one hurried. The doors between the houses I did not notice at all, it was just a gigantic row of rooms, and yet not only the differences between the individual apartments but also between the houses were recognizable. They were perhaps all rooms with beds through which I went. One typical bed has remained in my memory. It stood at the side to the left of me against the dark or dirty wall, which sloped like an attic's, perhaps had a low pile of bedclothes, and its cover, really only a coarse sheet crumpled by the feet of the person who had slept here, hung down in a point. I felt abashed to walk through people's rooms at a time when many of them were still lying in their beds, therefore took long strides on tiptoes, by which I somehow or other hoped to show that I was passing through only by compulsion, was as considerate of every-thing as was at all possible, walked softly, and that my passing through did not, as it were, count at all. Therefore, too, I never turned my head in any one room and saw only either what lay on the right toward the street or on the left toward the back wall.

The row of houses was often interrupted by brothels; and although I was making this journey seemingly because of them, I walked through them especially quickly so that I remember nothing except that they were there. However, the last room of all the houses was again a brothel, and here I remained. The wall across from the door through which I entered, therefore the last wall of the row of houses, was either of glass or merely broken through, and if I had walked on I should have fallen. It is even more probable that it was broken through, for the whores lay toward the edge of the floor. Two I saw clearly on the ground, the head of one hung down a little over the edge into the open air. To the left was a solid wall, on the other hand the wall on the right was not finished, you could see down into the court, even if not to the bottom of it, and a ramshackle gray staircase led down in several flights. To judge by the light in the room the ceiling was like that in the other rooms.

I occupied myself chiefly with the whore whose head was hanging down, Max with the one lying beside her on the left. I fingered her legs and then for a long time pressed the upper parts of her thighs in regular rhythm. My pleas-ure in this was so great that I wondered that for this enter-tainment, which was after all really the most beautiful kind, one still had to pay nothing. I was convinced that I (and I alone) deceived the world. Then the whore, without moving her legs, raised the upper part of her body and turned her back to me, which to my horror was covered with large sealing-wax-red circles with paling edges, and red splashes scattered among them. I now noticed that her whole body was full of them, that I was pressing my thumb to her thighs in just such spots and that there were these little red particles—as though from a crumbled seal—on my fingers too.

I stepped back among a number of men who seemed to be waiting against the wall near the opening of the stairway, on which there was a small amount of traffic. They were waiting in the way men in the country stand together in the market place on Sunday morning. Therefore it was Sunday too. It was here that the comic scene took place, when a man I and Max had reason to be afraid of went away, then came up the stairs, then stepped up to me, and while I and Max anxiously expected some terrible threat from him, put a ridiculously simple-minded question to me. Then I stood there and with apprehension watched Max, who, without fear in this place, was sitting on the ground somewhere to the left eating a thick potato soup out of which the potatoes peeped like large balls, especially one. He pushed them down into the soup with his spoon, perhaps with two spoons, or just turned them.

October 10. Wrote a sophistic article for the *Tetschen-Bodenbacher Zeitung* for and against my insurance institute.

Yesterday evening on the Graben. Three actresses coming toward me from a rehearsal. It is so difficult quickly to become familiar with the beauty of three women when in addition you also want to look at two actors who are approaching behind them with that too-swinging actors' walk. The two—of whom the one on the left, with his fat, youthful face and open overcoat wrapped around his strong body, is representative enough of both—overtake the ladies, the one on the left on the sidewalk, the one on the right down in the roadway. The one on the left grasps his hat high up near the top, seizes it with all five fingers, raises it high and calls (the one on the right recollects himself only now): Goodbye! Good night! But while this overtaking and greeting has separated the gentlemen, the ladies addressed, as though led by the one nearest the roadway who seems to be the weakest and tallest but also the youngest and most beautiful, continue on their way quite undisturbed, with an easy greeting which scarcely interrupts their harmonious conversation. The whole thing seemed to me at the moment to be strong proof that theatrical affairs here are orderly and well conducted.

Day before yesterday among the Jews in Café Savoy. *Die Sedernacht* by Feimann. At times (at the moment the consciousness of this pierced me) we did not interfere in the plot only because we were too moved, not because we were mere spectators.

October 12. Yesterday at Max's wrote in the Paris diary.[21] In the half-darkness of Rittergasse, in her fall outfit, fat, warm R. whom we have known only in her summer blouse and thin, blue summer jacket, in which a girl with a not entirely faultless appearance is, after all, worse than naked. Then you really were able to see the large nose in her bloodless face and the cheeks to which you could have pressed your hands for a long time before any redness appeared, the heavy blond down which heaped itself up on the cheek and upper lip, the railroad dust which had strayed between the nose and cheek, and the sickly whiteness where her blouse was cut away. Today, however, we ran after her respectfully, and when I had to make my farewells at the entrance to a house that went through to Ferdinand-strasse (I was unshaven and otherwise shabby in appearance), I afterward felt a few slight impulses of affection for her. And when I considered why, I had to keep telling myself: because she was so warmly dressed.

October 13. Inaesthetic transition from the taut skin of my boss's bald spot to the delicate wrinkles of his forehead. An obvious, very easily imitated fault of nature, bank notes should not be made so.

I didn't consider the description of R. good, but nevertheless it must have been better than I thought, or my impression of R. the day before yesterday must have been so incomplete that the description was adequate to it or even surpassed it. For when I went home last night the description came to my mind for a moment, imperceptibly replaced the original impression and I felt that I had seen R. only yesterday, and indeed without Max, so that I prepared myself to tell him about her just as I have described her here for myself.

Yesterday evening on Schützen Island, did not find my colleagues and left immediately. I made some stir in my short jacket with my crushed soft hat in my hand, because it was cold out, but too hot inside from the breath of the beer drinkers, smokers and the wind instrument players of the military band. This band was not very high up, could not be, either, because the hall is pretty low, and filled the one end of the hall to the side walls. The mass of musicians was crowded into this end of the room as though cut to size. This crowded impression was then lost a little in the hall, as the places near the band were pretty empty and the hall filled up only toward the middle.

Talkativeness of Dr. K. Walked around with him for two hours behind the Franz-Josef railroad station, begged him from time to time to let me leave, had clasped my hands in impatience and listened as little as possible. It seemed to me that a person who is good at his job, when he has got himself involved in talking shop, must become irresponsible; he becomes conscious of his proficiency, there are associations with every story, and indeed several, he surveys them all because he has experienced them, must in haste and out of consideration for me suppress many, some I also destroy by asking questions but remind him by these of others, show him thereby that he is also in control deep into my own thinking, he himself plays in most of the stories a handsome role which he just touches upon, because of which the suppressed seems even more significant to him, now he is however so certain of my admiration that he can also complain, for even in his misfortune, his trouble, his doubt, he is admirable, his opponents are also capable people and worth talking about; in an attorney's office which had four clerks and two chiefs there was a controversy in which he alone opposed this office, for weeks the daily subject of discussion of the six lawyers. Their best speaker, a sharp lawyer, opposed him—to this is attached the Supreme Court whose decisions are allegedly bad, contradictory; in a tone of farewell I say a word of defense for this court, now he produces proofs that the court cannot be defended, and once more we must walk up and down the street, I am immediately surprised at the badness of this court, whereupon he explains to me why it must be so, the court is overburdened, why and how, well, I must leave, but now the Court of Appeals is better and the Court of Administration much better still, and why and how, finally I can't be detained any longer, whereupon he brings in my own affairs (setting up the factory), which is what I had come to him about and which we had already fully discussed, he unconsciously hopes in this way to trap me and to be able to tempt me back to his stories again. I say something, but while speaking I hold out my hand in farewell and so escape.

He is a very good storyteller, by the way, in his stories the detailed expansiveness of the brief is mixed with the vivacious speech that one often finds in such fat, black Jews, healthy for the present, of medium height, excited by continuous smoking of cigarettes. Legal expressions give the speech steadiness, paragraphs are numbered to a high count that seems to banish them into a distance. Each story is developed from its very beginning, speech and counterspeech are produced and, as it were, shuffled up by personal asides, matters that are beside the point, that no one would think of, are first mentioned, then called beside the point and set aside ("A man, his name is beside the point"), the listener is personally drawn in, questioned, while alongside the plot of the story thickens, sometimes, preliminary to a story which cannot interest him at all, the listener is even questioned, uselessly of course, in order to establish some sort of provisional connection, the listener's interjected remarks are not immediately introduced, which would be annoying (Kubin), but are shortly put in the right place as the story goes on, so that the listener is flattered and drawn into the story and given a special right to be a listener.

October 14. Yesterday evening at the Savoy. *Sulamith* by A. Goldfaden. Really an opera, but every sung play is called an operetta, even this trifle seems to me to point to an artistic endeavor that is stubborn, hasty and passionate for the wrong reasons, that cuts across European art in a direction that is partly arbitrary.

The story: A hero saves a girl who is lost in the desert ("I pray thee, great, almighty God") and because of the torments of thirst has thrown herself into a well. They swear to be true to each other ("My dear one, my loved one, my diamond found in the desert") by calling upon the well and a red-eyed desert cat in witness. The girl, Sulamith (Mrs. Ts.), is taken back to Bethlehem to her father, Manoach (Ts.), by Cingitang, the savage servant of Absalom (P.), while Absalom (K.) goes on another journey to Jerusalem; there, however, he falls in love with Abigail, a rich girl of Jerusalem (Mrs. K.), forgets Sulamith and marries. Sulamith waits for her lover at home in Bethlehem. "Many people go to *Yerusholaim* and arrive *beshulim*." "He, the noble one, will be untrue to me!" By means of despairing outbursts she gains a confidence prepared for anything and determines to feign insanity in order not to have to marry and to be able to wait. "My will is of iron, my heart I make a fortress." And even in the insanity which she now feigns for years she enjoys sadly and aloud all her memories of her lover, for her insanity is concerned only with the desert, the well and the cat. By means of her insanity she immediately repels her three suitors with whom Manoach was able to get along in peace only by organizing a lottery: Joel Gedoni (U.), "I am the most powerful Jewish hero," Avidanov, the landowner (R.P.), and the potbellied priest, Nathan (Löwy), who feels superior to everyone, "Give her to me, I die for her." Absalom suffered a misfortune, one of his children was bitten to death by a desert cat, the other falls into a well. He remembers his guilt, confesses all to Abigail. "Restrain your crying." "Cease with your words to split my heart." "Alas, it is all *emes* that I speak." Some ideas seem on the point of taking shape around the two and then disappear. Is Absalom to return to Sulamith and desert Abigail? Sulamith too deserves *rachmones*. Finally Abigail releases him. In Bethlehem Manoach laments over his daughter: "Alas, oh, the years of my old age." Absalom cures her with his voice. "The rest, Father, I will tell thee later." Abigail collapses there in the Jerusalem vineyard, Absalom has as justification only his heroism.

At the end of the performance we still expect the actor Löwy, whom I would admire in the dust. He is supposed, as is customary, "to announce": "Dear guests, I thank you in all our names for your visit and cordially invite you to tomorrow's performance, when the world-famous masterpiece —— by —— will be produced. Until we meet again!" Exit with a flourish of his hat. Instead, we see the curtain first held tightly closed, then tentatively drawn apart a little. This goes on quite awhile. Finally it is drawn wide open, in the middle a button holds it together, behind it we see Löwy walking toward the footlights and, his face turned to us, the audience, defending himself with his hands against someone who is attacking him from behind, until suddenly the whole curtain with its wire supports on top is pulled down by Löwy who is looking for something to hold on to. Before our eyes P., who had played the savage and who is still bowed down as if the curtain were drawn, grabs Löwy (who is on his knees) by his head and pushes him sideways off the stage. Everyone runs together into the wing of the theater. "Close the curtain!" they shout on the almost completely exposed stage on which Mrs. Ts., with her pale Sulamith face, is standing pitiably. Little waiters on tables and chairs put the curtain somewhat in order, the landlord tries to calm the government representative who, however, wants only to get away and is being held back by this attempt to calm him, behind the curtain one hears Mrs. Ts.: "And we who claim to preach morals to the public from the stage. . . ." The association of Jewish office workers, Zukunft, which took over the next night under its own direction and before tonight's performance had held a regular membership meeting, decides because of this occurrence to call a special meeting within half an hour, a Czech member of the association prophesies complete ruin for the actors as a result of their scandalous behavior. Then suddenly one sees Löwy, who seemed to have disappeared, pushed toward a door by the headwaiter, R., with his hands, perhaps also with his knees. He is simply being thrown out. This headwaiter, who before and later stands before every guest, before us as well, like a dog, with a doglike muzzle which sags over a large mouth closed by humble wrinkles on the side, has his——

October 16. Strenuous Sunday yesterday. The whole staff gave Father notice. By soft words, cordiality, effective use of his illness, his size and former strength, his experience, his cleverness, he wins almost all of them back in group and individual discussions. An important clerk, F., wants time until Monday to think it over because he has given his word to our manager who is stepping out and would like to take the whole staff along into his newly-to-be established business. On Sunday the bookkeeper writes he cannot remain after all, R. will not release him from his promise.

I go to see him in Žižkov. His young wife with round cheeks, longish face and a small, thick nose of the sort that never spoils Czech faces. A too-long, very loose, flowered and spotted housecoat. It seems especially long and loose because she moves especially hurriedly in order to greet me, to place the album properly on the table in a final straightening of the room and to disappear in order to have her husband called. The husband enters with similar hurried movements, perhaps imitated by his very dependent wife, the upper part of his body bent forward and his arms swinging rapidly like pendulums while the lower part is noticeably behind it. Impression of a man you have known for ten years, seen often, regarded little, with whom you suddenly come into a closer relationship. The less success I have with my Czech arguments (indeed, he already had a signed contract with R., he was just so embarrassed by my father Saturday evening that he had not mentioned the contract), the more catlike his face becomes. Toward the end I act a little with a very pleasurable feeling, so I look silently around the room with my face drawn rather long and my eyes narrowed, as though I were pursuing something significant into the ineffable. Am, however, not unhappy when I see that it has little effect and that I, instead of being spoken to by him in a new tone, must begin afresh to persuade him. The conversation was begun with the fact that on the other side of the street another T. lives, it was concluded at the door with his surprise at my thin clothes in the cold weather. Indicative of my first hopes and final failure. I made him promise, however, to come to see Father in the afternoon. My arguments in places too abstract and formal. Mistake not to have called his wife into the room.

Afternoon to Radotin to keep the clerk. Miss, as a result, the meeting with Löwy of whom I think incessantly. In the carriage: pointed nose of the old woman with still almost youthful, taut skin. Does youth therefore end at the tip of the nose and death begin there? The swallowing of the passengers that glides down their throats, the widening of their mouths as a sign that in their judgment the railroad journey, the combination of the other passengers, their seating arrangements, the temperature in the carriage, even the copy of *Pan* that I hold on my knees and that several glance at from time to time (as it is after all something that they would not have expected in the compartment), are harmless, natural, unsuspicious, while at the same time they still believe that everything could have been much worse.

Up and down in Mr. H.'s yard, a dog puts his paw on the tip of my foot which I shake. Children, chickens, here and there adults. A children's nurse, occasionally leaning on the railing of the *Pawlatsche* [22] or hiding behind a door, has her eye on me. Under her eyes I do not know just what I am, whether indifferent, embarrassed, young or old, impudent or devoted, holding my hands behind or before me, animal lover or man of affairs, friend of H. or supplicant, superior to those gathered at the meeting who sometimes go from the tavern to the pissoir and back in an unbroken line, or ridiculous to them because of my thin clothes, Jew or Christian, etc. The walking around, wiping my nose, occasional reading of *Pan*, timid avoiding of the *Pawlatsche* with my eyes only suddenly to see that it is empty, watching the poultry, being greeted by a man, seeing through the tavern window the flat faces of the men set crookedly close together and turned toward a speaker, everything contributes to it. Mr. H. leaves the meeting from time to time and I ask him to use his influence for us with the clerk whom he had brought into our office. Black-brown beard growing around cheeks and chin, black eyes, between eyes and beard the dark shadings of his cheeks. He is a friend of my father's, I knew him even as a child and the idea that he was a coffee-roaster always made him even darker and more manly for me than he was.

October 17. I finish nothing because I have no time and it presses so within me. If the whole day were free and this morning restlessness could mount within me until midday and wear itself out by evening, then I could sleep. This way, however, there is left for this restlessness only an evening twilight hour at most, it gets somewhat stronger, is then suppressed, and uselessly and injuriously undermines the night for me. Shall I be able to bear it long? And is there any purpose in bearing it, shall I, then, be given time?

Napoleon is reminiscing at the royal table in Erfurt: When I was still a mere lieutenant in the Fifth Regiment . . . (the royal highnesses look at each other in embarrassment, Napoleon notices it and corrects himself), when I still had the honor to be a mere lieutenant. . . . When I think of this anecdote the arteries in my neck swell with the pride that I can easily feel with him and that vicariously thrills through me.

Again in Radotin: freezing, I then walked around alone in the garden, then recognized in an open window the children's nurse who had walked to this side of the house with me.

October 20. The 18th at Max's; wrote about Paris. Wrote badly, without really arriving at that freedom of true description which releases one's foot from the experienced.

I was also dull after the great exaltation of the previous day that had ended with Löwy's lecture. During the day I was not yet in any unusual frame of mind, went with Max to meet his mother who was arriving from Gablonz, was in the coffeehouse with them and then at Max's, who played a gypsy dance from *La Jolie Fille de Perth* for me. A dance in which for pages only the hips rock gently in a monotonous ticking and the face has a slow, cordial expression. Until finally, toward the end, briefly and late, the inner wildness that has been tempted outward arrives, shakes the body, overpowers it, compresses the melody so that it beats into the heights and depths (unusually bitter, dull tones are heard in it) and then comes to an unheeded close. At the beginning, and unmistakable through it all, a strong feeling of closeness to gypsydom, perhaps because a people so wild in the dance shows its tranquil side only to a friend. Impression of great truth of the first dance. Then leafed through *Aussprüche Napoleons*. How easily you become for the moment a little part of your own tremendous notion of Napoleon! Then, already boiling, I went home, I couldn't withstand one of my ideas, disordered, pregnant, disheveled, swollen, amidst my furniture which was rolling about me; overwhelmed by my pains and worries, taking up as much space as possible, for despite my bulk I was very nervous, I entered the lecture hall. From the way in which I was sitting, for instance, and very truly sat, I should as a spectator immediately have recognized my condition.

Löwy read humorous sketches by Sholom Aleichem, then a story by Peretz, the *Lichtverkäuferin* by Rosenfeld, a poem by Bialik (the one instance where the poet stooped from Hebrew to Yiddish, himself translating his original Hebrew poem into Yiddish, in order to popularize this poem which, by making capital out of the Kishinev pogrom, sought to further the Jewish cause). A recurrent widening of the eyes, natural to the actor, which are then left so for a while, framed by the arched eyebrows. Complete truth of all the reading; the weak raising of the right arm from the shoulder, the adjusting of the pince-nez that seems borrowed for the occasion, so poorly does it fit the nose; the position under the table of the leg that is stretched out in such a way that the weak joint between the upper and lower parts of the leg is particularly in motion; the crook of the back, weak and wretched-looking since the unbroken surface of a back cannot deceive an observer in the way that a face does, with its eyes, the hollows and projections of its cheeks, or even with some trifle be it only a stubble of beard. After the reading, while still on my way home, I felt all my abilities concentrated, and on that account complained to my sisters, even to my mother, at home.

On the 19th at Dr. K.'s about the factory. The little theoretical hostility that is bound to arise between contracting parties when contracts are being made. The way my eyes searched H.'s face, which was turned toward the lawyers. This hostility is bound to arise all the more between two people who otherwise are not accustomed to think through their mutual relationship and therefore make difficulties about every trifle. Dr. K.'s habit of walking diagonally up and down the room with the tense, forward rocking of the upper part of his body, as though in a drawing-room, at the same time telling stories and frequently, at the end of a diagonal, shaking off the ash of his cigarette into one of the three ash trays placed about the room.

This morning at N. N. Co. The way the boss leans back sideways in his armchair in order to get room and support for the Eastern Jewish gestures of his hand. The interaction and reciprocal re-enforcement of the play of his hands and face. Sometimes he combines the two, either by looking at his hands, or for the convenience of the listener, holding them close to his face. Temple melodies in the cadence of his speech; the melody is led from finger to finger as though through various registers, especially when enumerating several points. Then met Father at the Graben with Mr. Pr., who raises his hand to make his sleeve fall back a little (since he doesn't himself want to draw back the sleeve) and there in the middle of the Graben makes powerful screwing motions by opening up his hand and letting it fall away with the fingers spread.

I am probably sick, since yesterday my body has been itching all over. In the afternoon my face was so hot and blotched that I was afraid the assistant giving me a haircut, who could see me and my reflected image all the time, would recognize that I had a serious disease. Also the connection between stomach and mouth is partly disturbed, a lid the size of a gulden moves up or down, or stays down below from where it exerts an expanding effect of light pressure that spreads upward over my chest.

More on Radotin: Invited her to come down. The first answer was serious although until then, together with the girl entrusted to her, she had giggled and flirted across at me in a way she would never have dared from the moment we became acquainted. We then laughed a great deal together although I was freezing down below and she up above at the open window. She pressed her breasts against her crossed arms and, her knees apparently bent, pressed her whole body against the window sill. She was seventeen years old and took me to be fifteen or sixteen,[23] I couldn't make her change her mind throughout our entire conversation. Her small nose was a little crooked and threw an unusual shadow across her cheek, which, to be sure, wouldn't help me to recognize her again. She was not from Radotin but from Chuchle (the next station on the way to Prague), which she wouldn't let me forget.

Then a walk with the clerk (who even without my trip would have remained with our firm) in the dark out of Radotin on the highway and back to the railroad station. On one side waste hills used by a cement factory for its supply of chalky sand. Old mills. Story of a poplar whirled out of the earth by a tornado. Face of the clerk: doughlike reddish flesh on heavy bones, looks tired but robust within his limits. Does not show surprise even by his voice that we are walking here together. A clear moon over a large field, the chimney smoke looking like clouds in the light; the field, right in the middle of the town, bought up as a precaution by a factory but left unused for the time being, surrounded by factory buildings which were strongly but only partly lit up by electric lights. Train signals. Scuffling of rats near the path worn across the field by the townspeople in defiance of the will of the factory.

Examples of the way this writing, which is on the whole trivial, strengthens me after all:

Monday, the 16th, I was with Löwy at the National Theater to see *Dubrovačka Trilogjia*. Play and production were hopeless. Of the first act I remember the beautiful chime of a mantel clock; the singing of the "Marseillaise" by Frenchmen marching outside the window, the fading song is repeatedly taken up by the newcomers and rises again; a girl dressed in black carries her shadow through the streak of light that the setting sun throws on the parquet floor. Of the second act only the delicate throat of a girl, which rises out of shoulders dressed in red-brown, expands from between puffed sleeves and lengthens into a small head. Of the third act the crushed Prince Albert, the dark fancy vest of an old, stooped descendant of the former gospodars with the gold watch chain drawn diagonally across it. So it is not much. The seats were expensive, I was a poor benefactor to have thrown money away here while L. was in need; finally he was even somewhat more bored than I. In short, I had again demonstrated the misfortune that follows every undertaking that I begin by myself. But while I usually unite myself indivisibly with this misfortune, attract all earlier cases of misfortune up to me, all later ones down to me, I was this time almost completely independent, bore everything quite easily as something that happens just once, and for the first time in the theater even felt my head, as the head of a spectator, raised high out of the collective darkness of the seat and the body into a distinct light, independent of the bad occasion of this play and this production.

A second example: Yesterday evening I simultaneously held out both my hands to my two sisters-in-law on Mari-engasse with a degree of adroitness as if they were two right hands and I a double person.

October 21. A counterexample: When my boss confers with me about office matters (today the filing cabinet), I cannot look him in the eye for long without there coming into my eyes against my will a slight bitterness which forces either my look or his away. His look yields more

briefly but more often to every impulse to look away, since
he is not aware of the reason, but his glance immediately
returns as he considers it all only a momentary fatigue of
his eyes. I defend myself against it more vigorously, therefore hasten the zigzagging of my glance, look by prefer-
ence along his nose and across to the shadows of his cheeks,
often only keep my face toward him by the aid of the teeth
and tongue in my tight-shut mouth—when I must, I lower
my eyes, to be sure, but never farther than to his tie, but
get the most direct look immediately after he turns his eyes
away, when I follow him closely and without consideration.

The Jewish actors. Mrs. Tschissik has protuberances on
her cheeks near her mouth. Caused in part by hollow
cheeks as a result of the pains of hunger, childbed, journeys
and acting, in part by the relaxed unusual muscles she had
to develop for the actor's movements of her large, what
originally must have been a heavy mouth. Most of the time,
as Sulamith, she wore her hair loose, which covered her
cheeks so that her face sometimes looked like the face of
a girl out of the past. She has a large, bony, moderately
robust body and is tightly laced. Her walk easily takes on
a solemnity since she has the habit of raising, stretching and
slowly moving her long arms. Especially when she sang the
Jewish national anthem, gently rocked her large hips and
moved her arms, bent parallel to her hips, up and down with
hands cupped as though she were playing with a slowly flying ball.

October 22. Yesterday with the Jews. *Kol Nidre* by
Scharkansky, pretty bad play with a good, witty letter-
writing scene, a prayer by the lovers standing up beside

each other with hands clasped, the converted Grand Inquisitor pressing himself against the curtain of the Ark of the Covenant, he mounts the stairs and remains standing there, his head bowed, his lips against the curtain, holds the prayer book before his chattering teeth. For the first time on this fourth evening my distinct inability to get a clear impression. Our large company and the visits at my sisters' table were also responsible for it. Nevertheless, I needn't have been so weak. With my love for Mrs. Ts., who only thanks to Max sat beside me, I behaved wretchedly. I'll recover again, however, even now I feel better.

Mrs. Tschissik (I enjoy writing the name so much) likes to bow her head at the table even while eating roast goose, you believe you can get in under her eyelids with your glance if you first carefully look along her cheeks and then, making yourself small, slip in, in doing which you don't even first have to raise the lids, for they are raised and even let a bluish gleam through which lures you on to the attempt. Out of her truthful acting flourishes of her fist now and then emerge, turns of her arm that drape invisible trains about her body, she places her outspread fingers on her breast because the artless shriek does not suffice. Her acting is not varied: the frightened look at her antagonist, the seeking for a way out on the small stage, the soft voice that, without being raised, mounts heroically in even, short ascents aided only by a greater inner resonance, the joy that spreads through her face across her high forehead into her hair; the self-sufficiency and independence of all other means when she sings solos, the holding herself erect when she resists that compels the spectator to devote his attention to her whole body—but not much more. But there is the truth of the whole and as a result the conviction that the least of her effects cannot be taken from her, that she is independent of the play and of us.

The sympathy we have for these actors who are so good, who earn nothing and who do not get nearly enough gratitude and fame is really only sympathy for the sad fate of many noble strivings, above all of our own. Therefore, too, it is so immoderately strong, because on the surface it is attached to strangers and in reality belongs to us. Nevertheless, in spite of everything, it is so closely bound up with the actors that I cannot disengage it even now. Because I recognize this and in spite of it this sympathy attaches itself even more closely to them.

The striking smoothness of Mrs. Tschissik's cheeks alongside her muscular mouth. Her somewhat shapeless little girl.

Walking with Löwy and my sister for three hours.

October 23. The actors by their presence always convince me to my horror that most of what I've written about them until now is false. It is false because I write about them with steadfast love (even now, while I write it down, this too becomes false) but varying ability and this varying ability does not hit off the real actors loudly and correctly but loses itself dully in this love that will never be satisfied with the ability and therefore thinks it is protecting the actors by preventing this ability from exercising itself.

Quarrel between Tschissik and Löwy. Ts.: Edelstatt is the greatest Jewish writer. He is sublime. Rosenfeld is of course also a great writer, but not the foremost. Löwy: **Ts.**

is a socialist and because Edelstatt writes socialist poems, because he is editor of a Jewish socialist newspaper in London, therefore Ts. considers him the greatest. But who is Edelstatt, his party knows him, no one else, but the world knows Rosenfeld.—Ts.: It is not a question of recognition. Everything of Edelstatt's is sublime.—L.: Of course, I'm well acquainted with him too. The *Selbstmörder*, for example, is very good.—Ts.: What's the use of arguing. We won't agree. I'll repeat my opinion until tomorrow and you the same.—L.: I until the day after tomorrow.

Goldfaden, married, spendthrift, even if terribly badly off. About a hundred pieces. Stolen liturgical melodies made popular. The whole people sings them. The tailor at his work (is imitated), the maid, etc.

With so little room for dressing you are bound, as Ts. says, to get into quarrels. You come off the stage excited, everyone considers himself the greatest actor, then if someone, for example, steps on someone else's foot, which cannot be avoided, not only a quarrel but a good battle is ready to break out. But in Warsaw there were seventy-five small, individual dressing rooms, each one with light.

At six o'clock I met the actors in their coffeehouse seated around two tables, divided into the two hostile groups. A book by Peretz was on the table of the Ts. group. Löwy had just shut it and stood up to leave with me.

Until the age of twenty Löwy was a *bocher* who studied and spent the money of his well-to-do father. There was a society of young people of the same age who met in a locked tavern precisely on Saturday and, dressed in their caftans, smoked and otherwise sinned against the Sabbath commandments.

"The great Adler" from New York, the most famous Yiddish actor, who is a millionaire, for whom Gordin wrote *Der Wilde Mensch* and whom Löwy in Karlsbad had asked not to come to the performance because he didn't have the courage to act in his presence on their poorly equipped stage.—Real sets, not this miserable stage on which you cannot move. How shall we play the wild man! You need a sofa for it. In the Crystal Palace in Leipzig it was magnificent. Windows you could open, the sun shone in, you needed a throne in the play, good, there was a throne, I walked toward it through the crowd and was really a king. It is much easier to act there. Here everything confuses you.

October 24. Mother works all day, is merry and sad as the fancy strikes her, without taking advantage of her own condition in the slightest, her voice is clear, too loud for ordinary speech but does you good when you are sad and suddenly hear it after some time. For a long time now I have been complaining that I am always ill, but never have any definite illness that would compel me to go to bed. This wish certainly goes back chiefly to the fact that I know how comforting Mother can be when, for example, she comes from the lighted living room into the twilight of the sick room, or in the evening, when the day begins to change monotonously into night, returns from business and with her concerns and hurried instructions once more causes the day, already so late, to begin again and rouses the invalid to help her in this. I should wish that for myself

once more, because then I should be weak, therefore convinced by everything my mother did, and could enjoy
childish pleasure with age's keener capacity for gratifica-
tion. Yesterday it occurred to me that I did not always
love my mother as she deserved and as I could, only because the German language prevented it. The Jewish
mother is no "Mutter," to call her "Mutter" makes her a
little comic (not to herself, because we are in Germany),
we give a Jewish woman the name of a German mother,
but forget the contradiction that sinks into the emotions
so much the more heavily, "Mutter" is peculiarly German
for the Jew, it unconsciously contains, together with the
Christian splendor Christian coldness also, the Jewish
woman who is called "Mutter" therefore becomes not
only comic but strange. Mama would be a better name if
only one didn't imagine "Mutter" behind it. I believe that
it is only the memories of the ghetto that still preserve the
Jewish family, for the word "Vater" too is far from meaning the Jewish father.

Today I stood before Counselor L., who asked about
my illness unexpectedly, uninvited, childishly, lyingly, ridiculously and to the point where I lost patience. We
hadn't spoken so intimately for a long time, or perhaps
never at all—I felt my face, which had never before been
so closely observed by him, reveal parts to him in spurious
frankness that he hardly understood but that nevertheless
surprised him. I was unrecognizable to myself. I know
him quite well.

October 26. Thursday. All afternoon yesterday Löwy
read from *Gott, Mensch, Teufel* by Gordin and then from
his own Paris diaries. The day before yesterday I saw the

performance of *Der Wilde Mensch* by Gordin. Gordin is
better than Lateiner, Scharkansky, Feimann, etc., because
he has more detail, more order and more logical sequence
in this order, he therefore somehow lacks the immediate
Jewishness that is always being improvised in other plays,
the clamor of this Jewishness rings more dully and therefore in less detail. Of course, concessions are made to the
audience and sometimes you believe you must stretch in
order to see the play over the heads of the Jewish theater
audience of New York (the character of the wild man, the
whole story of Mrs. Selde), but worse is the fact that palpable concessions are made also to some vaguely felt art;
for example, in *Der Wilde Mensch* the plot rambles as a
result of hesitancy, the wild man delivers speeches hu-
manly unintelligible but dramatically so clumsy that one
would prefer to close one's eyes, the same is true of the
older girl in *Gott, Mensch, Teufel*. Parts of the plot of *Der
Wilde Mensch* are very spirited. A young widow marries
an old man with four children and immediately brings her
lover, Vladimir Vorobeitchik, along into the marriage.
The two proceed to ruin the whole family, Shmul Leiblich
(Pipes) must hand over all his money and becomes sick,
the oldest son, Simon (Klug), a student, leaves the house,
Alexander becomes a gambler and drunkard, Lise (Tschissik) becomes a prostitute and Lemech (Löwy), the idiot,
is driven to idiotic insanity by hate of Mrs. Selde, because
she takes the place of his mother, and by love, because she
is the first young woman to whom he feels close. At this
point the plot reaches a climax with the murder of Selde by
Lemech. All the others remain incomplete and helpless in
the spectator's memory. The conception of this woman
and her lover, a conception that asks no one's opinion, gave
me a vague, different self-confidence.

The discreet impression made by the playbill. One learns not only the names but a little more, yet only so much as the audience has to know, even a very cool audience with the best intentions, about a family exposed to their judgment. Shmul Leiblich is a "rich merchant," however, it is not said that he is old and infirm, that he is a ridiculous ladies' man, a bad father and an irreverent widower who remarries on the anniversary of his wife's death. And yet all these characterizations would be more accurate than that on the playbill, for at the end of the play he is no longer rich, because the Selde woman has thoroughly robbed him, he is also hardly a merchant any longer, since he has neglected his business. Simon is "a student" on the playbill, therefore something very vague, something we know many sons of our most distant acquaintances are. Alexander, this characterless young man, is just "Alexander," of Lise, the home-loving girl, we know also only that she is "Lise." Lemech is unfortunately "an idiot," for that is something that cannot be hushed up. Vladimir Vorobeitchik is only "Selde's lover," but not the corrupter of a family, not a drunkard, gambler, wastrel, idler, parasite. In the characterization, "Selde's lover," much of course is betrayed, but considering his behavior it is the least that can be said. In addition to this the scene of action is Russia, the scarcely assembled characters are scattered over a tremendous area, or assembled in a small, unrevealed place in this area, in short, the play has become impossible, the spectator will get to see nothing.

—Nevertheless, the play begins, the obviously great powers of the author begin to work, things come to light which one would not expect of the characters on the playbill but which fall to their lot with the greatest inevitability if one can only persuade oneself to believe in all the whipping, snatching away, beating, slapping on the shoulder, fainting, throat-cutting, limping, dancing in Russian top boots, dancing with raised skirts, rolling on the sofa, which are after all things that it does no good to contradict. Yet not even the climax of the spectator's excitement, remembered afterward, is necessary in order to recognize that the discreet impression made by the playbill is a false impression which can be formed only after the performance, and then is already inaccurate, yes, impossible, an impression which can originate only in some tired outsider, since for one who judges honestly no decent relationship can be seen between the playbill and the play after its performance.

From the dash on, written in despair, because today they are playing cards with unusual uproar, I must sit at the common table, O. laughs with all her mouth, gets up, sits down, reaches across the table, speaks to me, and I, to complete the misfortune, write so badly and must think of Löwy's Paris recollections, well-written with an uninterrupted feeling, which come out of an independent fire while I, at least now (mostly, I am certain, because I have so little time), am almost entirely under Max's influence, which sometimes, to cap it all, even spoils my enjoyment of his work as well. Because it consoles me I write down an autobiographical remark of Shaw's, although it actually is the opposite of consoling: As a boy he was apprentice in the office of a real-estate agency in Dublin. He soon gave up this position, went to London and became a writer. In the first nine years, from 1876 to 1885, he earned 140 kronen in all. "But although I was a strong young man and my family found itself in poor circumstances, I did not throw myself into the struggle for a livelihood; I threw my mother in and let her support me. I was no support for

my old father, on the contrary, I hung on to his coattails."
In the end this is little consolation for me. The free years
he spent in London are already past for me, the possible
happiness becomes ever more impossible, I lead a horrible
synthetic life and am cowardly and miserable enough to
follow Shaw only to the extent of having read the passage
to my parents. How this possible life flashes before my
eyes in colors of steel, with spanning rods of steel and airy
darkness between!

October 27. Löwy's stories and diaries: How Notre
Dame frightens him, how the tiger in the Jardin des Plantes
affects him as an image of one who despairs and hopes, ap-
peasing his despair and hope with food, how his pious
father in misapprehension questions him as to whether he
can now go for walks on Saturday, whether he now has
time to read modern books, whether he now may eat on
the fast days, while as a matter of fact he must work on
Saturdays, has no time for anything and fasts more than
any religion prescribed. When he walks through the
streets chewing his black beard it looks from a distance as
though he were eating chocolate. The work in the cap factory and his friend the socialist who considers everyone a
bourgeois who does not work exactly the way he does—
such as Löwy with his fine hands—who is bored on Sun-
days, who despises reading as something luxurious, cannot
read himself and ironically asks Löwy to read him a letter
that he had received.

The Jewish ritual bath that every Jewish community in
Russia has, which I picture to myself as a cabin with a basin
of exactly determined outline, with arrangements appointed and supervised by the rabbi, which must only

wash the earthly dirt from the soul, whose external condition is therefore a matter of indifference, that is, a symbol, therefore can be, and is, filthy and stinking, but still fulfils its purpose. The woman comes here to purify herself of her period, the Torah scribe to purify himself of all sinful thoughts before writing the last verse of a section of the Torah.

Custom, immediately after awakening, to dip the fingers three times in water, as the evil spirits have settled during the night on the second and third joints of the fingers. Rationalist explanation: To prevent the fingers directly touching the face, since, uncontrolled during sleep and dreams, they could after all have touched every possible part of the body, the armpits, the behind, the genitals.

The dressing room behind their stage is so narrow that if by chance you are standing in front of the mirror behind the portière on the set and someone else wants to pass by, he must raise the curtain and willy-nilly show himself for a moment to the audience.

Superstition: The evil spirits gain entry into a person who drinks out of an imperfect glass.

How bruised the actors appeared to me after the performance, how I feared to touch them with a word. How instead I quickly left after a hasty handshake, as though I were angry and dissatisfied, because the truth of my impression was so impossible to express. Everyone seemed false to me except Max, who quietly made some meaningless remark. And the person who asked about some irrelevant detail was false, the person who gave a facetious reply to a remark by an actor, the ironic one and the one who began to explain his varied impressions, all the rabble that had been crowded into the back of the auditorium where it belonged and now, late at night, got up and once more became aware of its importance. (Very far from correct.)

October 28. Of course, I had a similar feeling, but neither acting nor play came anywhere near seeming perfect to me that evening. For that very reason I owed the actors particular respect. When there are small, even if many deficiencies in one's impression, who knows whose fault they are? Mrs. Tschissik once stepped on the hem of her dress and tottered for a moment in her princess-style hussy's dress like a massive pillar, once she made a mistake in her lines and in order to calm her tongue turned in great agitation toward the back wall, despite the fact that this did not quite suit the words; it irritated me, but it did not prevent the sudden flutter of a shudder upon my cheekbone, which I always feel when I hear her voice. But because my acquaintances had got a much less pure impression than I, they seemed to me to owe even greater respect, because in my opinion their respect would have been much more effective than mine, so that I had double reason to curse their behavior.

"Axioms for the Drama" by Max in the *Schaubühne*. Has quite the character of a dream truth, which the expression "axioms" suits too. The more dreamlike it inflates itself, all the more coolly must you seize it. The following principles are formulated:

The thesis is, that the essence of the drama lies in a lack.

The drama (on the stage) is more exhaustive than the

novel, because we see everything about which we otherwise just read.

It only seems to be, for in the novel the author can show us only what is important, in the drama, on the other hand, we see everything, the actor, the settings, and so not just what is important, therefore less. From the point of view of the novel, therefore, the best drama would be entirely unstimulating, for example, a philosophical drama that would be read by seated actors in any set at all that represented a room.

And yet the best drama is that which is the most stimulating in time and space, frees itself of all the demands of life, limits itself only to the speeches, to the thoughts in the monologues, to the main points of what happens, everything else is left to the stimulation that has been aroused, and, raised high on a shield borne by the actors, painters, directors, obeys only its most extreme inspirations.

Error in this chain of reasoning: It changes its point of view without indicating it, sees things now from the writer's room, now from the audience. Granted that the audience does not see everything from the point of view of the author, that even he is surprised by the performance (October 29, Sunday), it is still the author who had the play with all its details within himself, who moved along from detail to detail, and who only because he assembled all the details in the speeches has given them dramatic weight and force. Because of this the drama in its highest development achieves an unbearable humanization which it is the task of the actor—with his role blowing loosely and in tatters about him—to draw down, to make bearable. The drama therefore hovers in the air, but not like a roof carried along on a storm, rather like a whole building whose foundation walls have been torn up out of the earth with a force which today is still close to madness.

Sometimes it seems that the play is resting up in the flies, the actors have drawn down strips of it the ends of which they hold in their hands or have wound about their bodies for the play, and that only now and then a strip that is difficult to release carries an actor, to the terror of the audience, up in the air.

I dreamed today of a donkey that looked like a greyhound, it was very cautious in its movements. I looked at it closely because I was aware how unusual a phenomenon it was, but remember only that its narrow human feet could not please me because of their length and uniformity. I offered it a bunch of fresh, dark-green cypress leaves which I had just received from an old Zurich lady (it all took place in Zurich), it did not want it, just sniffed a little at it; but then, when I left the cypress on a table, it devoured it so completely that only a scarcely recognizable kernel resembling a chestnut was left. Later there was talk that this donkey had never yet gone on all fours but always held itself erect like a human being and showed its silvery shining breast and its little belly. But actually that was not correct.

Besides this, I dreamed about an Englishman whom I met at a meeting like the one the Salvation Army held in Zurich. There were seats there like those in school, under the blackboard there was even an open shelf; once when I reached in to straighten something I wondered at the ease with which one makes friends on a trip. By this apparently was meant the Englishman, who shortly thereafter approached me. He had loose, light clothes in very good condition, but high up on the back of the arms, instead of the material of the clothing, or at least sewn on over it, there was a gray, wrinkled material, hanging a little, torn in strips, stippled as though by spiders, that reminded one as much of the leather re-enforcements on riding breeches as of the sleeve protectors of seamstresses, salesgirls, clerks. His face was also covered with a gray material that had very clever slits for mouth, eyes, probably also for the nose. But this material was new, napped, rather like flannel, very flexible and soft, of excellent English manufacture. All this pleased me so, that I was eager to become acquainted with the man. He wanted to invite me to his house too, but since I had to leave as soon as the day after tomorrow, that came to nothing. Before he left the meeting he put on several more apparently very practical pieces of clothing that made him look quite inconspicuous after he had buttoned them. Although he could not invite me to his home, he nevertheless asked me to go into the street with him. I followed him, we stopped across the street from the meeting place on the curb, I below, he above, and found again after some discussion that nothing could be done about the invitation.

Then I dreamed that Max, Otto [24] and I had the habit of packing our trunks only when we reached the railroad station. There we were, carrying our shirts, for example, through the main hall to our distant trunks. Although this seemed to be a general custom, it was not a good one in our case, especially since we had begun to pack only shortly before the arrival of the train. Then we were naturally excited and had hardly any hope of still catching the train, let alone getting good seats.

Although the regular guests and employees of the

coffeehouse are fond of the actors, they cannot remain respectful amid the depressing impressions, and despise the actors as starvelings, tramps, fellow Jews, exactly as in the past. Thus, the headwaiter wanted to throw Löwy out of the hall, the doorman, who used to work in a brothel and is now a pimp, shouted little Tschissik down when she, in the excitement of her sympathy during *Der Wilde Mensch*, wanted to pass something to the actors, and the day before yesterday, when I accompanied Löwy back to the coffeehouse after he had read me the first act of Gordin's *Eliezar ben Schevia* in the City Café, that fellow called to him (he squints, and between his crooked, pointed nose and his mouth there is a hollow out of which a small mustache bristles): "Come on, idiot. (Allusion to the role in *Der Wilde Mensch*.) Someone's waiting. There's a visitor you really don't deserve. An officer candidate in the artillery is here. Look." And he points to one of the curtained coffeehouse windows behind which the officer candidate is allegedly sitting. Löwy passes his hand over his forehead: "From Eliezar ben Schevia to this."

The sight of stairs moves me so today. Early in the day already, and several times since, I have enjoyed the sight from my window of the triangular piece cut out of the stone railing of the staircase that leads down on the right from the Czech Bridge to the quay level. Very steep, as though it were giving only a hasty suggestion. And now, over there across the river, I see a stepladder on the slope that leads down to the water. It has always been there, but is revealed only in the autumn and winter by the removal of the swimming school in front of it, and it lies there in the dark grass under the brown trees in the play of perspective.

Löwy: Four young friends became great Talmud scholars in their old age. But each had a different fate. One became mad, one died, Rabbi Eliezar became a free-thinker at forty and only the oldest one, Akiva, who had not begun his studies until the age of forty, achieved complete knowledge. The disciple of Rabbi Eliezar was Rabbi Meyer, a pious man whose piety was so great that he was not harmed by what the free-thinker taught him. He ate, as he said, the kernel of the nut, the shell he threw away. Once, on Saturday, Eliezar went for a ride, Rabbi Meyer followed on foot, the Talmud in his hand, of course only for two thousand paces, for you are not permitted to go any farther on Saturday. And from this walk emerged a symbolic demand and the reply to it. Come back to your people, said Rabbi Meyer. Rabbi Eliezar refused with a pun.

October 30. This craving that I almost always have, when for once I feel my stomach is healthy, to heap up in me notions of terrible deeds of daring with food. I especially satisfy this craving in front of pork butchers. If I see a sausage that is labeled as an old, hard sausage, I bite into it in my imagination with all my teeth and swallow quickly, regularly and thoughtlessly, like a machine. The despair that this act, even in the imagination, has as its immediate result, increases my haste. I shove the long slabs of rib meat unbitten into my mouth, and then pull them out again from behind, tearing through stomach and intestines. I eat dirty delicatessen stores completely empty. Cram myself with herrings, pickles and all the bad, old, sharp foods. Bonbons are poured into me like hail from their tin boxes. I enjoy in this way not only my healthy condition but also a suffering that is without pain and can pass at once.

It is an old habit of mine, at the point when an impression has reached its greatest degree of purity, whether of joy or pain, not to allow it to run its salutary course through all my being, but rather to cloud and dispel its purity by new, unexpected, weak impressions. It is not that I evilly intend my own harm, I am only too weak to bear the purity of that impression. Instead of admitting this weakness, which alone would be right, because in revealing itself it calls forth other forces to its support, I rather quietly and with seeming arbitrariness try to evoke new impressions in an effort to help myself.

On Saturday evening, for example, after hearing Miss T.'s [25] excellent story, which after all belongs more to Max, at least belongs to him to a greater extent than one of his own stories, and later after hearing the excellent play *Konkurrenz* by Baum, in which dramatic force can be seen in the work and in the effect quite as uninterruptedly as in the production of a living craftsman, after the hearing of both these works I was so cast down and my insides, already fairly empty for several days, quite without warning filled with such deep sorrow that I declared to Max on the way home that nothing can come of "Richard and Samuel." For this declaration too, not the smallest courage was needed at the time, as far as either I or Max was concerned. The discussion that followed confused me a little, as "Richard and Samuel" was then far from being my chief concern and I therefore did not find the right answers to Max's objections. But later, when I was alone, and not only the disturbance of my sorrow by the conversation but also the almost effective consolation of Max's presence had disappeared, my hopelessness grew to such an extent that it began to dissolve my thinking (at this point, while I am stopping for dinner, Löwy comes to the house and interrupts me and delights me from seven to ten o'clock). Still, instead of waiting at home for what would happen next, I carelessly read two issues of *Aktion*, a little in *Die Missge-schickten*,[26] finally also in my Paris notes, and went to bed, really more content than before, but obdurate. It was the same several days ago when I returned from a walk and found myself imitating Löwy to such a degree that the force of his enthusiasm, externally, worked toward my goal. Then, too, I read and spoke a great deal in confusion at home and slowly collapsed.

October 31. Despite the fact that today I have read here and there in the Fischer catalogue, in the *Insel Almanach*, in the *Rundschau*, I am now pretty sure that, whether I have assimilated everything either thoroughly or casually, I have in any case defended myself against all harm. And I should have enough self-confidence tonight if I didn't have to go out with Löwy again.

When on Sunday afternoon, just after passing three women, I stepped into Max's house, I thought: There are still one or two houses in which I have something to do, there are still women walking behind me who can see me turn in on a Sunday afternoon at a house door in order to work, talk, purposefully, hurriedly, only occasionally looking at the matter in this way. This must not remain so for long.

I read the stories of Wilhelm Schäfer, especially when aloud, with the same attentive enjoyment that I should get from drawing a piece of twine over my tongue. At first I did not like Valli [27] very much yesterday afternoon, but after I had lent her *Die Missgeschickten* and she had already read it a little while and must already have been properly under the influence of the story, I loved her because of this influence and caressed her.

In order not to forget it, should my father once again call me a bad son, I write it down that, in the presence of several relatives, without special occasion, whether it may have been simply to put me in my place, whether it was supposedly to rescue me, he called Max a *"meshuggener ritoch,"* [28] and that yesterday, when Löwy was in my room, ironically shaking his body and contorting his mouth, he referred to these strange people who were being let into the house, what could interest one in a strange person, why one enters into such useless relationships, etc. After all, I should not have written it down, for I have written myself almost into a hatred of my father, for which after all he has given no occasion today and which, at least as far as Löwy is concerned, is out of all proportion to what I have written down as having been said by my father, and which even increases because I cannot remember what was really wicked in my father's behavior yesterday.

November 1. Today, eagerly and happily began to read the *History of the Jews* by Graetz. Because my desire for it had far outrun the reading, it was at first stranger to me than I thought, and I had to stop here and there in order by resting to allow my Jewishness to collect itself. Toward the end, however, I was already gripped by the imperfection of the first settlements in the newly conquered Canaan and the faithful handing down of the imperfections of the popular heroes (Joshua, the Judges, Elijah).

Last night, goodbye to Mrs. Klug. We, I and Löwy, ran alongside the train and saw Mrs. Klug looking out from the darkness behind a closed window in the last coach. She quickly stretched her arm toward us while still in her compartment, stood up, opened the window, filling it for a moment with her unbuttoned cloak, until the dark Mr. Klug (all he can do is open up his mouth wide and bitterly and then snap it shut, as though forever) got up opposite her. During the fifteen minutes I spoke very little to Mr. Klug and looked at him for perhaps only two seconds, otherwise I could not, during the weak, uninterrupted conversation, turn my eyes away from Mrs. Klug. She was completely under the domination of my presence, but more in her imagination than in reality. When she turned to Löwy with the repeated introductory phrase, "You, Löwy," she spoke to me, when she leaned close against her husband who sometimes left her with only her right shoulder showing at the window and pressed against her dress and her baggy overcoat, she was attempting in that way to make me an empty sign.

The first impression I had at the performances, that she did not like me especially, was probably correct, she seldom invited me to sing with her; when, without real feeling, she asked me something, I unfortunately answered incorrectly ("Do you understand that?" "Yes," I said, but she wanted "No" in order to reply, "Neither do I"); she did not offer me her picture postcards a second time, I preferred Mrs. Tschissik, to whom I wanted to give some flowers in order to spite Mrs. Klug. To this disinclination, however, was joined a respect for my doctorate which was not impaired by my childish appearance, indeed, it was even increased by it. This respect was so great and it became so articulate in her frequent but by no means particularly stressed way of addressing me—"You know, Herr Doktor"—that I half unconsciously regretted that I deserved it so little and asked myself whether I had a right to be addressed like that by everyone. But while I was so respected by her as a person, as a spectator I was even more respected. I beamed when she sang, I laughed and looked at her all the time while she was on the stage, I sang the tunes with her, later the words, I thanked her after several performances; because of this, again, she naturally liked me very well. But if she spoke to me out of this feeling I was so embarrassed that she undoubtedly fell back into her original disinclination and remained there. She had to exert herself all the more to reward me as a spectator, and she was glad to do it because she is a vain actress and a good-natured woman.

She looked at me, especially when she was silent up there in the window of the compartment, with a mouth rapturously contorted by embarrassment and slyness and with twinkling eyes that swam on the wrinkles spreading from her mouth. She must have believed I loved her, as was indeed true, and with these glances she gave me the sole fulfilment that a young but experienced woman, a good wife and mother, could give to a doctor of her imagination. These glances were so urgent, and were supported by expressions like "There were such nice guests here, especially some of them," that I defended myself, and those were the moments when I looked at her husband. I had, when I compared the two, an unjustified sense of astonishment at the fact that they should depart from us together and yet concern themselves only with us and have no glance for one another. Löwy asked whether they had good seats. "Yes, if it remains as empty as this," Mrs. Klug answered, and looked casually into the inside of the compartment the warm air of which her husband will spoil with his smoking. We spoke of their children for whose sake they were leaving; they have four children, three boys among them, the oldest is nine years old, they haven't seen them for eighteen months now. When a gentleman got hurriedly into a nearby compartment, the train seemed about to leave, we quickly said goodbye, shook each other's hands, I tipped my hat and then held it against my chest, we stepped back as one does when trains leave, by which one means to show that everything is finished and one has come to terms with it. The train did not leave yet, however, we stepped up close again, I was rather happy about it, she asked after my sisters. Surprisingly, the train began to move slowly. Mrs. Klug prepared to wave her handkerchief, I must write her, she called, do I know her address, she was already too far away for me to be able to answer her, I pointed to Löwy from whom I could get the address, that's good, she nodded to me and him quickly, and let her handkerchief float in the wind, I tipped my hat, at first awkwardly, then, the farther away she was, the more freely.

Later I remembered that I had had the impression that the train was not really leaving but only moving the short length of the railroad station in order to put on a play for us, and then was swallowed up. In a doze that same evening, Mrs. Klug appeared to me unnaturally short, almost without legs, and wrung her hands with her face distorted as though a great misfortune had befallen her.

This afternoon the pain occasioned by my loneliness came upon me so piercingly and intensely that I became aware that the strength which I gain through this writing thus spends itself, a strength which I certainly have not intended for this purpose.

As soon as Mr. Klug comes to a new city one can see how his and his wife's jewels disappear into the pawnshop. As their departure draws near he gradually redeems them again.

Favorite saying of the wife of the philosopher Mendelssohn: *Wie mies ist mir vor tout l'univers!*

One of the most important impressions at the departure of Mrs. Klug: I was always forced to think that, as a simple middle-class woman, she holds herself by force below the level of her true human destiny and requires only a jump, a tearing open of the door, a turned-up light, in order to be an actress and to subjugate me. Actually, even, she stood above and I below, as in the theater.—She married at sixteen, is twenty-six years old.

November 2. This morning, for the first time in a long time, the joy again of imagining a knife twisted in my heart.

In the newspapers, in conversation, in the office, the impetuosity of language often leads one astray, also the hope, springing from temporary weakness, for a sudden and stronger illumination in the very next moment, also mere strong self-confidence, or mere carelessness, or a great present impression that one wishes at any cost to shift into the future, also the opinion that true enthusiasm in the present justifies any future confusion, also delight in sentences that are elevated in the middle by one or two jolts and open the mouth gradually to its full size even if they let it close much too quickly and tortuously, also the slight possibility of a decisive and clear judgment, or the effort to give further flow to the speech that has really ended, also the desire to escape from the subject in a hurry, one's belly if it must be, or despair that seeks a way out for its heavy breath, or the longing for a light without shadow —all this can lead one astray to sentences like: "The book which I have just finished is the most beautiful I have ever read," or, "is more beautiful than any I have ever read."

In order to prove that everything I write and think about them is false, the actors (aside from Mr. and Mrs. Klug) have again remained here, as Löwy, whom I met yesterday evening, told me; who knows whether for the same reason they will not depart again today, for Löwy did not call at the office despite the fact that he promised to.

November 3. In order to prove that both things that I wrote were false, a proof that seems almost impossible, Löwy himself came yesterday evening and interrupted me while I was writing.

N.'s habit of repeating everything in the same tone of voice. He tells someone a story about his business, of course not with so many details that it would in itself completely kill the story, but nevertheless in a slow manner, thorough only because of that, it is a communication which is not intended to be anything else and is therefore done with when it is finished. A short time passes with something else, suddenly he finds a transition to his story and produces it again in its old form, almost without additions, but also almost without omissions, with the innocence of a person who carries about the room a ribbon that someone has treacherously tied to his back. Now my parents like him particularly, therefore feel his habit more strongly than they notice it, and so it happens that they, especially my mother, unconsciously give him opportunities to repeat. If some evening the moment for repeating a story cannot quite be found, then Mother is there, she asks a question, and indeed with a curiosity that does not end even after the question is asked, as one might expect. As for stories that have already been repeated and could not return again by their own strength, Mother hunts after them with her questions even several evenings later. N.'s habit is, however, so obsessive that it often has the power to justify itself completely. No one else gets with such regular frequency into the position of having to tell members of the family individually a story that basically concerns all of them. The story must then be told, almost as often as there are persons, to the family circle that in such cases assembles slowly, at intervals, one person at a time. And because I am the one who alone has recognized N.'s habit, I am also usually the one who hears the story first and for whom the repetitions provide only the small pleasure of confirming an observation.

Envy at nominal success of Baum whom I really like so much. With this, the feeling of having in the middle of my body a ball of wool that quickly winds itself up, its innumerable threads pulling from the surface of my body to itself.

Löwy. My father about him: "Whoever lies down with dogs gets up with fleas." I could not contain myself and said something uncontrolled. To which Father with unusual quietness (to be sure, after a long interval which was otherwise occupied): "You know that I should not get excited and must be treated with consideration. And now you speak to me like that. I really have enough excitement, quite enough. So don't bother me with such talk." I say: "I make every effort to restrain myself," and sense in my father, as always in such extreme moments, the existence of a wisdom of which I can grasp only a breath.

Death of Löwy's grandfather, a man who had an open hand, knew several languages, had made long journeys deep into Russia and who once on a Saturday refused to eat at the house of a wonder-rabbi in Ekaterinoslav because the long hair and colored neckerchief of the rabbi's son made him suspect the piety of the house.

The bed was set up in the middle of the room, the candlesticks were borrowed from friends and relatives, the room therefore full of the light and smoke of the candles. Some forty men stood around his bed all day to receive inspiration from the death of a pious man. He was conscious until the end and at the right moment, his hand on his breast, he began to repeat the death prayers. During his suffering and after his death the grandmother, who was with the women gathered in the next room, wept incessantly, but while he was dying she was completely calm because it is a commandment to ease the death of the dying man as much as one can. "With his own prayers he passed away." He was much envied for this death that followed so pious a life.

Pesach festival. An association of rich Jews rents a bakery, its members take over for the heads of the families all the tasks of producing the so-called eighteen-minute matzos: the fetching of water, the koshering, the kneading, the cutting, the piercing.

November 5. Yesterday slept, with Löwy after *Bar Kokhba* from seven on, read a letter from his father. Evening at Baum's.

I want to write, with a constant trembling on my forehead. I sit in my room in the very headquarters of the uproar of the entire house. I hear all the doors close, because
of their noise only the footsteps of those running between
them are spared me, I hear even the slamming of the oven
door in the kitchen. My father bursts through the doors of
my room and passes through in his dragging dressing
gown, the ashes are scraped out of the stove in the next
room, Valli asks, shouting into the indefinite through the
anteroom as though through a Paris street, whether Father's hat has been brushed yet, a hushing that claims to be
friendly to me raises the shout of an answering voice. The
house door is unlatched and screeches as though from a
catarrhal throat, then opens wider with the brief singing
of a woman's voice and closes with a dull manly jerk that
sounds most inconsiderate. My father is gone, now begins
the more delicate, more distracted, more hopeless noise led
by the voices of the two canaries. I had already thought of
it before, but with the canaries it comes back to me again,
that I might open the door a narrow crack, crawl into the
next room like a snake and in that way, on the floor, beg
my sisters and their governess for quiet.

The bitterness I felt yesterday evening when Max read
my little automobile story at Baum's. I was isolated from
everyone and in the face of the story I kept my chin
pressed against my breast, as it were. The disordered sentences of this story with holes into which one could stick
both hands; one sentence sounds high, one sentence sounds
low, as the case may be; one sentence rubs against another
like the tongue against a hollow or false tooth; one sentence comes marching up with so rough a start that the
entire story falls into sulky amazement; a sleepy imitation

of Max (reproaches muffled—stirred up) seesaws in, sometimes it looks like a dancing course during its first quarter-hour. I explain it to myself by saying that I have too little time and quiet to draw out of me all the possibilities of my talent. For that reason it is only disconnected starts that always make an appearance, disconnected starts, for instance, all through the automobile story. If I were ever able to write something large and whole, well shaped from beginning to end, then in the end the story would never be able to detach itself from me and it would be possible for me calmly and with open eyes, as a blood relation of a healthy story, to hear it read, but as it is, every little piece of the story runs around homeless and drives me away from it in the opposite direction.—At the same time I can still be happy if this explanation is correct.

Performance of Goldfaden's *Bar Kokhba*. False judgment of the play throughout the hall and on the stage.

I had brought along a bouquet for Mrs. Tschissik, with an attached visiting card inscribed "in gratitude," and waited for the moment when I could have it presented to her. The performance had begun late, Mrs. Tschissik's big scene was promised me only in the fourth act, in impatience and fear that the flowers might wilt I had them unwrapped by the waiter as early as during the third act (it was eleven o'clock), they lay on a table, the kitchen help and several dirty regular guests handed them from one to another and smelled them, I could only look on worriedly and angrily, nothing else, I loved Mrs. Tschissik during her big scene in the prison, but still, I was anxious for her to bring it to its end, finally the act, unnoticed by me in my distraction, was finished, the headwaiter handed up the flowers, Mrs. Tschissik took them between final curtains, she bowed in a narrow opening of the curtains and did not return again. No one noticed my love and I had intended to reveal it to all and so make it valuable in the eyes of Mrs. Tschissik, the bouquet was hardly noticed. Meanwhile it was already past two o'clock, everyone was tired, several people had already left, I should have enjoyed throwing my glass at them.

With me was Comptroller P. from our firm, a Gentile. He, whom I usually like, disturbed me. My worry was the flowers, not his affairs. At the same time I knew that he understood the play incorrectly, while I had no time, desire or ability to force upon him assistance which he did not think he needed. Finally I was ashamed of myself before him because I myself was paying so little attention. Also he disturbed me in my conversation with Max and even by the recollection that I had liked him before, would again like him afterward, and that he could take my behavior today amiss.

But not only I was disturbed. Max felt responsible because of his laudatory article in the paper. It was getting too late for the Jews in Bergmann's convoy. The members of the Bar Kokhba Association had come because of the name of the play and could not help being disappointed. From what I know of Bar Kokhba from this play, I would not have named any association after him. In the back of the hall there·were two shopgirls in their best clothes with their sweethearts and had to be silenced by loud shouts during the death scenes. Finally people on the street struck the huge panes in annoyance that they saw so little of the stage.

The two Klugs were missing from the stage. Ridiculous extras. "Vulgar Jews," as Löwy said. Traveling salesmen who weren't paid. Most of the time they were concerned only with concealing their laughter or enjoying it, even if aside from this they meant well. A round-cheeked fellow with a blond beard at the sight of whom you could scarcely keep from laughing looked especially funny when he laughed. His false beard shook unnaturally, because of his laughter it was no longer pasted in its right place on his cheeks. Another fellow laughed only when he wanted to, but then a lot. When Löwy died, singing, in the arms of these two elders and was supposed to slip slowly to earth with the fading song, they put their heads together behind his back in order finally to be able to laugh their fill for once, unseen by the audience (as they thought). Yesterday, when I remembered it at lunch, I still had to laugh.

Mrs. Tschissik in prison must take the helmet off the drunken Roman governor (young Pipes) who is visiting her and then put it on herself. When she takes it off, a crushed towel falls out which Pipes had apparently stuffed in because the helmet pinched too much. Although he certainly must have known that the helmet would be taken off his head on the stage, he looks reproachfully at Mrs. Tschissik, forgetting his drunkenness.

Beautiful: the way Mrs. Tschissik, under the hands of the Roman soldiers (whom, however, she first had to pull to her, for they obviously were afraid to touch her), writhed while the movements of the three actors by her care and art almost, only almost, followed the rhythm of the singing; the song in which she proclaims the appearance of the Messiah, and, without destroying the illusion, sheerly by the spell she casts, represents the playing of a harp by the motions of bowing a violin; in the prison where at the frequent approach of footsteps she breaks off her song of lamentation, hurries to her treadmill and turns it to the accompaniment of a work song, then again escapes to her song and again to the mill, the way she sings in her sleep when Papus visits her and her mouth is open like a twinkling eye, the way in general the corners of her mouth in opening remind one of the corners of her eyes. In the white veil, as in the black, she was beautiful.

New among her familiar gestures: pressing her hand deep into her not very good bodice, abrupt shrug of her shoulders and hips in scorn, especially when she turns her back on the one scorned.

She led the whole performance like the mother of a family. She prompted everyone but never faltered herself; she instructed the extras, implored them, finally shoved them if need be; her clear voice, when she was off stage, joined in the ragged chorus on stage; she held up the folding screen (which in the last act was supposed to represent a citadel) that the extras would have knocked down ten times.

I had hoped, by means of the bouquet of flowers, to appease my love for her a little, it was quite useless. It is possible only through literature or through sleeping together. I write this not because I did not know it, but rather because it is perhaps well to write down warnings frequently.

November 7. Tuesday. Yesterday the actors and Mrs. Tschissik finally left. I went with Löwy to the coffee-house in the evening, but waited outside, did not want to go in, did not want to see Mrs. Tschissik. But while I was walking up and down I saw her open the door and come out with Löwy, I went toward them with a greeting and met them in the middle of the street. Mrs. Tschissik thanked me for my bouquet in the grand but natural vocables of her speech, she had only just now learned that it was from me. This liar Löwy had therefore said nothing to her. I was worried about her because she was wearing only a thin, dark blouse with short sleeves and I asked her—I almost touched her in order to force her—to go into the restaurant so that she would not catch cold. No, she said, she does not catch cold, indeed she has a shawl, and she raised it a little to show it and then drew it together more closely about her breast. I could not tell her that I was not really concerned about her but was rather only happy to have found an emotion in which I could enjoy my love, and therefore I told her again that I was worried.

Meanwhile her husband, her little girl and Mr. Pipes had also come out and it turned out that it had by no means been decided that they would go to Brünn as Löwy had convinced me, on the contrary, Pipes was even determined to go to Nuremberg. That would be best, a hall would be easy to get, the Jewish community is large, moreover, the trip to Leipzig and Berlin very comfortable. Furthermore they had discussed it all day and Löwy, who had slept until four, had simply kept them waiting and made them miss the seven-thirty for Brünn. Amidst these arguments we entered the tavern and sat down at a table, I across from Mrs. Tschissik. I should so have liked to distinguish myself, this would not have been so difficult, I should just have had to know several train connections, tell the railroad stations apart, bring about a choice between Nuremberg and Brünn, but chiefly shout down Pipes who was behaving like his Bar Kokhba. To Pipes' shouting Löwy very reasonably, if unintentionally, counterposed a very quick, uninterruptable chatter in his normal voice that was, at least for me, rather incomprehensible at the time. So instead of distinguishing myself I sat sunk in my chair, looked from Pipes to Löwy, and only now and then caught Mrs. Tschissik's eye on the way, but when she answered me with her glance (when she smiled at me because of Pipes' excitement, for instance) I looked away. This had its sense. Between us there could be no smiling at Pipes' excitement. Facing her, I was too serious for this, and quite tired by this seriousness. If I wanted to laugh at something I could look across her shoulder at the fat woman who had played the governor's wife in *Bar Kokhba*. But really I could not look at her seriously either. For that would have meant that I loved her. Even young Pipes behind me, in all his innocence, would have had to recognize that. And that would have been really unheard of. A young man whom everyone takes to be eighteen years old declares in the presence of the evening's guests at the Café Savoy, amidst the surrounding waiters, in the presence of the table full of actors, declares to a thirty-year-old woman whom hardly anyone even considers pretty, who has two children, ten and eight years old, whose husband is sitting beside her, who is a model of respectability and economy—declares to this woman his love to which he has completely fallen victim and, now comes the really remarkable part which of course no one else would have observed, immediately renounces the woman, just as he would renounce her if she were young and single. Should I be grateful or should I curse the fact that despite all misfortune I can still feel love, an unearthly love but still for earthly objects.

Mrs. Tschissik was beautiful yesterday. The really normal beauty of small hands, of light fingers, of rounded forearms which in themselves are so perfect that even the unaccustomed sight of this nakedness does not make one think of the rest of the body. The hair separated into two waves, brightly illumined by the gaslight. Somewhat bad complexion around the right corner of her mouth. Her

mouth opens as though in childish complaint, running
above and below into delicately shaped curves, one im-
agines that the beautiful shaping of words, which spreads
the light of the vowels throughout the words and preserves
their pure contours with the tip of the tongue, can succeed
only once, and admires how everlasting it is. Low, white
forehead. The powdering that I have so far seen I hate, but
if this white color, this somewhat cloudy milk-colored veil
hovering low over the skin is the result of powder, then
every woman should powder. She likes to hold two fingers
to the right corner of her mouth, perhaps she even stuck
the tips of her fingers into her mouth—yes, perhaps she
even put a toothpick into her mouth; I didn't look closely
at these fingers, but it seemed almost as though she were
poking in a hollow tooth with a toothpick and let it stay
there a quarter of an hour.

November 8. All afternoon at the lawyer's about the
factory.

The girl who only because she was walking arm in arm
with her sweetheart looked quietly around.

The clerk in N.'s office reminded me of the actress who
played Manette Salomon at the Odéon in Paris a year and a
half ago. At least when she was sitting. A soft bosom,
broader than it was high, encased in a woolly material. A
broad face down to the mouth, but then rapidly narrowing. Neglected, natural curls in a flat hair-do. Zeal and
calm in a strong body. The resemblance was strengthened
too, as I see now, because she worked on unmoved (the
keys flew—Oliver system—on her typewriter like old-time
knitting needles), also walked about, but scarcely spoke

two words in half an hour, as though she had Manette Salomon within her.

When I was waiting at the lawyer's I looked at the one typist and thought how hard it was to make out her face even while looking at it. The relationship between a hairdo standing out almost at the same distance all around her head, and the straight nose that most of the time seemed too long, was especially confusing. When the girl who was reading a document made a more striking movement, I was almost confounded by the observation that through my contemplation I had remained more of a stranger to the girl than if I had brushed her skirt with my little finger.

When the lawyer, in reading the agreement [about the shares in the factory] to me, came to a passage concerning my possible future wife and possible children, I saw across from me a table with two large chairs and a smaller one around it. At the thought that I should never be in a position to seat in these or any other three chairs myself, my wife and my child, there came over me a yearning for this happiness so despairing from the very start that in my excitement I asked the lawyer the only question I had left after the long reading, which at once revealed my complete misunderstanding of a rather long section of the agreement that had just been read.

Continuation of the farewell: In Pipes, because I felt oppressed by him, I saw first of all the jagged and darkly spotted tips of his teeth. Finally I got half an idea: "Why go as far as Nuremberg in one jump?" I asked. "Why not give one or two performances at a smaller way station?"

"Do you know one?" asked Mrs. Tschissik, not nearly as sharply as I write it, and in this way forced me to look at her. All that part of her body which was visible above the table, all the roundness of shoulders, back and breast, was soft despite her (in European dress, on the stage) bony, almost coarse build. Ridiculously, I mentioned Pilsen. Some regular guests at the next table very reasonably mentioned Teplitz. Mr. Tschissik would have been in favor of any way station, he has confidence only in small undertakings, Mrs. Tschissik agreed without their having consulted much with one another, aside from that she asks around about the fares. Several times they said that if they just earned enough for *parnusse*,[29] it would be sufficient. Her daughter rubs her cheek against her arm; she certainly does not feel it, but to the adult there comes the childish conviction that nothing can happen to a child who is with its parents, even if they are traveling actors, and that if you think about it, real troubles are not to be met with so close to the earth but only at the height of an adult's face. I was very much in favor of Teplitz because I could give them a letter of recommendation to Dr. P. and so use my influence for Mrs. Tschissik. In face of the objection of Pipes, who himself prepared the lots to be drawn for the three possible cities and conducted the drawing with great liveliness, Teplitz was drawn for the third time. I went to the next table and excitedly wrote the letter of recommendation. I took my leave with the excuse that I had to go home to get the exact address of Dr. P., which was not necessary, however, and which they didn't know at home, either. In embarrassment, while Löwy prepared to accompany me, I played with the hand of the woman, the chin of her little girl.

November 9. A dream the day before yesterday: Everything theater, I now up in the balcony, now on the stage, a girl whom I had liked a few months ago was playing a part, tensed her lithe body when she held on to the back of a chair in terror; from the balcony I pointed to the girl who was playing a male role, my companion did not like her. In one act the set was so large that nothing else was to be seen, no stage, no auditorium, no dark, no footlights; instead, great crowds of spectators were on the set which represented the Altstädter Ring, probably seen from the opening of Niklasstrasse. Although one should really not have been able to see the square in front of the Rathaus clock and the small Ring, short turns and slow rockings of the stage floor nevertheless made it possible to look down, for example, on the small Ring from Kinsky Palace. This had no purpose except to show the whole set whenever possible, since it was already there in such perfection anyhow, and since it would have been a crying shame to miss seeing any of this set which, as I was well aware, was the most beautiful set in all the world and of all time. The lighting was that of dark, autumnal clouds. The light of the dimmed sun was scatteredly reflected from one or another stained-glass window on the southeast side of the square. Since everything was executed in life size and without the smallest false detail, the fact that some of the casement windows were blown open and shut by the slight breeze without a sound because of the great height of the houses, made an overwhelming impression. The square was very steep, the pavement almost black, the Tein Church was in its place, but in front of it was a small imperial castle in the courtyard of which all the monuments that ordinarily stood in the square were assembled in perfect order: the Pillar of St. Mary, the old fountain in front of the Rathaus that I myself have never seen, the fountain before the Niklas Church, and a board fence that has now been put up around the excavation for the Hus memorial.

They acted—in the audience one often forgets that it is only acting, how much truer is this on the stage and behind the scenes—an imperial fete and a revolution. The revolution, with huge throngs of people sent back and forth, was probably greater than anything that ever took place in Prague; they had apparently located it in Prague only because of the set, although really it belonged in Paris. Of the fete one saw nothing at first, in any event, the court had ridden off to a fete, meanwhile the revolution had broken out, the people had forced its way into the castle, I myself ran out into the open right over the ledges of the fountain in the churchyard, but it was supposed to be impossible for the court to return to the castle. Then the court carriages came from Eisengasse at so wild a pace that they had to brake while still far from the castle entrance, and slid across the pavement with locked wheels. They were the sort of carriages—one sees them at festivals and processions—on which living tableaux are shown, they were therefore flat, hung with garlands of flowers, and from the carriage floors a colored cloth covering the wheels hung down all around. One was all the more aware of the terror that their speed indicated. As though unconsciously, the horses, which reared before the entrance, pulled the carriages in a curve from Eisengasse to the castle. Just then many people streamed past me out into the square, mostly spectators whom I knew from the street and who perhaps had arrived this very moment. Among them there was also a girl I know, but I do not know which; beside her walked a young, elegant man in a yellowish-brown ulster with small checks, his right hand deep in his pocket. They walked toward Niklasstrasse. From this moment on I saw nothing more.

Schiller some place or other: The chief thing is (or something similar) "to transform emotion into character."

November 11. Saturday. Yesterday all afternoon at Max's. Decided on the sequence of the essays for "The Beauty of Ugly Pictures." Without good feeling. It is just then, however, that Max loves me most, or does it only seem so because then I am so clearly conscious how little deserving I am. No, he really loves me more. He wants to include my "Brescia" in the book too.[30] Everything good in me struggles against it. I was supposed to go to Brünn with him today. Everything bad and weak in me held me back. For I cannot believe that I shall really write something good tomorrow.

The girls, tightly wrapped up in their work aprons, especially behind. One at Löwy's and Winterberg's this morning whose apron flaps, which closed only on her behind, did not tie together as they usually do, but instead closed over each other so that she was wrapped up like a child in swaddling clothes. Sensual impression like that which, even unconsciously, I always had of children in swaddling clothes who are so squeezed in their wrappings and beds and so laced with ribbons, quite as though to satisfy one's lust.

Edison, in an American interview, told of his trip through Bohemia, in his opinion the relatively higher development of Bohemia (in the suburbs there are broad streets, gardens in front of the houses, in traveling through the country you see factories being built) is due to the fact that the emigration of Czechs to America is so large, and

that those returning from there one by one bring new am-
bition back.

As soon as I become aware in any way that I leave abuses
undisturbed which it was really intended that I should correct (for example, the extremely satisfied, but from my
point of view dismal life of my married sister), I lose all
sensation in my arm muscles for a moment.

I will try, gradually, to group everything certain in me,
later the credible, then the possible, etc. The greed for
books is certain in me. Not really to own or to read them,
but rather to see them, to convince myself of their actuality
in the stalls of a bookseller. If there are several copies of the
same book somewhere, each individual one delights me. It
is as though this greed came from my stomach, as though
it were a perverse appetite. Books that I own delight me
less, but books belonging to my sisters do delight me. The
desire to own them is incomparably less, it is almost absent.

November 12. Sunday. Yesterday lecture by Richepin:
"La légende de Napoléon" in the Rudolphinum. Pretty
empty. As though on sudden inspiration to test the manners
of the lecturer, a large piano is standing in the way between
the small entrance door and the lecturer's table. The lecturer enters, he wants, with his eyes on the audience, to
reach his table by the shortest route, therefore comes close
to the piano, is startled, steps back and walks around it
softly without looking at the audience again. In the enthusiasm at the end of his speech and in the loud applause,
he naturally forgot the piano, as it did not call attention to
itself during the lecture. With his hands on his chest he
wants to turn his back on the audience as late as possible,

therefore takes several elegant steps to the side, naturally bumps gently into the piano and, on tiptoe, must arch his back a little before he gets into the clear again. At least that is the way Richepin did it.

A tall, powerful man of fifty with a waistline. His hair is stiff and tousled (Daudet's, for example) although pressed fairly close to his skull. Like all old Southerners with their thick nose and the broad, wrinkled face that goes with it, from whose nostrils a strong wind can blow as from a horse's muzzle, and of whom you know very well that this is the final state of their faces, it will not be replaced but will endure for a long time; his face also reminded me of the face of an elderly Italian woman wearing a very natural, definitely not false beard.

The freshly painted light gray of the podium rising behind him was distracting at first. His white hair blended with the color and there was no outline to be seen. When he bent his head back the color was set in motion, his head almost sank in it. Only toward the middle of the lecture, when your attention was fully concentrated, did this disturbance come to an end, especially when he raised his large, black-clad body during a recitation and, with waving hands, conducted the verses and put the gray color to flight.—In the beginning he was embarrassing, he scattered so many compliments in all directions. In telling about a Napoleonic soldier whom he had known personally and who had had fifty-seven wounds, he remarked that the variety of colors on the torso of this man could have been imitated only by a great colorist such as his friend Mucha, who was present.

I observed in myself a continual increase in the degree to which I am affected by people on a podium. I gave no thought to my pains and cares. I was squeezed into the left corner of my chair, but really into the lecture, my clasped hands between my knees. I felt that Richepin had an effect upon me such as Solomon must have felt when he took young girls into his bed. I even had a slight vision of Napoleon who, in a connected fantasy, also stepped through the little entrance door although he could really have stepped out of the wood of the podium or out of the organ. He overwhelmed the entire hall, which was tightly packed at that moment. Near as I actually was to him, I had and would have had even in reality never a doubt of his effect. I should perhaps have noticed any absurdity in his dress, as in the case of Richepin as well, but noticing it would not have disturbed me. How cool I had been, on the other hand, as a child! I often wished to be brought face to face with the Emperor to show him how little effect he had. And that was not courage, it was just coolness.

He recited poems as though they were speeches in the Chamber. An impotent onlooker at battles, he pounded the table, he flung out his outstretched arms to clear a path for the guards through the middle of the hall, "Empereur!" he shouted, with his raised arm become a banner, and in repeating it made it echo as though an army was shouting down in the plain. During the description of a battle, a little foot kicked against the floor somewhere, the matter was looked into, it was his foot that had had too little confidence in itself. But it did not disturb him. After "The Grenadiers," which he read in a translation by Gérard de Nerval and which he thought very highly of, there was the least applause.

In his youth the tomb of Napoleon had been opened once a year and the embalmed face was displayed to disabled soldiers filing past in procession; the face was bloated and greenish, more a spectacle of terror than of admiration; this is why they later stopped opening the tomb. But nevertheless Richepin saw the face from the arm of his granduncle, who had served in Africa and for whose sake the Commandant opened the tomb.

He announces long in advance that a poem he intends to recite (he has an infallible memory, which a strong temperament must really always have), discusses it, the coming verses already cause a small earthquake under his words, in the case of the first poem he even said he would recite it with all his fire. He did.

He brought things to a climax in the last poem by getting imperceptibly into the verses (by Victor Hugo), standing up slowly, not sitting down again even after he finished the verses, picking up and carrying on the sweeping movements of the recitation with the final force of his own prose. He closed with the vow that even after a thousand years each grain of dust of his corpse, if it should have consciousness, would be ready to answer the call of Napoleon.

The French, short-winded from the quick succession of its escaping breaths, withstood even the most unskilful improvisations, did not break down even under his frequent talking about poets who beautify everyday life, about his own imagination (eyes closed) being that of a poet's, about his hallucinations (eyes reluctantly wrenched open on the distance) being those of a poet's, etc. At the same time he sometimes covered his eyes and then slowly uncovered them, taking away one finger after another.

He served in the army, his uncle in Africa, his grandfather under Napoleon, he even sang two lines of a battle song.—November 13. And this man is, I learned today, sixty-two years old.

November 14. Tuesday. Yesterday at Max's who returned from his Brünn lecture.

In the afternoon while falling asleep. As though the solid skullcap encircling the insensitive cranium had moved more deeply inward and left a part of the brain exposed to the free play of light and muscles.

To awaken on a cold autumn morning full of yellowish light. To force your way through the half-shut window and while still in front of the panes, before you fall, to hover, arms extended, belly arched, legs curved backward, like the figures on the bows of ships in old times.

Before falling asleep.

It seems so dreadful to be a bachelor, to become an old man struggling to keep one's dignity while begging for an invitation whenever one wants to spend an evening in company, having to carry one's meal home in one's hand, unable to expect anyone with a lazy sense of calm confidence, able only with difficulty and vexation to give a gift to someone, having to say good night at the front door, never being able to run up a stairway beside one's wife, to lie ill and have only the solace of the view from one's window when one can sit up, to have only side doors in one's room leading into other people's living rooms, to feel estranged from one's family, with whom one can keep on close terms only by marriage, first by the marriage of one's parents, then, when the effect of that has worn off, by one's own, having to admire other people's children and not even being allowed to go on saying: "I have none myself," never to feel oneself grow older since there is no family growing up around one, modeling oneself in appearance and behavior on one or two bachelors remembered from our youth.

This is all true, but it is easy to make the error of unfolding future sufferings so far in front of one that one's eye must pass beyond them and never again return, while in reality, both today and later, one will stand with a palpable body and a real head, a real forehead that is, for smiting on with one's hand.[31]

Now I'll try a sketch for the introduction to "Richard and Samuel."

November 15. Yesterday evening, already with a sense of foreboding, pulled the cover off the bed, lay down and again became aware of all my abilities as though I were holding them in my hand; they tightened my chest, they set my head on fire, for a short while, to console myself for not getting up to work, I repeated: "That's not healthy, that's not healthy," and with almost visible purpose tried to draw sleep over my head. I kept thinking of a cap with a visor which, to protect myself, I pulled down hard over my forehead. How much did I lose yesterday, how the blood pounded in my tight head, capable of anything and restrained only by powers which are indispensable for my very life and are here being wasted.

It is certain that everything I have conceived in advance, even when I was in a good mood, whether word for word or just casually, but in specific words, appears dry, wrong, inflexible, embarrassing to everybody around me, timid, but above all incomplete when I try to write it down at my desk, although I have forgotten nothing of the original conception. This is naturally related in large part to the fact that I conceive something good away from paper only in a time of exaltation, a time more feared than longed for, much as I do long for it; but then the fulness is so great that I have to give up. Blindly and arbitrarily I snatch handfuls out of the stream so that when I write it down calmly, my acquisition is nothing in comparison with the fulness in which it lived, is incapable of restoring this fulness, and thus is bad and disturbing because it tempts to no purpose.

November 16. This noon, before falling asleep, but I did not fall asleep, the upper part of the body of a wax woman lay on top of me. Her face was bent back over mine, her left forearm pressed against my breast.

No sleep for three nights, at the slightest effort to do anything my strength is immediately exhausted.

From an old notebook: "Now, in the evening, after having studied since six o'clock in the morning, I noticed that my left hand had already for some time been sympathetically clasping my right hand by the fingers." [32]

November 18. Yesterday in the factory. Rode back on the trolley, sat in a corner with legs stretched out, saw people outside, lights in stores, walls of viaducts through which we passed, backs and faces over and over again, a highway leading from the business street of the suburb with nothing human on it save people going home, the glaring electric lights of the railroad station burned into the darkness, the low, tapering chimneys of a gas works, a poster announcing the guest appearance of a singer, de Treville, that gropes its way along the walls as far as an alley near the cemeteries, from where it then returned with me out of the cold of the fields into the livable warmth of the city. We accept foreign cities as a fact, the inhabitants live there without penetrating our way of life, just as we cannot penetrate theirs, a comparison must be made, it can't be helped, but one is well aware that it has no moral or even psychological value, in the end one can often even omit the comparison because the difference in the conditions of life is so great that it makes it unnecessary.

The suburbs of our native city, however, are also foreign to us, but in this case comparisons have value, a half-hour's walk can prove it to us over and over again, here live people partly within our city, partly on the miserable, dark edge of the city that is furrowed like a great ditch, although they all have an area of interest in common with us that is greater than any other group of people outside the city. For this reason I always enter and leave the suburb with a weak, mixed feeling of anxiety, of abandonment, of sympathy, of curiosity, of conceit, of joy in traveling, of fortitude, and return with pleasure, seriousness and calm, especially from Žižkov.

November 19. Sunday. Dream: In the theater. Performance of *Das Weite Land* by Schnitzler, adapted by Utitz.[33] I sit all the way up front, think I am sitting in the first row until it finally appears that it is the second. The back of the row is turned toward the stage so that one can see the auditorium comfortably, the stage only by turning. The author is somewhere nearby, I can't hold back my poor opinion of the play which I seem to know from before, but add that the third act is supposed to be witty. With this "supposed to be," however, I mean to say that if one is speaking of the good parts, I do not know the play and must rely on hearsay; therefore I repeat this remark once more, not just for myself, but nevertheless it is disregarded by the others. There is a great crush around me. The audience seems to have come in its winter clothes, everyone fills his seat to overflowing. People beside me, behind me, whom I do not see, interrupt me, point out new arrivals, mention their names, my attention is called especially to a married couple forcing their way along a row of seats, since the woman has a dark-yellow, mannish, long-nosed face and besides, as far as one can see in the crowd out of which her head towers, is wearing men's clothes; near me, remarkably free, the actor Löwy, but very unlike the real one, is standing and making excited speeches in which the word "principium" is repeated, I keep expecting the words "tertium compara-tionis," they do not come. In a box in the second tier, really only in a right-hand corner (seen from the stage) of the balcony that connects with the boxes there, a third son of the Kisch family,[34] dressed in a beautiful Prince Albert with its flaps opened wide, stands behind his mother, who is seated, and speaks out into the theater. Löwy's speeches have a connection with these speeches. Among other things, Kisch points high up to a spot on the curtain and says, There sits the German Kisch, by this he means my schoolmate who studied Germanics. When the curtain goes up the theater begins to darken, and Kisch, in order to indi-cate that he would disappear in any case, marches up and away from the balcony with his mother, again with all his arms, coats and legs spread wide.

The stage is somewhat lower than the auditorium, you look down with your chin on the back of the seat. The set consists chiefly of two low, thick pillars in the middle of the stage. The scene is a banquet in which girls and young men take part. Despite the fact that when the play began many people in the first rows left, apparently to go back-stage, I can see very little, for the girls left behind block the view with their large, flat hats, most of which are blue, that move back and forth along the whole length of the row. Nevertheless, I see a small ten- to fifteen-year-old boy unusually clearly on the stage. He has dry, parted, straight-cut hair. He cannot even place his napkin properly on his lap, must look down carefully when he does, and is sup-posed to be a man-about-town in this play. In consequence, I no longer have much confidence in this theater. The com-pany on the stage now waits for various newcomers who come down onto the stage from the first rows of the audi-torium. But the play is not well rehearsed, either. Thus, an actress named Hackelberg has just entered, an actor, leaning back in his chair like a man of the world, addresses her as "Hackel," then becomes aware of his mistake and corrects himself. Now a girl enters whom I know (her name is Frankel, I think), she climbs over the back of the seat right where I am sitting, her back, when she climbs over, is entirely naked, the skin not very good, over the right hip there is even a scratched, bloodshot spot the size of a doorknob. But then, when she turns around on the stage and stands there with a clean face, she acts very well. Now a singing horseman is supposed to approach out of the distance at a gallop, a piano reproduces the clatter of hoofs, you hear the stormy song approaching, finally I see the singer too, who, to give the singing the natural swelling that takes place in a rapid approach, is running along the balcony up above toward the stage. He is not yet at the stage or through with the song and yet he has already passed the climax of haste and shrieking song, and the piano too can no longer reproduce distinctly the sound of hoofs striking against the stones. Both stop, therefore, and the singer approaches quietly, but he makes himself so small that only his head rises above the railing of the balcony, so that you cannot see him very clearly.

With this, the first act is over, but the curtain doesn't come down, the theater remains dark too. On the stage two critics sit on the floor, writing, with their backs resting against a piece of scenery. A dramatic coach or stage manager with a blond, pointed beard jumps onto the stage, while still in the air he stretches one hand out to give some instructions, in the other hand he has a bunch of grapes that had been in a fruit dish on the banquet table and which he now eats.

Again facing the auditorium I see that it is lit by simple petroleum lanterns that are stuck up on simple chandeliers, like those in the streets, and now, of course, burn only very low. Suddenly, impure petroleum or a damaged wick is probably the cause, the light spurts out of one of these lanterns and sparks pour down in a broad gush on the crowded audience that forms a mass as black as earth. Then a gentleman rises up out of this mass, walks on it toward the lantern, apparently wants to fix the lantern, but first looks up at it, remains standing near it for a short while and, when nothing happens, returns quietly to his place in which he is swallowed up. I take him for myself and bow my face into the darkness.

I and Max must really be different to the very core. Much as I admire his writings when they lie before me as a whole, resisting my and anyone else's encroachment (a few small book reviews even today), still, every sentence he writes for "Richard and Samuel" is bound up with a reluctant concession on my part which I feel painfully to my very depths. At least today.

This evening I was again filled with anxiously restrained abilities.

November 20. Dream of a picture, apparently by Ingres. The girls in the woods in a thousand mirrors, or rather: the virgins, etc. To the right of the picture, grouped in the same way and airily drawn like the pictures on theater curtains, there was a more compact group, to the left they sat and lay on a gigantic twig or flying ribbon, or soared by their own power in a chain that rose slowly toward the sky. And now they were reflected not only toward the spectator but also away from him, became more indistinct and multitudinous; what the eye lost in detail it gained in fulness. But in front stood a naked girl untouched by the reflections, her weight on one leg, her hip thrust forward. Here Ingres' draftsmanship was to be admired, but I actually found with satisfaction that there was too much real nakedness left in this girl even for the sense of touch. From behind her came a gleam of pale, yellowish light.

My repugnance for antitheses is certain. They are unexpected, but do not surprise, for they have always been there; if they were unconscious, it was at the very edge of consciousness. They make for thoroughness, fulness, completeness, but only like a figure on the "wheel of life";[35] we have chased our little idea around the circle. They are as undifferentiated as they are different, they grow under one's hand as though bloated by water, beginning with the prospect of infinity, they always end up in the same medium size. They curl up, cannot be straightened out, are mere clues, are holes in wood, are immobile assaults, draw antitheses to themselves, as I have shown. If they would only draw all of them, and forever.

For the drama: Weise, English teacher, the way he hurried by with squared shoulders, his hands deep in his pockets, his yellowish overcoat tightly folded, crossing the tracks with powerful strides right in front of the trolley that still stood there but was already signaling its departure with its bell. Away from us.

E: Anna!
A (*looking up*): Yes.
E: Come here.
A (*long, quiet steps*): What do you want?
E: I wanted to tell you that I have been dissatisfied with you for some time.
A: Really!
E: It is so.
A: Then you must certainly give me notice, Emil.
E: So quickly? And don't you even ask the reason?
A: I know it.
E: You do?
A: You don't like the food.
E (*stands up quickly, loud*): Do you or don't you know that Kurt is leaving this evening?
A (*inwardly undisturbed*): Why yes, unfortunately he is leaving, you didn't have to call me here for that.

November 21. My former governess, the one with the black-and-yellow face, with the square nose and a wart on her cheek which used to delight me so, was at our house today for the second time recently to see me. The first time I wasn't home, this time I wanted to be left in peace and to sleep and had them tell her I was out. Why did she bring me up so badly, after all I was obedient, she herself is saying so now to the cook and the governess in the anteroom, I was good and had a quiet disposition. Why didn't she use this to my advantage and prepare a better future for me? She is a married woman or a widow, has children, has a lively way of speaking that doesn't let me sleep, thinks I am a tall, healthy gentleman at the beautiful age of twenty-eight who likes to remember his youth and in general knows what to do with himself. Now, however, I lie here on the sofa, kicked out of the world, on the lookout for the sleep that refuses to come and will only graze me when it does, my joints ache with fatigue, my dried-up body trembles toward its own destruction in turmoils of which I dare not become fully conscious, in my head are astonishing convulsions. And there stand the three women before my door, one praises me as I was, two as I am. The cook says I shall go straight—she means without any detour—to heaven. Thus it shall be.

Löwy: A rabbi in the Talmud made it a principle, in this case very pleasing to God, to accept nothing, not even a glass of water, from anyone. Now it happened, however, that the greatest rabbi of his time wanted to make his acquaintance and therefore invited him to a meal. To refuse the invitation of such a man, that was impossible. The first rabbi therefore set out sadly on his journey. But because his principle was so strong, a mountain raised itself up between the two rabbis.

ANNA (*sits at the table, reading the paper*).
KARL (*walks around the room, when he comes to the window he stops and looks out, once he even opens the inner window*).
ANNA: Please leave the window closed, it's really freezing.

KARL (*closes the window*): Well, we have different things to worry about.

(November 22) ANNA: No, but you have developed a new habit, Emil, one that's quite horrible. You know how to catch hold of every trifle and use it to find something bad in me.

KARL (*rubs his fingers*): Because you have no consideration, because in general you are incomprehensible.

It is certain that a major obstacle to my progress is my physical condition. Nothing can be accomplished with such a body. I shall have to get used to its perpetual balking. As a result of the last few nights spent in wild dreams but with scarcely a few snatches of sleep, I was so incoherent this morning, felt nothing but my forehead, saw a halfway bearable condition only far beyond my present one, and in sheer readiness to die would have been glad simply to have curled up in a ball on the cement floor of the corridor with the documents in my hand. My body is too long for its weakness, it hasn't the least bit of fat to engender a blessed warmth, to preserve an inner fire, no fat on which the spirit could occasionally nourish itself beyond its daily need without damage to the whole. How shall the weak heart that lately has troubled me so often be able to pound the blood through all the length of these legs. It would be labor enough to the knees, and from there it can only spill with a senile strength into the cold lower parts of my legs. But now it is already needed up above again, it is being waited for, while it is wasting itself down below. Everything is pulled apart throughout the length of my body. What could it accomplish then, when it perhaps wouldn't have enough strength for what I want to achieve even if it were shorter and more compact.

From a letter of Löwy's to his father: When I come to Warsaw I will walk about among you in my European clothes like "a spider before your eyes, like a mourner at a wedding."

Löwy tells a story about a married friend who lives in Postin, a small town near Warsaw, and who feels isolated in his progressive interests and therefore unhappy.

"Postin, is that a large city?"

"This large," he holds out the palm of his hand to me. It is covered by a rough yellow-brown glove and looks like a wasteland.

November 23. On the 21st, the hundredth anniversary of Kleist's death, the Kleist family had a wreath placed on his grave with the epitaph: "To the best of their house."

On what circumstances my way of life makes me dependent! Tonight I slept somewhat better than in the past week, this afternoon even fairly well, I even feel that drowsiness which follows moderately good sleep, consequently I am afraid I shall not be able to write as well, feel individual abilities turning more deeply inward and am prepared for any surprise, that is, I already see it.

November 24. *Shechite* (one who is learning the slaughterer's art). Play by Gordin. In it quotations from the Talmud, for example:

If a great scholar commits a sin during the evening or the night, by morning you are no longer permitted to reproach him with it, for in his scholarship he has already repented of it himself.

If you steal an ox then you must return two, if you

slaughter the stolen ox then you must return four, but if you slaughter a stolen calf then you must return only three because it is assumed that you had to carry the calf away, therefore had done hard work. This assumption influences the punishment even if the calf was led away without any difficulty.

Honesty of evil thoughts. Yesterday evening I felt especially miserable. My stomach was upset again. I had written with difficulty. I had listened with effort to Löwy's reading in the coffeehouse (which at first was quiet so that we had to restrain ourselves, but which then became full of bustle and gave us no peace), the dismal future immediately before me seemed not worth entering, abandoned, I walked through Ferdinandstrasse. Then at the junction with the Bergstein I once more thought about the more distant future. How would I live through it with this body picked up in a lumber room? The Talmud too says: A man without a woman is no person. I had no defense this evening against such thoughts except to say to myself: "It is now that you come, evil thoughts, now, because I am weak and have an upset stomach. You pick this time for me to think you. You have waited for your advantage. Shame on you. Come some other time, when I am stronger. Don't exploit my condition in this way." And, in fact, without even waiting for other proofs, they yielded, scattered slowly and did not again disturb me during the rest of my walk, which was, naturally, not too happy. They apparently forgot, however, that if they were to respect all my evil moments, they would seldom get their chance.

The odor of gasoline from an automobile driving toward me from the theater made me notice how visibly a beautiful home life (and were it lit only by a single candle, that is all one needs before going to bed) is waiting for the theater-goers coming toward me who are giving their cloaks and dangling opera glasses a last tug into place, but also how it seems that they are being sent home from the theater like subordinates before whom the curtain has gone down for the last time and behind whom the doors have opened through which—full of pride because of some ridiculous worry or another—they had entered the theater before the beginning of or during the first act.

November 28. Have written nothing for three days.

Spent all afternoon of the 25th in the Café City persuading M. to sign a declaration that he was just a clerk with us, therefore not covered by insurance, so that Father would not be obliged to make the large payment on his insurance. He promises it, I speak fluent Czech, I apologize for my mistakes with particular elegance, he promises to send the declaration to the office Monday, I feel that if he does not like me then at least he respects me, but on Monday he sends nothing, nor is he any longer in Prague, he has left.

Dull evening at Baum's without Max. Reading of *Die Hässliche*, a story that is still too disorganized, the first chapter is rather the building site of a story.

On Sunday, November 26th, "Richard and Samuel" with Max morning and afternoon until five. Then to N., a collector from Linz, recommended by Kubin, fifty, gigantic, towerlike movements; when he is silent for any length of time one bows one's head, for he is entirely silent, while when he speaks he does not speak entirely; his life consists of collecting and fornicating.

Collecting: He began with a collection of postage stamps, then turned to drawings, then collected everything, then saw the aimlessness of this collection which could never be completed and limited himself to amulets, later to pilgrimage medals and pilgrimage tracts from lower Austria and southern Bavaria. These are medals and tracts which are issued anew for each pilgrimage, most of them worthless in their material and also artistically, but often have nice pictures. He now also began industriously to write about them, and indeed was the first to write on this subject, for the systematization of which he first established the points of reference. Naturally, those who had been collecting these objects and had put off publishing were furious, but had to put up with it nevertheless. Now he is an acknowledged expert on these pilgrimage medals, requests come from all over for his opinion and decision on these medals, his voice is decisive. Besides, he collects everything else as well, his pride is a chastity belt that, together with his amulets, was exhibited at the Dresden Hygienic Exhibition. (He has just been there to have everything packed for shipment.) Then a beautiful knight's sword of the Falkensteiners. His relationship to art is unambiguous and clear in that bad way which collecting makes possible.

From the coffeehouse in the Hotel Graf he takes us up to his overheated room, sits down on the bed, we on two chairs around him, so that we form a quiet group. His first question: "Are you collectors?"

"No, only poor amateurs."

"That doesn't matter." He pulls out his wallet and practically showers us with bookplates, his own and others', jumbled with announcements of his next book, "Magic and Superstition in the Mineral Kingdom." He has already written much, especially on "Motherhood in Art," he considers the pregnant body the most beautiful, for him it is also the most pleasant to f———. He has also written about amulets.

He was also in the employ of the Vienna Court Museum, was in charge of excavations in Braila at the mouth of the Danube, invented a process, named after him, for restoring excavated vases, is a member of thirteen learned societies and museums, his collection is willed to the Germanic Museum in Nuremberg, he often sits at his desk until one or two o'clock at night and is back at eight o'clock in the morning. We have to write something in a lady friend's album which he has brought along to fill up on his journey. Those who themselves create come first. Max writes a complicated verse which Mr. N. tries to render by the proverb, "Every cloud has a silver lining." Before this, he had read it aloud in a wooden voice. I write down:

> Little soul,
> Boundest in dancing, etc.

He reads aloud again, I help, finally he says: "A Persian rhythm? Now what is that called? Ghazel? Right." We are not in a position to agree with this nor even to guess at what he means. Finally he quotes a "*ritornello* by Rückert." Yes, he meant *ritornello*. However, it is not that either. Very well, but it has a certain melody.

He is a friend of Halbe. He likes to talk about him. We would much rather talk about Blei. There is not much to say about him, however, Munich literary society does not think much of him because of his intellectual doublecrossing, he is divorced from his wife who had had a large practice as a dentist and supported him, his daughter, sixteen, blond, with blue eyes, is the wildest girl in Munich. In Sternheim's *Hose*—N. was at the theater with Halbe—Blei played an aging man-about-town. When N. met him the next day he said: "Herr Doktor, yesterday you played Dr. Blei."

"What? What?" he said in embarrassment, "but I was playing so-and-so."

When we leave he throws open the bed so that it may thoroughly take on the warmth of the room, he arranges for additional heating besides.

November 29. From the Talmud: When a scholar goes to meet his bride, he should take an *am ha-aretz* [36] along, he is too deeply sunk in his scholarliness, he would not observe what should be observed.

As a result of bribery the telephone and telegraph wires around Warsaw were put up in a complete circle, which in the sense of the Talmud makes the city a bounded area, a courtyard, as it were, so that on Saturday it is possible even for the most pious person to move about, carry trifles (like handkerchiefs) on his person, within this circle.

The parties of the Hasidim where they merrily discourse on talmudic problems. If the entertainment runs down or if someone does not take part, they make up for it by singing. Melodies are invented, if one is a success, members of the family are called in and it is repeated and rehearsed with them. At one such entertainment a wonder-rabbi who often had hallucinations suddenly laid his face on his arms, which were resting on the table, and remained in that position for three hours while everyone was silent. When he awoke he wept and sang an entirely new, gay, military march. This was the melody with which the angels of the dead had just escorted to heaven the soul of a wonder-rabbi who had died at this time in a far-off Russian city.

On Friday, according to the Kabbalah, the pious get a new, more delicate soul, entirely divine, which remains with them until Saturday evening.

On Friday evening two angels accompany each pious

man from the synagogue to his home; the master of the house stands while he greets them in the dining room; they stay only a short time.

The education of girls, their growing up, getting used to the ways of the world, was always especially important to me. Then they no longer run so hopelessly out of the way of a person who knows them only casually and would like to speak casually with them, they have begun to stop for a moment, even though it be not quite in that part of the room in which you would have them, you need no longer hold them with glances, threats or the power of love; when they turn away they do so slowly and do not intend any harm by it, then their backs have become broader too. What you say to them is not lost, they listen to the whole question without your having to hurry, and they answer, jokingly to be sure, but directly to the point. Yes, with their faces lifted up they even ask questions themselves, and a short conversation is not more than they can stand. They hardly ever let a spectator disturb them any more in the work they have just undertaken, and therefore pay less attention to him, yet he may look at them longer. They withdraw only to dress for dinner. This is the only time when you may be insecure. Aside from this, however, you need no longer run through the streets, lie in wait at house doors, and wait over and over again for a lucky chance, even though you have really long since learned that such chances can't be forced.

But despite this great change that has taken place in them it is no rarity for them to come toward us with mournful faces when we meet them unexpectedly, to put their hands flatly in ours and with slow gestures invite us to enter their homes as though we were business acquaintances. They walk heavily up and down in the next room; but when we penetrate there too, in desire and spite, they crouch in a window seat and read the paper without a glance to spare for us.

December 3. I have now read a part of Schäfer's *Karl Stauffers Lebensgang. Eine Chronik der Leidenschaft,* and am so caught up and held fast by this powerful impression forcing its way into that inner part of me which I listen to and learn from only at rare intervals, but at the same time am driven to such a pass by the hunger imposed on me by my upset stomach and by the usual excitements of the free Sunday, that I must write, just as one can get relief from external excitement forced upon one from the outside only by flailing one's arms.

The unhappiness of the bachelor, whether seeming or actual, is so easily guessed at by the world around him that he will curse his decision, at least if he has remained a bachelor because of the delight he takes in secrecy. He walks around with his coat buttoned, his hands in the upper pockets of his jacket, his arms akimbo, his hat pulled down over his eyes, a false smile that has become natural to him is supposed to shield his mouth as his glasses do his eyes, his trousers are tighter than seem proper for his thin legs. But everyone knows his condition, can detail his sufferings. A cold breeze breathes upon him from within and he gazes inward with the even sadder half of his double face. He moves incessantly, but with predictable regularity, from one apartment to another. The farther he moves away from the living, for whom he must still—and this is the worst mockery—work like a conscious slave who dare not express his consciousness, so much the smaller a space is considered sufficient for him. While it is death that must still strike down the others, though they may have spent all their lives in a sickbed—for even though they would have gone down by themselves long ago from their own weakness, they nevertheless hold fast to their loving, very healthy relatives by blood and marriage—he, this bachelor, still in the midst of life, apparently of his own free will resigns himself to an ever smaller space, and when he dies the coffin is exactly right for him.

My recent reading of Mörike's autobiography to my sisters began well enough but improved as I went on, and finally, my fingertips together, it conquered inner obstacles with my voice's unceasing calm, provided a constantly expanding panorama for my voice, and finally the whole room round about me dared admit nothing but my voice. Until my parents, returning from business, rang.

Before falling asleep felt on my body the weight of the fists on my light arms.

December 8. Friday, have not written for a long time, but this time it was really in part because of satisfaction, as I have finished the first chapter of "Richard and Samuel" and consider it, particularly the original description of the sleep in the train compartment, a success. Even more, I think that something is happening within me that is very close to Schiller's transformation of emotion into character. Despite all the resistance of my inner being I must write this down.

Walk with Löwy to the Lieutenant-Governor's castle, which I called Fort Zion. The entrance gates and the color of the sky matched very well.

Another walk to Hetz Island. Story about Mrs. Tschissik, how they took her into the company in Berlin out of pity, at first an insignificant singer of duets in an antiquated dress and hat. Reading of a letter from Warsaw in which a young Warsaw Jew complains about the decline of the Jewish theater and writes that he prefers to go to the "Nowosti," the Polish operetta theater, rather than to the Jewish one, for the miserable equipment, the indecencies, the "moldy" couplets, etc., are unbearable. Just imagine the big scene of a Jewish operetta in which the prima donna, with a train of small children behind her, marches through the audience onto the stage. Each of them is carrying a small scroll of the Torah and is singing: *Toire iz di beste s'khoire*—the Torah is the best merchandise.

Beautiful lonely walk over the Hradschin and the Belvedere after those successful parts of "Richard and Samuel." In the Nerudagasse a sign: Anna Křižová, Dressmaker, Trained in France by the Aid of the Dowager Duchess Ahrenberg, née Princess Ahrenberg.—In the middle of the first castle court I stood and watched the calling out of the castle guard.

The last section I wrote hasn't pleased Max, probably because he regards it as unsuitable for the whole, but possibly also because he considers it bad in itself. This is very probable because he warned me against writing such long passages and regards the effect of such writing as somewhat jellylike.

In order to be able to speak to young girls I need older persons near me. The slight disturbance emanating from them enlivens my speech, I immediately feel that the demands made on me are diminished; what I speak out of myself without previous consideration can always, if it is not suitable for the girl, be directed to the older person, from whom I can also, if it becomes necessary, draw an abundance of help.

Miss H. She reminds me of Mrs. Bl., only her long, slightly double-curved and relatively narrow nose looks like the ruined nose of Mrs. Bl. But aside from that there is also in her face a blackness, hardly caused externally, that can be driven into the skin only by a strong character. Broad back, well on the way to being a woman's swelling back; heavy body that seems thin in the well-cut jacket and on which the narrow jacket is even loose. She raises her head freely to show that she has found a way out of the embarrassing moments of the conversation. Indeed, I was not put down in this conversation, had not surrendered even inwardly, but had I just looked at myself from the outside, I should not have been able to explain my behavior in any other way. In the past I could not express myself freely in the company of new acquaintances because the presence of sexual wishes unconsciously hindered me, now their conscious absence hinders me.

Ran into the Tschissik couple at the Graben. She was wearing the hussy's dress she wore in *Der Wilde Mensch*. When I break down her appearance into its details as I saw it then at the Graben, she becomes improbable. (I saw her only for a moment, for I became frightened at the sight of her, did not greet her, nor did she see me and I did not immediately dare to turn around.) She seemed much smaller than usual, her left hip was thrust forward, not just at the moment, but permanently, her right leg was bent in at the knee, the movements of her throat and head, which she brought close to her husband, were very quick, with her right arm crooked outward she tried to take the arm of her husband. He was wearing his little summer hat with the brim turned down in front. When I turned they were gone. I guessed that they had gone to the Café Central, waited awhile on the other side of the Graben and was lucky enough after a long interval to see her come to the window. When she sat down at the table only the rim of her cardboard hat, covered with blue velvet, was visible.

I then dreamed that I was in a very narrow but not very tall glass-domed house with two entrances like the impassable passageways in the paintings of Italian primitives, also resembling from the distance an arcade leading off from the Rue des Petits Champs that we saw in Paris. Except that the one in Paris was really wider and full of stores, but this one ran along between blank walls, appeared to have scarcely enough room for two people to walk side by side, but when one really entered it, as I did with Mrs. Tschissik, there was a surprising amount of room, which did not really surprise us. While I left by one exit with Mrs. Tschissik in the direction of a possible observer of all this, and Mrs. Tschissik at the same time apologized for some offense or other (it seemed to be drunkenness) and begged me not to believe her detractors, Mr. Tschissik, at the second of the house's two exits, whipped a shaggy, blond St. Bernard which stood opposite him on its hind legs. It was not quite clear whether he was just playing with the dog and neglected his wife because of it, or whether he had himself been attacked by the dog in earnest, or whether he wished to keep the dog away from us.

With L. on the quay. I had a slight spell of faintness that

stifled all my being, got over it and remembered it after a short time as something long forgotten.

Even if I overlook all other obstacles (physical condition, parents, character), the following serves as a very good excuse for my not limiting myself to literature in spite of everything: I can take nothing on myself as long as I have not achieved a sustained work that satisfies me completely. That is of course irrefutable.

I have now, and have had since this afternoon, a great yearning to write all my anxiety entirely out of me, write it into the depths of the paper just as it comes out of the depths of me, or write it down in such a way that I could draw what I had written into me completely. This is no artistic yearning. Today, when Löwy spoke of his dissatisfaction with and of his indifference to everything that the troupe does, I explained his condition as due to homesickness, but in a sense did not give him this explanation even though I voiced it, instead kept it for myself and enjoyed it in passing as a sorrow of my own.

December 9. Stauffer-Bern: "The sweetness of creation begets illusions about its real value."

If one patiently submits to a book of letters or memoirs, no matter by whom, in this case it is Karl Stauffer-Bern, one doesn't make him one's own by main strength, for to do this one has to employ art, and art is its own reward; but rather one suffers oneself to be drawn away—this is easily done, if one doesn't resist—by the concentrated otherness of the person writing and lets oneself be made into his counterpart. Thus it is no longer remarkable, when one is brought back to one's self by the closing of the book, that one feels the better for this excursion and this recreation, and, with a clearer head, remains behind in one's own being, which has been newly discovered, newly shaken up and seen for a moment from the distance. Only later are we surprised that these experiences of another person's life, in spite of their vividness, are faithfully described in the book—our own experience inclines us to think that nothing in the world is further removed from an experience (sorrow over the death of a friend, for instance) than its description. But what is right for us is not right for the other person. If our letters cannot match our own feelings—naturally, there are varying degrees of this, passing imperceptibly into one another in both directions—if even at our best, expressions like "indescribable," "inexpressible," or "so sad," or "so beautiful," followed by a rapidly collapsing "that"-clause, must perpetually come to our assistance, then as if in compensation we have been given the ability to comprehend what another person has written with at least the same degree of calm exactitude which we lack when we confront our own letter-writing. Our ignorance of those feelings which alternately make us crumple up and pull open again the letter in front of us, this very ignorance becomes knowledge the moment we are compelled to limit ourselves to this letter, to believe only what it says, and thus to find it perfectly expressed and perfect in expression, as is only right, if we are to see a clear road into what is most human. So Karl Stauffer's letters contain only an account of the short life of an artist——

December 10. Sunday. I must go to see my sister and her little boy. When my mother came home from my sister's at one o'clock at night the day before yesterday with the news of the boy's birth, my father marched through the house in his nightshirt, opened all the doors, woke me, the maid and my sisters and proclaimed the birth as though the child had not only been born, but as though it had already lived an honorable life and been buried too.

December 13. Because of fatigue did not write and lay now on the sofa in the warm room and now on the one in the cold room, with sick legs and disgusting dreams. A dog lay on my body, one paw near my face. I woke up because of it but was still afraid for a little while to open my eyes and look at it.

Biberpelz. Bad play, flowing along without climax. Scenes with the police superintendent not true. Delicate acting by the Lehmann woman of the Lessing Theater. The way her skirt folds between her thighs when she bends. The thoughtful look of the people when she raises her two hands, places them one under the other on the left in front of her face, as though she wanted to weaken the force of the denying or protesting voice. Bewildered, coarse acting of the others. The comedian's impudence toward the play (draws his saber, exchanges hats). My cold aversion. Went home, but while still there sat with a feeling of admiration that so many people take upon themselves so much excitement for an evening (they shout, steal, are robbed, harass, slander, neglect), and that in this play, if one only looks at it with blinking eyes, so many disordered human voices and exclamations are thrown together. Pretty girls. One with a flat face, unbroken surfaces of skin, rounded cheeks, hair beginning high up, eyes lost in this smoothness and protruding a little.—Beautiful passages of the play in which the Wulffen woman shows herself at once a thief and an honest friend of the clever, progressive, democratic people. A Wehrhahn in the audience might feel himself justified.—Sad parallelism of the four acts. In the first act there is stealing, in the second act is the judgment, the same in the third and fourth acts.

Der Schneider als Gemeinderat at the Jews. Without the Tschissiks but with two new, terrible people, the Liebgold couple. Bad play by Richter. The beginning like Molière, the purse-proud alderman hung with watches. The Liebgold woman can't read, her husband has to rehearse with her.

It is almost a custom for a comedian to marry a serious actress and a serious actor a comedienne, and in general to take along with them only married women or relatives. The way once, at midnight, the piano player, probably a bachelor, slipped out the door with his music.

Brahms concert by the Singing Society. The essence of my unmusicalness consists in my inability to enjoy music connectedly, it only now and then has an effect on me, and how seldom it is a musical one. The natural effect of music on me is to circumscribe me with a wall, and its only constant influence on me is that, confined in this way, I am different from what I am when free.

There is, among the public, no such reverence for literature as there is for music. The singing girls. It was only the melody that held open the mouths of many of them. The throat and head of one with a clumsy body quivered when she sang.

Three clerics in a box. The middle one, wearing a red skullcap, listens with calm and dignity, unmoved and heavy, but not stiff; the one on the right is sunken into himself, with a pointed, rigid, wrinkled face; the one on the left, stout, holds his face propped at an angle on his half-opened fist.

Played: *Tragic Overture.* (I hear only slow, solemn beats, now here, now there. It is instructive to watch the music pass from one group of players to another and to follow it with the ear. The disheveled hair of the conductor.) "Beherzigung" by Goethe, "Nänie" by Schiller, "Gesang der Parzen," "Triumphlied."

The singing women who stood up on the low balustrade as though on a piece of early Italian architecture.

Despite the fact that for a considerable time I have been standing deep in literature and it has often broken over me, it is certain that for the past three days, aside from a general desire to be happy, I have felt no genuine desire for literature. In the same way I considered Löwy my indispensable friend last week, and now I have easily dispensed with him for three days.

When I begin to write after a rather long interval, I draw the words as if out of the empty air. If I capture one, then I have just this one alone and all the toil must begin anew.

December 14. My father reproached me at noon because I don't bother with the factory. I explained that I had accepted a share because I expected profit but that I cannot take an active part so long as I am in the office. Father quarreled on, I stood silently at the window. This evening, however, I caught myself thinking, as a result of that noontime discussion, that I could put up with my present situation very contentedly, and that I only had to be careful

not to have all my time free for literature. I had scarcely
exposed this thought to a closer inspection when it became
no longer astonishing and already appeared accustomed. I
disputed my ability to devote all my time to literature.
This conviction arose, of course, only from the momentary situation, but was stronger than it. I also thought of
Max as of a stranger despite the fact that today he has an
exciting evening of reading and acting in Berlin; it occurs
to me now that I thought of him only when I approached
Miss Taussig's house on my evening walk.

Walk with Löwy down by the river. The one pillar of
the vault rising out of the Elizabeth Bridge, lit on the inside by an electric light, looked—a dark mass between light
streaming from the sides—like a factory chimney, and the
dark wedge of shadow stretching over it to the sky was
like ascending smoke. The sharply outlined green areas of
light at the side of the bridge.

The way, during the reading of *Beethoven und das Lie-
bespaar* by W. Schäfer, various thoughts (about dinner,
about Löwy, who was waiting) unconnected with what I
was reading passed through my mind with great distinct-
ness without disturbing my reading, which just today was
very pure.

December 16. Sunday, 12 noon. Idled away the morning
with sleeping and reading newspapers. Afraid to finish a
review for the *Prager Tagblatt*. Such fear of writing always expresses itself by my occasionally making up, away
from my desk, initial sentences for what I am to write
which immediately prove unusable, dry, broken off long

before their end and pointing with their towering fragments to a sad future.

The old tricks at the Christmas Fair. Two cockatoos on
a crossbar pull fortunes. Mistakes: a girl has a ladylove pre-
dicted. A man offers artificial flowers for sale in rhyme: *To
jest ruže udělená z kuže* [This is a rose, made of leather].

Young Pipes when singing. As sole gesture, he rolls his
right forearm back and forth at the joint, he opens his
hands a little and then draws them together again. Sweat
covers his face, especially his upper lip, as though with
splinters of glass. A buttonless dickey has been hurriedly
tucked into the vest under his straight black coat.
The warm shadow in the soft red of Mrs. Klug's mouth
when she sings.

Jewish streets in Paris, Rue Rosier, sidestreet of Rue de
Rivoli.

If a disorganized education having only that minimum
coherence indispensable for the merest uncertain existence
is suddenly challenged to a task limited in time, therefore
necessarily arduous, to self-development, to articulate
speech, then the response can only be a bitterness in which
are mingled arrogance over achievements which could be
attained only by calling upon all one's untrained powers, a
last glance at the knowledge that escapes in surprise and
that is so very fluctuating because it was suspected rather
than certain, and, finally, hate and admiration for the
environment.

Before falling asleep yesterday I had an image of a drawing in which a group of people were isolated like a moun-

tain in the air. The technique of the drawing seemed to me completely new and, once discovered, easily executed.

A company was assembled around a table, the earth extended somewhat beyond the circle of people, but of all these people, at the moment, I saw with a powerful glance only one young man in ancient dress. His left arm was propped on the table, the hand hung loosely over his face, which was playfully turned up toward someone who was solicitously or questioningly bent over him. His body, especially the right leg, was stretched out in careless youthfulness, he lay rather than sat. The two distinct pairs of lines that outlined his legs crossed and softly merged with the lines outlining his body. His pale, colored clothes lay heaped up between these lines with feeble corporeality. In astonishment at this beautiful drawing, which begot in my head an excitement that I was convinced was that same and indeed permanent excitement which would guide the pencil in my hand when I wished, I forced myself out of my twilight condition in order better to be able to think the drawing through. Then it soon turned out, of course, that I had imagined nothing but a small, gray-white porcelain group.

In periods of transition such as the past week has been for me and as this moment at least still is, a sad but calm astonishment at my lack of feeling often grips me. I am divided from all things by a hollow space and I don't even push myself to the limits of it.

Now, in the evening, when my thoughts begin to move more freely and I would perhaps be capable of something, I must go to the National Theater to the first night of *Hippodamie* by Vrchlicky.

It is certain that Sunday can never be of more use to me than a weekday because its special organization throws all my habits into confusion and I need the additional free time to adjust myself halfway to this special day.

The moment I were set free from the office I would yield at once to my desire to write an autobiography. I would have to have some such decisive change before me as a preliminary goal when I began to write in order to be able to give direction to the mass of events. But I cannot imagine any other inspiriting change than this, which is itself so terribly improbable. Then, however, the writing of the autobiography would be a great joy because it would move along as easily as the writing down of dreams, yet it would have an entirely different effect, a great one, which would always influence me and would be accessible as well to the understanding and feeling of everyone else.

December 18. Day before yesterday *Hippodamie*. Bad play. A rambling about in Greek mythology without rhyme or reason. Kvapil's essay in the program which expresses between the lines the view apparent throughout the whole performance, that a good production (which here, however, was nothing but an imitation of Reinhardt) can make a bad play into a great theatrical work. All this must be sad for a Czech who knows even a little of the world.

The Lieutenant-Governor, who during the intermission snatched air from the corridor through the open door of his box.

The appearance of the dead Axiocha, called up in the shape of a phantom, who soon disappears because, having died only a short time ago, she relives her old human sorrows too keenly at the sight of the world.

I hate Werfel, not because I envy him, but I envy him too. He is healthy, young and rich, everything that I am not. Besides, gifted with a sense of music, he has done very good work early and easily, he has the happiest life behind him and before him, I work with weights I cannot get rid of, and I am entirely shut off from music.

I am not punctual because I do not feel the pains of waiting. I wait like an ox. For if I feel a purpose in my momentary existence, even a very uncertain one, I am so vain in my weakness that I would gladly bear anything for the sake of this purpose once it is before me. If I were in love, what couldn't I do then. How long I waited, years ago, under the arcades of the Ring until M. came by, even to see her walk by with her lover. I have been late for appointments partly out of carelessness, partly out of ignorance of the pains of waiting, but also partly in order to attain new, complicated purposes through a renewed, uncertain search for the people with whom I had made the appointments, and so to achieve the possibility of long, uncertain waiting. From the fact that as a child I had a great nervous fear of waiting one could conclude that I was destined for something better and that I foresaw my future.

My good periods do not have time or opportunity to live themselves out naturally; my bad ones, on the other hand, have more than they need. As I see from the diary, I have now been suffering from such a state since the 9th, for almost ten days. Yesterday I once again went to bed with my head on fire, and was ready to rejoice that the bad time was over and ready to fear that I would sleep badly. It passed, however, I slept fairly well and feel badly when I'm awake.

December 19. Yesterday *Davids Geige* by Lateiner. The disinherited son, a good violinist, returns home a rich man, as I used to dream of doing in my early days at the Gymnasium. But first, disguised as a beggar, his feet bound in rags like a snow-shoveller, he tests his relatives who have never left home: his poor, honest daughter, his rich brother who will not give his son in marriage to his poor cousin and who despite his age himself wants to marry a young woman. He reveals himself later on by tearing open a Prince Albert under which, on a diagonal sash, hang decorations from all the princes of Europe. By violin playing and singing he turns all the relatives and their hangers-on into good people and straightens out their affairs.

Mrs. Tschissik acted again. Yesterday her body was more beautiful than her face, which seemed narrower than usual so that the forehead, which is thrown into wrinkles at her first word, was too striking. The beautifully rounded, moderately strong, large body did not belong with her face yesterday, and she reminded me vaguely of hybrid beings like mermaids, sirens, centaurs. When she stood before me then, with her face distorted, her complexion spoiled by make-up, a stain on her dark-blue short-sleeved blouse, I felt as though I were speaking to a statue in a circle of pitiless onlookers.

Mrs. Klug stood near her and watched me. Miss Weltsch watched me from the left. I said as many stupid things as possible. I did not stop asking Mrs. Tschissik why she had gone to Dresden, although I knew that she had quarreled with the others and for that reason had gone away, and that this subject was embarrassing to her. In the end it was even more embarrassing to me, but nothing else occurred to me. When Mrs. Tschissik joined us while I was speaking to Mrs. Klug, I turned to Mrs. Tschissik, saying "Pardon!" to Mrs. Klug as though I intended to spend the rest of my life with Mrs. Tschissik. Then while I was speaking with Mrs. Tschissik I observed that my love had not really grasped her, but only flitted about her, now nearer, now farther. Indeed, it can find no peace.

Mrs. Liebgold acted a young man in a costume that tightly embraced her pregnant body. As she does not obey her father (Löwy), he presses the upper part of her body down on a chair and beats her over her very tightly trousered behind. Löwy said that he touched her with the same repugnance that he would a mouse. Seen from the front, however, she is pretty, it is only in profile that her nose slants down too long, too pointed and too cruel.

I first arrived at ten, took a walk and tasted to the full the slight nervousness of having a seat in the theater and going for a walk during the performance, that is, while the soloists were trying to sing me into my seat. I missed Mrs. Klug too. Listening to her always lively singing does nothing less than prove the solidity of the world, which is what I need, after all.

Today at breakfast I spoke with my mother by chance about children and marriage, only a few words, but for the first time saw clearly how untrue and childish is the conception of me that my mother builds up for herself. She considers me a healthy young man who suffers a little from the notion that he is ill. This notion will disappear by itself with time; marriage, of course, and having children would put an end to it best of all. Then my interest in literature would also be reduced to the degree that is perhaps necessary for an educated man. A matter-of-fact, undisturbed interest in my profession or in the factory or in whatever may come to hand will appear. Hence there is not the slightest, not the trace of a reason for permanent despair about my future. There is occasion for temporary despair, which is not very deep, however, whenever I think my stomach is upset, or when I can't sleep because I write too much. There are thousands of possible solutions. The most probable is that I shall suddenly fall in love with a girl and will never again want to do without her. Then I shall see how good their intentions toward me are and how little they will interfere with me. But if I remain a bachelor like my uncle in Madrid, that too will be no misfortune because with my cleverness I shall know how to make adjustments.

December 23. Saturday. When I look at my whole way of life going in a direction that is foreign and false to all my relatives and acquaintances, the apprehension arises, and my father expresses it, that I shall become a second Uncle Rudolf, the fool of the new generation of the family, the fool somewhat altered to meet the needs of a different period; but from now on I'll be able to feel how my mother (whose opposition to this opinion grows continually weaker in the course of the years) sums up and enforces everything that speaks for me and against Uncle Rudolf, and that enters like a wedge between the conceptions entertained about the two of us.

Day before yesterday in the factory. In the evening at

Max's where the artist, Novak, was just then displaying the lithographs of Max. I could not express myself in their presence, could not say yes or no. Max voiced several opinions which he had already formed, whereupon my thinking revolved about them without result. Finally I became accustomed to the individual lithographs, overcame at least the surprise of my unaccustomed eye, found a chin round, a face compressed, a chest armorlike, or rather he looked as though he were wearing a giant dress shirt under his street clothes. The artist replied to this with something which was not to be understood either at the first or second attempt, weakening its significance only by saying it to us of all people who thus, if his opinions were proved to be genuinely correct, were in the position of having spoken the cheapest nonsense.

He asserted that it is the felt and even conscious task of the artist to assimilate his subject to his own art form. To achieve this he had first prepared a portrait sketch in color, which also lay before us and which in dark colors showed a really too sharp, dry likeness (this too-great-sharpness I can acknowledge only now), and was declared by Max to be the best portrait, as, aside from its likeness about the eyes and mouth, it showed nobly composed features brought out in the right degree by the dark colors. If one were asked about it, one couldn't deny it. From this sketch the artist now worked at home on his lithographs, endeavoring in lithograph after lithograph to get farther and farther away from the natural phenomenon but at the same time not only not to violate his own art form but rather to come closer to it stroke by stroke. So, for instance, the ear lost its human convolutions and its clearly defined edge and became a sunken semicircular whorl around a small, dark opening. Max's bony chin, starting from the ear itself, lost its simple boundary, indispensable as it seems, and a new one was as little created for the observer as a new truth is created by the removal of the old. The hair flowed in sure, understandable outlines and remained human hair no matter how the artist denied it.

After having demanded from us understanding of these transformations, the artist indicated only hastily, but with pride, that everything on these sheets had significance and that even the accidental was necessary because its effect influenced everything that followed. Thus, alongside one head a narrow, pale coffee stain extended almost the entire length of the picture, it was part of the whole, so intended, and not to be removed without damage to all the proportions. There was in the left corner of another sheet a thinly stippled, scarcely noticeable, large blue stain; this stain had even been placed there intentionally, for the sake of the slight illumination that passed from it across the picture, and which the artist had taken advantage of when he continued his work. His next objective was now chiefly the mouth on which something, but not enough, had already been done, and then he intended to transform the nose too. In response to Max's complaint that in this way the lithograph would move farther and farther away from the beautiful color sketch, he observed that it wasn't at all impossible that it should again approach it.

One certainly could not overlook the sureness with which the artist relied throughout the discussion on the unexpected in his inspiration, and that only this reliance gave his work its best title to being almost a scientific one. —Bought two lithographs, "Apple Seller," and "Walk."

One advantage in keeping a diary is that you become aware with reassuring clarity of the changes which you constantly suffer and which in a general way are naturally believed, surmised and admitted by you, but which you'll unconsciously deny when it comes to the point of gaining hope or peace from such an admission. In the diary you find proof that in situations which today would seem unbearable, you lived, looked around and wrote down observations, that this right hand moved then as it does today, when we may be wiser because we are able to look back upon our former condition, and for that very reason have got to admit the courage of our earlier striving in which we persisted even in sheer ignorance.

All yesterday morning my head was as if filled with mist from Werfel's poems. For a moment I feared the enthusiasm would carry me along straight into nonsense.

Tormenting discussion with Weltsch [37] evening before last. My startled gaze ran up and down his face and throat for an hour. Once, in the midst of a facial distortion caused by excitement, weakness and bewilderment, I was not sure that I would get out of the room without permanent damage to our relationship. Outside, in the rainy weather intended for silent walking, I drew a deep breath of relief and then for an hour waited contentedly for M. in front of the Orient. I find this sort of waiting, glancing slowly at the clock and walking indifferently up and down, almost as pleasant as lying on the sofa with legs stretched out and hands in my trouser pockets. (Half asleep, one then thinks one's hands are no longer in the trouser pockets at all, but are lying clenched on top of one's thighs.)

December 24. Sunday. Yesterday it was gay at Baum's. I was there with Weltsch. Max is in Breslau. I felt myself free, could carry every moment to its conclusion, I answered and listened properly, made the most noise, and if I occasionally said something stupid it did not loom large but blew over at once. The walk home in the rain with Weltsch was the same; despite puddles, wind and cold it passed as quickly for us as though we had ridden. And we were both sorry to say goodbye.

As a child I was anxious, and if not anxious then uneasy, when my father spoke—as he often did, since he was a businessman—of the last day of the month (called the "ultimo"). Since I wasn't curious, and since I wasn't able —even if I sometimes did ask about it—to digest the answer quickly enough with my slow thinking, and since a weakly stirring curiosity once risen to the surface is often already satisfied by a question and an answer without requiring that it understand as well, the expression "the last day of the month" remained a disquieting mystery for me, to be joined later (the result of having listened more attentively) by the expression "ultimo," even if the latter expression did not have the same great significance. It was bad too that the last day, dreaded so long in advance, could never be completely done away with. Sometimes, when it passed with no special sign, indeed with no special attention (I realized only much later that it always came after about thirty days), and when the first had happily arrived, one again began to speak of the last day, not with special dread, to be sure, but it was still something that I put without examination beside the rest of the incomprehensible.

When I arrived at W.'s yesterday noon I heard the voice of his sister greeting me, but I did not see her herself until her fragile figure detached itself from the rocking chair standing in front of me.

This morning my nephew's circumcision. A short, bow-legged man, Austerlitz, who already has 2,800 circumcisions behind him, carried the thing out very skilfully. It is an operation made more difficult by the fact that the boy, instead of lying on a table, lies on his grandfather's lap, and by the fact that the person performing the operation, instead of paying close attention, must whisper prayers. First the boy is prevented from moving by wrappings which leave only his member free, then the surface to be operated on is defined precisely by putting on a perforated metal disc, then the operation is performed with what is almost an ordinary knife, a sort of fish knife. One sees blood and raw flesh, the *moule* [38] bustles about briefly with his long-nailed, trembling fingers and pulls skin from some place or other over the wound like the finger of a glove. At once everything is all right, the child has scarcely cried. Now there remains only a short prayer during which the *moule* drinks some wine and with his fingers, not yet entirely unbloody, carries some wine to the child's lips. Those present pray: "As he has now entered into the covenant, so may he enter into knowledge of the Torah, a happy marriage and the performance of good deeds."

Today when I heard the *moule*'s assistant say the grace after meals and those present, aside from the two grandfathers, spent the time in dreams or boredom with a complete lack of understanding of the prayer, I saw Western European Judaism before me in a transition whose end is clearly unpredictable and about which those most closely affected are not concerned, but, like all people truly in transition, bear what is imposed upon them. It is so indisputable that these religious forms which have reached their final end have merely a historical character, even as they are practiced today, that only a short time was needed this very morning to interest the people present in the obsolete custom of circumcision and its half-sung prayers by describing it to them as something out of history.

Löwy, whom I keep waiting half an hour almost every evening, said to me yesterday: For several days I have been looking up at your window while waiting. First I see a light there; if I have come early, as I usually do, I assume that you are still working. Then the light is put out, in the next room the light stays on, you are therefore having dinner; then the light goes on again in your room, you are therefore brushing your teeth; then the light is put out, you are therefore already on the stairs, but then the light is put on again.

December 25. What I understand of contemporary Jewish literature in Warsaw through Löwy, and of contemporary Czech literature partly through my own insight, points to the fact that many of the benefits of literature—the stirring of minds, the coherence of national consciousness, often unrealized in public life and always tending to disintegrate, the pride which a nation gains from a literature of its own and the support it is afforded in the face of the hostile surrounding world, this keeping of a diary by a nation which is something entirely different from historiography and results in a more rapid (and yet always closely scrutinized) development, the spiritualization of the broad area of public life, the assimilation of dissatisfied elements that are immediately put to use precisely in this sphere where only stagnation can do harm, the constant integration of a people with respect to its whole that the incessant bustle of the magazines creates, the narrowing down of the attention of a nation upon itself and the accepting of what is foreign only in reflection, the birth of a respect for those active in literature, the transitory awakening in the younger generation of higher aspirations, which nevertheless leaves its permanent mark, the acknowledgment of literary events as objects of political solicitude, the dignification of the antithesis between fathers and sons and the possibility of discussing this, the presentation of national faults in a manner that is very painful, to be sure, but also liberating and deserving of forgiveness, the beginning of a lively and therefore self-respecting book trade and the eagerness for books—all these effects can be produced even by a literature whose development is not in actual fact unusually broad in scope, but seems to be, because it lacks outstanding talents. The liveliness of such a literature exceeds even that of one rich in talent, for, as it has no writer whose great gifts could silence at least the majority of cavilers, literary competition on the greatest scale has a real justification.

A literature not penetrated by a great talent has no gap through which the irrelevant might force its way. Its claim to attention thereby becomes more compelling. The independence of the individual writer, naturally only within the national boundaries, is better preserved. The lack of irresistible national models keeps the completely untalented away from literature. But even mediocre talent would not suffice for a writer to be influenced by the unstriking qualities of the fashionable writers of the moment, or to introduce the works of foreign literatures, or to imitate the foreign literature that has already been introduced; this is plain, for example, in a literature rich in great talents, such as the German is, where the worst writers limit their imitation to what they find at home. The creative and beneficent force exerted in these directions by a literature poor in its component parts proves especially effective when it begins to create a literary history out of the records of its dead writers. These writers' undeniable influence, past and present, becomes so matter of fact that it can take the place of their writings. One speaks of the latter and means the former, indeed, one even reads the latter and sees only the former. But since that effect cannot be forgotten, and since the writings themselves do not act independently upon the memory, there is no forgetting and no remembering again. Literary history offers an unchangeable, dependable whole that is hardly affected by the taste of the day.

A small nation's memory is not smaller than the memory of a large one and so can digest the existing material more thoroughly. There are, to be sure, fewer experts in literary history employed, but literature is less a concern of literary history than of the people, and thus, if not purely, it is at least reliably preserved. For the claim that the national consciousness of a small people makes on the individual is such that everyone must always be prepared to know that part of the literature which has come down to him, to support it, to defend it—to defend it even if he does not know it and support it.

The old writings acquire a multiplicity of interpretations; despite the mediocre material, this goes on with an energy that is restrained only by the fear that one may too easily exhaust them, and by the reverence they are accorded by common consent. Everything is done very honestly, only within a bias that is never resolved, that refuses to countenance any weariness, and is spread for miles around when a skilful hand is lifted up. But in the end bias interferes not only with a broad view but with a close insight as well—so that all these observations are canceled out.

Since people lack a sense of context, their literary activities are out of context too. They depreciate something in order to be able to look down upon it from above, or they praise it to the skies in order to have a place up there beside it. (Wrong.) Even though something is often thought through calmly, one still does not reach the boundary where it connects up with similar things, one reaches this boundary soonest in politics, indeed, one even strives to see it before it is there, and often sees this limiting boundary everywhere. The narrowness of the field, the concern too for simplicity and uniformity, and, finally, the consideration that the inner independence of the literature makes the external connection with politics harmless, result in the dissemination of literature within a country on the basis of political slogans.

There is universal delight in the literary treatment of petty themes whose scope is not permitted to exceed the capacity of small enthusiasms and which are sustained by their polemical possibilities. Insults, intended as literature, roll back and forth, among the more violent temperaments they fly back and forth. What in great literature goes on down below, constituting a not indispensable cellar of the structure, here takes place in the full light of day, what is there a matter of passing interest for a few, here absorbs everyone no less than as a matter of life and death.

A character sketch of the literature of small peoples. Good results in both cases.

Here the results in individual instances are even better.

1. Liveliness:
   a. Conflict.
   b. Schools.
   c. Magazines.
2. Less constraint:
   a. Absence of principles.
   b. Minor themes.
   c. Easy formation of symbols.
   d. Throwing off of the untalented.
3. Popularity.
   a. Connection with politics.
   b. Literary history.
   c. Faith in literature, can make up their own laws.

It is difficult to readjust when one has felt this useful, happy life in all one's being.

Circumcision in Russia. Throughout the house, wherever there is a door, tablets the size of a hand printed with Kabbalistic symbols are hung up to protect the mother from evil spirits during the time between the birth and the circumcision. The evil spirits are especially dangerous to her and the child at this time, perhaps because her body is so very open and therefore offers an easy entrance to everything evil and because the child too, so long as it has not been accepted into the covenant, can offer no resistance to evil. That is also the reason why a female attendant is taken in, so that the mother may not remain alone for a moment. For seven days after the birth, except on Friday, also in order to ward off evil spirits, ten to fifteen children, always different ones, led by the *belfer* (assistant teacher), are admitted to the bedside of the mother, there repeat the

Shema Israel, and are then given candy. These innocent, five- to eight-year-old children are supposed to be especially effective in driving back the evil spirits, who press forward most strongly toward evening. On Friday a special celebration is held, just as in general one banquet follows another during this week. Before the day of the circumcision the evil ones are wildest, and so the last night is a night of wakefulness and until morning someone watches beside the mother. The circumcision follows, often in the presence of more than a hundred relatives and friends. The most distinguished person present is permitted to carry the child. The circumciser, who performs his office without payment, is usually a drinker—busy as he is, he has no time for the various holiday foods and so simply pours down some brandy. Thus they all have red noses and reeking breaths. It is therefore not very pleasant when, after the operation has been performed, they suck the bloody member with this mouth, in the prescribed manner. The member is then sprinkled with sawdust and heals in about three days.

A close-knit family life does not seem to be so very common among and characteristic of the Jews, especially those in Russia. Family life is also found among Christians, after all, and the fact that women are excluded from the study of the Talmud is really destructive of Jewish family life; when the man wants to discuss learned talmudic matters— the very core of his life—with guests, the women withdraw to the next room even if they need not do so—so it is even more characteristic of the Jews that they come together at every possible opportunity, whether to pray or to study or to discuss divine matters or to eat holiday meals whose basis is usually a religious one and at which alcohol is drunk only very moderately. They flee to one another, so to speak.

Goethe probably retards the development of the German language by the force of his writing. Even though prose style has often traveled away from him in the interim, still, in the end, as at present, it returns to him with strengthened yearning and even adopts obsolete idioms found in Goethe but otherwise without any particular connection with him, in order to rejoice in the completeness of its unlimited dependence.

In Hebrew my name is Amschel, like my mother's maternal grandfather, whom my mother, who was six years old when he died, can remember as a very pious and learned man with a long, white beard. She remembers how she had to take hold of the toes of the corpse and ask forgiveness for any offense she may have committed against her grandfather. She also remembers her grandfather's many books which lined the walls. He bathed in the river every day, even in winter, when he chopped a hole in the ice for his bath. My mother's mother died of typhus at an early age. From the time of this death her grandmother became melancholy, refused to eat, spoke with no one, once, a year after the death of her daughter, she went for a walk and did not return, her body was found in the Elbe. An even more learned man than her grandfather was my mother's great-grandfather, Christians and Jews held him in equal honor; during a fire a miracle took place as a result of his piety, the flames jumped over and spared his house while the houses around it burned down. He had four sons, one was converted to Christianity and became a doctor. All but my mother's grandfather died young. He had one son, whom my mother knew as crazy Uncle Nathan, and one daughter, my mother's mother.

To run against the window and, weak after exerting all one's strength, to step over the window sill through the splintered wood and glass.

December 26. Slept badly again, the third night now. So the three holidays during which I had hoped to write things which were to have helped me through the whole year, I spent in a state requiring help. On Christmas Eve, walk with Löwy in the direction of Stern. Yesterday *Blümale oder die Perle von Warschau*. For her steadfast love and loyalty Blümale is distinguished by the author with the honorific title, "Pearl of Warsaw," in the name of the play. Only the exposed, long, delicate throat of Mrs. Tschissik explains the shape of her face. The glint of tears in Mrs. Klug's eyes when singing a monotonously rhythmic melody into which the audience lets their heads hang, seemed to me by far to surpass in significance the song, the theater, the cares of all the audience, indeed my imagination. View through the back curtain into the dressing room, directly to Mrs. Klug, who is standing there in a white petticoat and a short-sleeved shirt. My uncertainty about the feelings of the audience and therefore my strenuous inner spurring on of its enthusiasm. The skilful, amiable manner in which I spoke to Miss T. and her escort yesterday. It was part of the freedom of the good spirits which I felt yesterday and even as early as Saturday, that, although it was definitely not necessary, because of a certain complaisance toward the world and a reckless modesty I made use of a few seemingly embarrassed words and gestures. I was alone with my mother, and that too I took easily and well; looked at everyone with steadiness.

List of things which today are easy to imagine as ancient: the crippled beggars on the way to promenades and picnic places, the unilluminated atmosphere at night, the crossed girders of the bridge.

A list of those passages in *Dichtung und Wahrheit* that, by a peculiarity on which one cannot place one's finger, give an unusually strong impression of liveliness not essentially consistent with what is actually described; for instance, call up the image of the boy Goethe, how—curious, richly dressed, loved and lively—he makes his way into the homes of all his acquaintances so that he may see and hear everything that is to be seen and heard. Now, when I leaf through the book, I cannot find any such passages, they all seem clear to me and have a liveliness that cannot be heightened by any accident. I must wait until some time when I am reading innocently along and then stop at the right passages.

It is unpleasant to listen to Father talk with incessant insinuations about the good fortune of people today and especially of his children, about the sufferings he had to endure in his youth. No one denies that for years, as a result of insufficient winter clothing, he had open sores on his legs, that he often went hungry, that when he was only ten he had to push a cart through the villages, even in winter and very early in the morning—but, and this is something he will not understand, these facts, taken together with the further fact that I have not gone through all this, by no means lead to the conclusion that I have been happier than he, that he may pride himself on these sores on his legs, which is something he assumes and asserts from the very beginning, that I cannot appreciate his past sufferings, and that, finally, just because I have not gone through the same sufferings I must be endlessly grateful to him. How gladly I would listen if he would talk on about his youth and parents, but to hear all this in a boastful and quarrelsome tone is torment. Over and over again he claps his hands together: "Who can understand that today! What do the children know! No one has gone through that! Does a child understand that today!" He spoke again in the same way today to Aunt Julie, who was visiting us. She too has the huge face of all Father's relatives. There is something wrong and somewhat disturbing about the set or color of her eyes. At the age of ten she was hired out as a cook. In a skimpy wet skirt, in the severe cold, she had to run out for something, the skin on her legs cracked, the skimpy skirt froze and it was only that evening, in bed, that it dried.

December 27. An unfortunate man, one who is condemned to have no children, is terribly imprisoned in his misfortune. Nowhere a hope for revival, for help from luckier stars. He must live his life afflicted by his misfortune, and when its circle is ended must resign himself to it and not start out again to see whether, on a longer path, under other circumstances of body and time, the misfortune which he has suffered could disappear or even produce something good.

My feeling when I write something that is wrong might be depicted as follows: In front of two holes in the ground a man is waiting for something to appear that can rise up only out of the hole on his right. But while this hole remains covered over by a dimly visible lid, one thing after another rises up out of the hole on his left, keeps trying to attract his attention, and in the end succeeds in doing this without any difficulty because of its swelling size, which, much as the man may try to prevent it, finally covers up even the right hole. But the man—he does not want to leave this place, and indeed refuses to at any price —has nothing but these appearances, and although—fleeting as they are, their strength is used up by their merely appearing—they cannot satisfy him, he still strives, whenever out of weakness they are arrested in their rising up, to drive them up and scatter them into the air if only he can thus bring up others; for the permanent sight of one is unbearable, and moreover he continues to hope that after the false appearances have been exhausted, the true will finally appear.

How weak this picture is. An incoherent assumption is thrust like a board between the actual feeling and the metaphor of the description.

December 28. The torment that the factory causes me. Why didn't I object when they made me promise to work there in the afternoons. No one used force to make me do it, but my father compels me by his reproaches, Karl by his silence and I by my consciousness of guilt. I know nothing about the factory, and this morning, when the committee made an inspection, I stood around uselessly with my tail between my legs. I deny that it is possible for me to fathom all the details of the operation of the factory. And if I should succeed in doing it by endlessly questioning and pestering all those concerned, what would I have achieved? I would be able to do nothing practical

with this knowledge, I am fit only for spectacular performances to which the sound common sense of my boss
adds the salt that makes it look like a really good job. But
through this empty effort spent on the factory I would, on
the other hand, rob myself of the use of the few afternoon
hours that belong to me, which would of necessity lead to
the complete destruction of my existence, which, even
apart from this, becomes more and more hedged in.

This afternoon, while taking a walk, for the duration
of a few steps I saw coming toward me or crossing my
path entirely imaginary members of the committee that
caused me such anxiety this morning.

December 29. Those lively passages in Goethe. Page
265, "I therefore led my friend into the woods."
Goethe: 307. "Now I heard during these hours no other
conversation save what concerned medicine or natural
history, and my imagination was drawn in quite another
direction."

The difficulties of bringing to an end even a short essay
lie not in the fact that we feel the end of the piece demands
a fire which the actual content up to that point has not
been able to produce out of itself, they arise rather from
the fact that even the shortest essay demands of the
author a degree of self-satisfaction and of being lost in
himself out of which it is difficult to step into the everyday air without great determination and an external incen-
tive, so that, before the essay is rounded to a close and one
might quietly slip away, one bolts, driven by unrest, and
then the end must be completed from the outside with

hands which must not only do the work but hold on as well.

December 30. My urge to imitate has nothing of the actor in it, its chief lack is unity. The whole range of those characteristics which are rough and striking, I cannot imitate at all, I have always failed when I attempted it, it is contrary to my nature. On the other hand, I have a decided urge to imitate them in their details, the way certain people manipulate walking sticks, the way they hold their hands, the movements of their fingers, and I can do it without any effort. But this very effortlessness, this thirst for imitation, sets me apart from the actor, because this effortlessness reflects itself in the fact that no one is aware that I am imitating. Only my own satisfied, or more often reluctant, appreciation shows me that I have been successful. Far beyond this external imitation, however, goes the inner, which is often so striking and strong that there is no room at all within me to observe and verify it, and it first confronts me in my memory. But here the imitation is so complete and replaces my own self with so immediate a suddenness that, even assuming it could be made visible at all, it would be unbearable on the stage. The spectator cannot be asked to endure what passes beyond the bounds of play-acting. If an actor who is supposed to thrash another according to the plot really does thrash him, out of excitement, out of an excess of emotion, and the other actor screams in pain, then the spectator must become a man and intervene. But what seldom happens in this way happens countless times in lesser ways. The essence of the bad actor consists not in the fact that he imitates too little, but rather in the fact that as a result of gaps in his education, experience and talent he imitates the wrong models.

But his most essential fault is still that he does not observe the limits of the play and imitates too much. His hazy notion of the demands of the stage drives him to this, and even if the spectator thinks one actor or another is bad because he stands around stiffly, toys with his fingers at the edge of his pocket, puts his hands on his hips improperly, listens for the prompter, in spite of the fact that things have changed completely maintains an anxious solemnity regardless, still, even this actor who suddenly dropped from nowhere on the stage is bad only because he imitates too much, even if he does so only in his mind. (December 31.) For the very reason that his abilities are so limited, he is afraid to give less than all he has. Even though his ability may not be so small that it cannot be divided up, he does not want to betray the fact that under certain circumstances, by the exercise of his own will, he can dispose of less than all his art.

In the morning I felt so fresh for writing, but now the idea that I am to read to Max in the afternoon blocks me completely. This shows too how unfit I am for friendship, assuming that friendship in this sense is even possible. For since a friendship without interruption of one's daily life is unthinkable, a great many of its manifestations are blown away time and again, even if its core remains undamaged. From the undamaged core they are formed anew, but as every such formation requires time, and not everything that is expected succeeds, one can never, even aside from the change in one's personal moods, pick up again where one left off last time. Out of this, in friendships that have a deep foundation, an uneasiness must arise before every fresh meeting which need not be so great that it is felt as such, but which can disturb one's conversation and behavior to such a degree that one is consciously astonished, especially as one is not aware of, or cannot believe, the reason for it. So how am I to read to M. or even think, while writing down what follows, that I shall read it to him.

Besides, I am disturbed by my having leafed through the diary this morning to see what I could read to M. In this examination I have found neither that what I have written so far is especially valuable nor that it must simply be thrown away. My opinion lies between the two and closer to the first, yet it is not of such a nature that, judging by the value of what I have written, I must, in spite of my weakness, regard myself as exhausted. Despite that, the sight of the mass of what I had written diverted me almost irrecoverably from the fountainhead of my writing for the next hour, because my attention was to a certain extent lost downstream, as it were, in the same channel.

While I sometimes think that all through the time I was at the Gymnasium and before that, as well, I was able to think unusually clearly, and only the later weakening of my memory prevents me from judging it correctly today, I still recognize at other times that my poor memory is only trying to flatter me and that I was mentally inert, at least in things themselves insignificant but having serious consequences. So I remember that when I was at the Gymnasium I often—even if not very thoroughly, I probably tired easily even then—argued the existence of God with Bergmann in a talmudic style either my own or imitated from him. At the time I liked to begin with a theme I had found in a Christian magazine (I believe it was *Die christliche Welt*) in which a watch and the world and the watchmaker and God were compared to one another, and the existence of the watchmaker was supposed to prove that of God. In my opinion I was able to refute this very well as far as Bergmann was concerned, even though this refutation was not firmly grounded in me and I had to piece it together for myself like a jigsaw puzzle before using it. Such a refutation once took place while we were walking around the Rathaus tower. I remember this clearly because once, years ago, we reminded each other of it.

But while I thought I was distinguishing myself—I had no other motive than the desire to distinguish myself and my joy in making an impression and in the impression itself—it was only as a result of giving it insufficient thought that I endured always having to go around dressed in the wretched clothes which my parents had made for me by one customer after another, longest by a tailor in Nusle. I naturally noticed—it was obvious—that I was unusually badly dressed, and even had an eye for others who were well dressed, but for years on end my mind did not succeed in recognizing in my clothes the cause of my miserable appearance. Since even at that time, more in tendency than in fact, I was on the way to underestimating myself, I was convinced that it was only on me that clothes assumed this appearance, first looking as stiff as a board, then hanging in wrinkles. I did not want new clothes at all, for if I was going to look ugly in any case, I wanted at least to be comfortable and also to avoid exhibiting the ugliness of the new clothes to the world that had grown accustomed to the old ones. These always long-drawn-out refusals on the frequent occasions when my mother (who with the eyes of an adult was still able to find differences between these new clothes and the old ones) wanted to have new clothes of this sort made for me, had this effect upon me that, with my parents concurring, I had to conclude that I was not at all concerned about my appearance.

January 2. As a result I let the awful clothes affect even my posture, walked around with my back bowed, my shoulders drooping, my hands and arms at awkward angles, was afraid of mirrors because they showed in me an ugliness which in my opinion was inevitable, which moreover could not have been an entirely truthful reflection, for had I actually looked like that, I certainly would have attracted even more attention, suffered gentle pokes in the back from my mother on Sunday walks and admonitions and prophecies which were much too abstract for me to be able to relate them to the worries I then had. In general I lacked principally the ability to provide even in the slightest detail for the real future. I thought only of things in the present and their present condition, not because of thoroughness or any special, strong interest, but rather, to the extent that weakness in thinking was not the cause, because of sorrow and fear—sorrow, because the present was so sad for me that I thought I could not leave it before it resolved itself into happiness; fear, because, like my fear of the slightest action in the present, I also considered myself, in view of my contemptible, childish appearance, unworthy of forming a serious, responsible opinion of the great, manly future which usually seemed so impossible to me that every short step forward appeared to me to be counterfeit and the next step unattainable.

I admitted the possibility of miracles more readily than that of real progress, but was too detached not to keep the sphere of miracles and that of real progress sharply divided. I was therefore able to spend a good deal of time before falling asleep in imagining that someday, a rich man in a coach and four, I would drive into the Jewish quarter, with a magic word set free a beautiful maiden who was being beaten unjustly, and carry her off in my coach; but untouched by this silly make-believe, which probably fed only on an already unhealthy sexuality, I remained convinced that I would not pass my final examinations that year, and if I did, I would not get on in the next class, and if by some swindle I could avoid even that, then I would certainly fail decisively in my graduation examination, convinced also that I would all at once—the precise moment did not matter —reveal some unheard-of inability and very definitely surprise my parents as well as the rest of the world, who had been lulled to sleep by my outwardly regular progress. Since I always looked only to my inability as my guide into the future—only seldom to my feeble literary work—considering the future never did me any good; it was only a spinning out of my present grief. If I chose to, I could of course walk erect, but it made me tired, nor could I see how a crooked back would hurt me in the future. If I should have a future, then, I felt, everything will straighten itself out of its own accord. I did not choose such a principle because it involved a confidence in a future in whose existence I did not believe, its purpose was only to make living easier for me, to walk, to dress, to wash, to read, above all to coop myself up at home in a way that took the least effort and required the least spirit. If I went beyond that I could think only of ridiculous solutions.

Once it seemed impossible to get along without a black dress suit, especially as I also had to decide whether I would join a dancing class. The tailor in Nusle was sent for and the cut of the suit discussed. I was undecided, as I always was in such cases, they made me afraid that by a definite statement I would be swept away not only into an immediate unpleasantness, but beyond that into something even worse. So at first I didn't want a dress suit, but when they shamed me before the stranger by pointing out that I had no dress suit, I put up with having a tail coat discussed; but since I regarded a tail coat as a fearful revolution one could forever talk about but on which one could never decide, we agreed on a tuxedo, which, because of its similarity to the usual sack coat, seemed to me at least bearable. But when I heard that the vest of the tuxedo had to be cut low and I would therefore have to wear a stiff shirt as well, my determination almost exceeded my strength, since something like this had to be averted. I did not want such a tuxedo, rather, if I had to have one, a tuxedo lined and trimmed with silk indeed, but one that could be buttoned high. The tailor had never heard of such a tuxedo, but he remarked that no matter what I intended to do with such a jacket, it couldn't be worn for dancing. Good, then it couldn't be worn for dancing, I didn't want to dance anyhow, that hadn't been decided on yet in any case, on the contrary, I wanted the jacket made for me as I had described it. The tailor's stubbornness was increased by the fact that until now I had always submitted with shamed haste to being measured for new clothes and to having them tried on, without expressing any opinions or wishes. So there was nothing else for me to do, and also since my mother insisted on it, but to go with him, painful as it was, across the Altstädter Ring to a second-hand clothing store in the window of which I had for quite some time seen displayed a simple tuxedo and had recognized it as suitable for me. But unfortunately it had already been removed from the window, I could not see it inside the store even by looking my hardest, I did not dare to go into the store just to look at the tuxedo, so we returned, disagreeing as before. I felt as though the future tuxedo was already cursed by the uselessness of this errand, at least I used my annoyance with the pros and cons of the argument as an excuse to send the tailor away with some small order or other and an indefinite promise about the tuxedo while I, under the reproaches of my mother, remained wearily behind, barred forever—everything happened to me forever —from girls, an elegant appearance and dances. The instantaneous cheerfulness that this induced in me made me miserable, and besides, I was afraid that I had made myself ridiculous before the tailor as none of his customers ever had before.

January 3. Read a good deal in *Die Neue Rundschau*. Beginning of the novel *Der nackte Mann*.[39] The clarity of the whole a little too thin, sureness in the details. *Gabriel Schillings Flucht* by Hauptmann. Education of people. Instructive in the bad and the good.

New Year's Eve I had planned to read to Max from the diaries in the afternoon, I looked forward to it, and it did not come off. We were not in tune, I felt a calculating pettiness and haste in him that afternoon, he was almost not my friend but nevertheless still dominated me to the extent that through his eyes I saw myself uselessly leafing through the notebooks over and over again, and found this leafing back and forth, which continually showed the same pages flying by, disgusting. It was naturally impossible to work together in this mutual tension, and the one page of "Richard and Samuel" that we finished amidst mutual resistance is simply proof of Max's energy, but otherwise bad. New Year's Eve at Čada's. Not so bad, because Weltsch, Kisch and someone else added new blood so that finally, although only within the limits of that group, I again found my way back to Max. I then pressed his hand on the crowded Graben, though without looking at him, and with my three notebooks pressed to me, as I remember, proudly went straight home.

The fern-shaped flames blazing up from a melting pot on the street in front of a building under construction.

It is easy to recognize a concentration in me of all my forces on writing. When it became clear in my organism that writing was the most productive direction for my being to take, everything rushed in that direction and left empty all those abilities which were directed toward the joys of sex, eating, drinking, philosophical reflection and above all music. I atrophied in all these directions. This was necessary because the totality of my strengths was so slight that only collectively could they even halfway serve the purpose of my writing. Naturally, I did not find this purpose independently and consciously, it found itself, and is now interfered with only by the office, but that interferes with it completely. In any case I shouldn't complain that I can't put up with a sweetheart, that I understand almost exactly as much of love as I do of music and have to resign myself to the most superficial effects I may pick up, that on New Year's Eve I dined on parsnips and spinach, washed down with a glass of Ceres, and that on Sunday I was unable to take part in Max's lecture on his philosophical work—the compensation for all this is clear as day. My development is now complete and, so far as I can see, there is nothing left to sacrifice; I need only throw my work in the office out of this complex in order to begin my real life in which, with the progress of my work, my face will finally be able to age in a natural way.

The sudden turn a conversation takes when in the discussion, which at first has dealt in detail with worries of the inner existence, the question is raised (not really breaking the conversation off, but naturally not growing out of it,

either) of when and where one will meet the next time and
the circumstances that must be considered in deciding this.
And if the conversation also ends with a shaking of hands,
then one takes one's leave with momentary faith in the pure,
firm structure of our life and with respect for it.

In an autobiography one cannot avoid writing "often"
where truth would require that "once" be written. For one
always remains conscious that the word "once" explodes
that darkness on which the memory draws; and though it is
not altogether spared by the word "often," either, it is at
least preserved in the opinion of the writer, and he is carried across parts which perhaps never existed at all in his life
but serve him as a substitute for those which his memory
can no longer even guess at.

January 4. It is only because of my vanity that I like so
much to read to my sisters (so that today, for instance, it
is already too late to write). Not that I am convinced that
I shall achieve something significant in the reading, it is
only that I am dominated by the passion to get so close to
the good works I read that I merge with them, not through
my own merit, indeed, but only through the attentiveness
of my listening sisters, which has been excited by what is
being read and is unresponsive to unessentials; and therefore too, under the concealment my vanity affords me, I
can share as creator in the effect which the work alone has
exercised. That is why I really read admirably to my sisters
and stress the accents with extreme exactness just as I feel
them, because later I am abundantly rewarded not only by
myself but also by my sisters.

But if I read to Brod or Baum or others, just because of
my pretensions my reading must appear horribly bad to

everyone, even if they know nothing of the usual quality of my reading; for here I know that the listener is fully aware of the separation between me and what is being read, here I cannot merge completely with what I read without becoming ridiculous in my own opinion, an opinion which can expect no support from the listener; with my voice I flutter around what is being read, try to force my way in here and there because they want me to, but don't intend this seriously because they don't expect that much from me at all; but what they really want me to do, to read without vanity, calmly and distantly, and to become passionate only when a genuine passion demands it, that I cannot do; but although I believe that I have resigned myself to reading badly to everyone except my sisters, my vanity, which this time has no justification, still shows itself: I feel offended if anyone finds fault with my reading, I become flushed and want to read on quickly, just as I usually strive, once I have begun, to read on endlessly, out of an unconscious yearning that during the course of the long reading there may be produced, at least in me, that vain, false feeling of integration with what I read which makes me forget that I shall never be strong enough at any one moment to impose my feelings on the clear vision of the listener and that at home it is always my sisters who initiate this longed-for substitution.

January 5. For two days I have noticed, whenever I choose to, an inner coolness and indifference. Yesterday evening, during my walk, every little street sound, every eye turned toward me, every picture in a showcase, was more important to me than myself.

Uniformity. History.

When it looks as if you had made up your mind finally to stay at home for the evening, when you have put on your house jacket and sat down after supper with a light on the table to the piece of work or the game that usually precedes your going to bed, when the weather outside is unpleasant so that staying indoors seems natural, and when you have already been sitting quietly at the table for so long that your departure must occasion not only paternal anger but surprise to everyone, when besides, the stairs are in darkness and the front door locked and in spite of all that you have started up in a sudden fit of restlessness, changed your jacket, abruptly dressed yourself for the street, explained that you must go out and with a few curt words of leave-taking actually gone out, banging the flat door more or less hastily according to the degree of displeasure you think you have left behind you and so cut off the general discussion of your departure, and when you find yourself once more in the street with limbs swinging extra freely in answer to the unexpected liberty you have procured for them, when as a result of this decisive action you feel aroused within yourself all the potentialities of decisive action, when you recognize with more than usual significance that your strength is greater than your need to accomplish effortlessly the swiftest of changes, that left alone you grow in understanding and calm, and in the enjoyment of them—then for that evening you have so completely got away from your family that the most distant journey could not take you farther and you have lived through what is for Europe so extreme an experience of solitude that one can only call it Russian. All this is still heightened if at such a late hour in the evening you look up a friend to see how he is getting on.[40]

A Manuscript Page of the *Diaries*

(SEE FACING PAGE)

Invited Weltsch to come to Mrs. Klug's benefit. Löwy, with his severe headaches that probably indicate a serious head ailment, leaned against a wall down in the street where he was waiting for me, his right hand pressed in despair against his forehead. I pointed him out to Weltsch who, from his sofa, leaned out of the window. I thought it was the first time in my life that I had so easily observed from the window an incident down in the street that concerned me so closely. In and of itself, this kind of observation is familiar to me from Sherlock Holmes.

January 6. Yesterday *Vizekönig* by Feimann. My receptivity to the Jewishness in these plays deserts me because they are too monotonous and degenerate into a wailing that prides itself on isolated, violent outbreaks. When I saw the first plays it was possible for me to think that I had come upon a Judaism on which the beginnings of my own rested, a Judaism that was developing in my direction and so would enlighten and carry me farther along in my own clumsy Judaism, instead, it moves farther away from me the more I hear of it. The people remain, of course, and I hold fast to them.

Mrs. Klug was giving a benefit and therefore sang several new songs and made a few new jokes. But only her opening song held me wholly under her influence, after that I had the strongest reaction to every detail of her appearance, to her arms, stretched out when she sings, and her snapping fingers, to the tightly twisted curls at her temples, to her thin shirt, flat and innocent under her vest, to her lower lip that she pursed once while she savored the effect of a joke ("Look, I speak every language, but in Yiddish"), to her fat little feet in their thick white stockings. But when she sang new songs yesterday she spoiled the main effect she had on me, which lay in the fact that here was a person exhibiting herself who had discovered a few jokes and songs that revealed her temperament and all its strong points to the utmost perfection. When this display is a success, everything is a success, and if we like to let this person affect us often, we will naturally—and in this, perhaps, all the audience agrees with me—not let ourselves be misled by the constant repetition of the songs, which are always the same, we will rather approve of it as an aid to concentration, like the darkening of the hall, for example, and, as far as the woman is concerned, recognize in her that fearlessness and self-awareness which are exactly what we are seeking. So when the new songs came along, songs that could reveal nothing new in Mrs. Klug since the old ones had done their duty so completely, and when these songs, without any justification at all, claimed one's attention purely as songs, and when they in this way distracted one's attention from Mrs. Klug but at the same time showed that she herself was not at ease in them either, part of the time making a failure of them and part of the time exaggerating her grimaces and gestures, one had to become annoyed and was consoled only by the fact that the memory of her perfect performances in the past, resulting from her unshakable integrity, was too firm to be disturbed by the present sight.

January 7. Unfortunately Mrs. Tschissik always has parts which show only the essence of her character, she always plays women and girls who all at once are unhappy, despised, dishonored, wronged, but who are not allowed time to develop their characters in a natural sequence. The explosive, natural strength with which she plays these roles makes them climactic only when she acts them, in the play as it is written, because of the wealth of acting they require, these roles are only suggestions, but this shows what she would be capable of. One of her important gestures begins as a shudder in her trembling hips, which she holds somewhat stiffly. Her little daughter seems to have one hip completely stiff. When the actors embrace, they hold each other's wigs in place.

Recently, when I went up to Löwy's room with him so that he could read me the letter he had written to the Warsaw writer, Nomberg, we met the Tschissik couple on the landing. They were carrying their costumes for *Kol Nidre*, wrapped in tissue paper like matzos, up to their room. We stopped for a little while. The railing supported my hands and the intonations of my sentences. Her large mouth, so close in front of me, assumed surprising but natural shapes. It was my fault that the conversation threatened to end hopelessly, for in my effort hurriedly to express all my love and devotion I only remarked that the affairs of the troupe were going wretchedly, that their repertoire was exhausted, that they could therefore not remain much longer and that the lack of interest that the Prague Jews took in them was incomprehensible. Monday I must—she asked me—come to see *Sedernacht*, although I already know the play. Then I shall hear her sing the song ("Hear, O Israel") which, she remembers from a remark I once made, I love especially.

"Yeshivahs" are talmudic colleges supported by many communities in Poland and Russia. The cost is not very great because these schools are usually housed in old, unusable buildings in which, besides the rooms where the students study and sleep, is found the apartment of the Rosh Yeshivah, who also performs other services in the community, and of his assistant. The students pay no tuition and take their meals in turn with the various members of the community. Although these schools are based on the most severely orthodox principles, it is precisely in them that apostate progress has its source: since young people from distant places come together here, precisely the poor, the energetic and those who want to get away from their homes; since the supervision is not very strict and the young people are entirely thrown upon one another, and since the most essential part of the instruction is common study and mutual explanation of difficult passages; since the orthodoxy in the various home towns of the students is always the same and therefore not much of a topic for conversation, while the suppressed progressive tendencies take the most varied forms, differing in strength according to the varying circumstances of the towns, so that there is always a lot to talk about; since, furthermore, one person always lays hands on only one or another copy of the forbidden progressive literature, while in the Yeshivah many such copies are brought together from everywhere and exercise a particularly telling effect because every possessor of a copy propagates not only the text but also his own zeal—because of all these reasons and their immediate consequences, in the recent past all the progressive writers, politicians, journalists and scholars have come out of these schools. The reputation of these schools among the orthodox has therefore deteriorated very much, while on the other hand young people of advanced inclinations stream to them more than ever.

One famous Yeshivah is in Ostro, a small place eight hours by train from Warsaw. All Ostro is really only a bracket around a short stretch of the highway. Löwy insists it's no longer than his stick. Once, when a count stopped in Ostro with his four-horse traveling carriage, the two lead horses stood outside one end of the place and the rear of the carriage outside the other.

Löwy decided, about the age of fourteen when the constraint of life at home became unbearable for him, to go to Ostro. His father had just slapped him on the shoulder as he was leaving the *klaus* toward evening and had casually told him to see him later, he had something to discuss with him. Because he could obviously expect nothing but the usual reproaches, Löwy went directly from the *klaus* to the railroad station, with no baggage, wearing a somewhat better caftan than usual because it was Saturday evening, and carrying all his money, which he always had with him. He took the ten o'clock train to Ostro where he arrived at seven the next morning. He went straight to the Yeshivah where he made no special stir, anyone can enter a Yeshivah, there are no special entrance requirements. The only striking thing was his entering just at this time—it was summer—which was not customary, and the good caftan he was wearing. But all this was soon settled too, because very young people such as these were, bound to each other by their Jewishness in a degree unknown to us, get to know each other easily. He distinguished himself in his studies, for he had acquired a good deal of knowledge at home. He liked talking to the strange boys, especially as, when they found out about his money, they all crowded around him offering to sell him things. One, who wanted to sell him "days," astonished him especially. Free board was called "days." They were a salable commodity because the members of the community, who wanted to perform a deed pleasing to God by providing free board for no matter what student, did not care who sat at their tables. If a student was unusually clever, it was possible for him to provide himself with two sets of free meals for one day. He could bear up under these double meals so much the better because they were not very ample, after the first meal, one could still swallow down the second with great pleasure, and because it might also happen that one day was doubly provided for while other days were empty. Nevertheless, everyone was happy, naturally, if he found an opportunity to sell such an additional set of free meals advantageously. Now if someone arrived in summer, as Löwy did, at a time when the free board had long since been distributed, the only possible way to get any was to buy it, as the additional sets of free meals which had been available at first had all been reserved by speculators.

The night in the Yeshivah was unbearable. Of course, all the windows were open since it was warm, but the stench and the heat would not stir out of the rooms, the students, who had no real beds, lay down to sleep without undressing, in their sweaty clothes, wherever they happened to be sitting last. Everything was full of fleas. In the morning everyone hurriedly wet his hands and face with water and resumed his studies. Most of the time they studied together, usually two from one book. Debates would often draw a number into a circle. The Rosh Yeshivah explained only the most difficult passages here and there. Although Löwy later—he stayed in Ostro ten days, but slept and ate at the inn—found two like-minded friends (they didn't find one another so easily, because they always first had carefully to test the opinions and reliability of the other person), he nevertheless was very glad to return home because he was accustomed to an orderly life and couldn't stand the homesickness.

In the large room there was the clamor of card playing

and later the usual conversation which Father carries on when he is well, as he is today, loudly if not coherently. The words represented only small shapes in a formless clamor. Little Felix slept in the girls' room, the door of which was wide open. I slept across the way, in my own room. The door of this room, in consideration of my age, was closed. Besides, the open door indicated that they still wanted to lure Felix into the family while I was already excluded.

Yesterday at Baum's. Strobl was supposed to be there, but was at the theater. Baum read a column, "On the Folk-song"; bad. Then a chapter from *Des Schicksals Spiele und Ernst;* very good. I was indifferent, in a bad mood, got no clear impression of the whole. On the way home in the rain Max told me the present plan of "Irma Polak." I could not admit my mood, as Max never gives it proper recognition. I therefore had to be insincere, which finally spoiled everything for me. I was so sorry for myself that I preferred to speak to Max when his face was in the dark, although mine, in the light, could then betray itself more easily. But then the mysterious end of the novel gripped me in spite of all the obstacles. On the way home, after saying good night, regret because of my falsity and pain because of its inevitability. Plan to start a special notebook on my relationship with Max. What is not written down swims before one's eyes and optical accidents determine the total impression.

When I lay on the sofa the loud talking in the room on either side of me, by the women on the left, by the men on the right, gave me the impression that they were coarse, savage beings who could not be appeased, who did not know what they were saying and spoke only in order to set the air in motion, who lifted their faces while speaking and followed the spoken words with their eyes.

So passes my rainy, quiet Sunday, I sit in my bedroom and am at peace, but instead of making up my mind to do some writing, into which I could have poured my whole being the day before yesterday, I have been staring at my fingers for quite a while. This week I think I have been completely influenced by Goethe, have really exhausted the strength of this influence and have therefore become useless.

From a poem by Rosenfeld describing a storm at sea: "The souls flutter, the bodies tremble." When he recites, Löwy clenches the skin on his forehead and the bridge of his nose the way one would think only hands could be clenched. At the most gripping passages, which he wants to bring home to the listener, he himself comes close to us, or rather he enlarges himself by making his appearance more distinct. He steps forward only a little, opens his eyes wide, plucks at his straight black coat with his absent-minded left hand and holds the right out to us, open and large. And we are supposed, even if we are not gripped, to acknowledge that he is gripped and to explain to him how the misfortune which has been described was possible.

I am supposed to pose in the nude for the artist Ascher, as a model for a St. Sebastian.

If I should now, in the evening, return to my relatives, I shall, since I have written nothing that I could enjoy, not appear stranger, more despicable, more useless to them than

I do to myself. All this, naturally, only in my feelings
(which cannot be deceived even by the most precise observation), for actually they all respect me and love me,
too.

January 24. Wednesday. For the following reasons have
not written for so long: I was angry with my boss and
cleared it up only by means of a good letter; was in the
factory several times; read, and indeed greedily, Pines'
L'histoire de la Littérature Judéo-Allemande, 500 pages,
with such thoroughness, haste and joy as I have never yet
shown in the case of similar books; now I am reading
Fromer, *Organismus des Judentums;* finally I spent a lot of
time with the Jewish actors, wrote letters for them, prevailed on the Zionist society to inquire of the Zionist
societies of Bohemia whether they would like to have guest
appearances of the troupe; I wrote the circular that was
required and had it reproduced; saw *Sulamith* once more
and Richter's *Herzele Mejiches* for the first time, was at the
folksong evening of the Bar Kokhba Society, and day before yesterday saw *Graf von Gleichen* by Schmidtbonn.

Folksong evening: Dr. Nathan Birnbaum is the lecturer.
Jewish habit of inserting "my dear ladies and gentlemen"
or just "my dear" at every pause in the talk. Was repeated
at the beginning of Birnbaum's talk to the point of being
ridiculous. But from what I know of Löwy I think that
these recurrent expressions, which are frequently found in
ordinary Yiddish conversation too, such as "Weh ist mir!"
or "S'ist nischt," or "S'ist viel zu reden," are not intended
to cover up embarrassment but are rather intended, like
ever-fresh springs, to stir up the sluggish stream of speech
that is never fluent enough for the Jewish temperament.

January 26. The back of Mr. Weltsch and the silence of the entire hall while listening to the bad poems. Birnbaum: His hair, worn somewhat longish, is cut off abruptly at his neck, which is very erect either in itself or because of its sudden nudity. Large, crooked nose, not too narrow and yet with broad sides, which looks handsome chiefly because it is in proper proportion to his large beard.—Gollanin, the singer. Peaceful, sweetish, beatific, patronizing face turned to the side and down, prolonged smile somewhat sharpened by his wrinkled nose, which may be only part of his breathing technique.

Pines: *Histoire de la Littérature Judéo-Allemande*. Paris 1911.

Soldiers' song: They cut off our beards and earlocks. And they forbid us to keep the Sabbath and holy days.

Or: At the age of five I entered the "Heder" and now I must ride a horse.

> *Wos mir seinen, seinen mir*
> *Ober jüden seinen mir.*
> [What we are, we are,
> But Jews we are.]

Haskalah movement introduced by Mendelssohn at the beginning of the nineteenth century, adherents are called Maskilim, are opposed to the popular Yiddish, tend toward Hebrew and the European sciences. Before the pogroms of 1881 it was not nationalist, later strongly Zionist. Principle formulated by Gordon: "Be a man on the street and a Jew at home." To spread its ideas the Haskalah must use Yiddish and, much as it hates the latter, lays the foundation of its literature.

Other aims are "la lutte contre le chassidisme, l'exaltation de l'instruction et des travaux manuels."

Badchan, the sad folk and wedding minstrel (Eliakum Zunser), talmudic trend of thought.

Le Roman populaire: Eisik Meir Dick (1808–1894) instructive, haskalic. Schomer, still worse, title, for example, "Der podriatechik (l'entrepreneur), ein höchst interessanter Roman. Ein richtiger fach fun leben," or "Die eiserne Frau oder das verkaufte Kind. Ein wunderschöner Roman." Further, in America serial novels, "Zwischen Menschenfressern," twenty-six volumes.

S. J. Abramowitsch (Mendele Mocher Sforim), lyric, subdued gaiety, confused arrangement. *Fishke der Krummer,* Jewish habit of biting the lips.

End of Haskalah 1881. New nationalism and democracy. Flourishing of Yiddish literature.

S. Frug, lyric writer, life in the country by all means. *Délicieux est le sommeil du seigneur dans sa chambre. Sur des oreillers doux, blancs comme la neige. Mais plus délicieux encore est le repos dans le champ sur du foin frais à l'heure du soir, après le travail.*

Talmud: He who interrupts his study to say, "How beautiful is this tree," deserves death.

Lamentations at the west wall of the Temple. Poem: "La fille du Shammes." The beloved rabbi is on his deathbed. The burial of a shroud the size of the rabbi and other mystical measures are of no avail. Therefore at night the elders of the congregation go from house to house with a list and collect from the members of the congregation renunciations of days or weeks of their lives in favor of the rabbi. Deborah, la fille du Shammes, gives "the rest of her life." She dies, the rabbi recovers. At night, when he is studying alone in the synagogue, he hears the voice of Deborah's whole aborted life. The singing at her wedding, her screams in childbed, her lullabies, the voice of her son studying the

Torah, the music at her daughter's wedding. While the songs of lamentation sound over her corpse the rabbi, too, dies.

Peretz: bad Heine lyrics and social poems. Né 1851. Rosenfeld: The poor Yiddish public took up a collection to assure him of a livelihood.

S. Rabinowitz (Sholom Aleichem), né 1859. Custom of great jubilee celebrations in Yiddish literature. Kasrilevke, Menachem Mendel, who emigrated and took his entire fortune with him; although previously he had only studied Talmud, he begins to speculate in the stock market in the big city, comes to a new decision every day and always reports it to his wife with great self-satisfaction; until finally he must beg for traveling expenses.

Peretz: The figure of the *batlan* frequent in the ghettos, lazy and grown clever through idling, lives in the circle of the pious and learned. Many marks of misfortune on them, as they are young people who, although they enjoy idleness, also waste away in it, live in dreams, under the domination of the unrestrained force of unappeased desires.

Mitat neshika, death by a kiss: reserved only for the most pious.

Baal Shem: Before he became a rabbi in Miedzyboz he lived in the Carpathians as a vegetable gardener, later he was his brother-in-law's coachman. His visions came to him on lonely walks. Zohar, "Bible of the Kabbalists."

Jewish theater. Frankfort Purim play, 1708. *Ein schön neu Achashverosh-spiel*, Abraham Goldfaden, 1876–7 Russo-Turkish War, Russian and Galician army contractors had gathered in Bucharest, Goldfaden had also come there in search of a living, heard the crowds in the stores singing Yiddish songs and was encouraged to found a theater. He was not yet able to put women on the stage.

Yiddish performances were forbidden in Russia 1883. They began in London and New York 1884.

J. Gordin 1897 in a jubilee publication of the Jewish theater in New York: The Yiddish theater has an audience of hundreds of thousands, but it cannot expect to see a writer of great talent emerge as long as the majority of its authors are people like me who have become dramatic authors only by chance, who write plays only by force of circumstance and remain isolated and see about them only ignorance, envy, enmity and spite.

January 31. Wrote nothing. Weltsch brings me books about Goethe that provoke in me a distracted excitement that can be put to no use. Plan for an essay, "Goethe's Frightening Nature," fear of the two hours' walk which I have now begun to take in the evening.

February 4. Three days ago Wedekind: *Erdgeist*. Wedekind and his wife, Tilly, act in it. Clear, precise voice of the woman. Narrow, crescent-shaped face. The lower part of the leg branching off to the left when she stood quietly. The play clear even in retrospect, so that one goes home peaceful and aware of oneself. Contradictory impression of what is thoroughly well established and yet remains strange.

On my way to the theater I felt well. I savored my innermost being as though it were honey. Drank it in an uninterrupted draught. In the theater this passed away at once. *Orpheus in the Underworld* with Pallenberg. The performance was so bad, applause and laughter around me in the standing-room so great, that I could think of no way out but to run away after the second act and so silence it all.

Day before yesterday wrote a good letter to Trautenau about a guest appearance for Löwy. Each fresh reading of the letter calmed and strengthened me, there was in it so much unspoken indication of everything good in me.

The zeal, permeating every part of me, with which I read about Goethe (Goethe's conversations, student days, hours with Goethe, a visit of Goethe's to Frankfort) and which keeps me from all writing.

S., merchant, thirty-five years old, member of no religious community, educated in philosophy, interested in literature for the most part only to the extent that it pertains to his writing. Round head, black eyes, small, energetic mustache, firm flesh on his cheeks, thickset body. For years has been studying from nine to one o'clock at night. Born in Stanislau, knows Hebrew and Yiddish. Married to a woman who gives the impression of being limited only because of the quite round shape of her face.

For two days coolness toward Löwy. He asks me about it. I deny it.

Quiet, restrained conversation with Miss T. in the balcony between the acts of *Erdgeist*. In order to achieve a good conversation one must, as it were, push one's hand more deeply, more lightly, more drowsily under the subject to be dealt with, then it can be lifted up astonishingly. Otherwise one breaks one's fingers and thinks of nothing but one's pains.

Story: The evening walks, discovery of quick walking. Introduction, a beautiful, dark room.

Miss T. told me about a scene in her new story where a girl with a bad reputation enters the sewing school. The impression on the other girls. I say that they, who feel clearly in themselves the capacity and desire to earn a bad reputation and who at the same time are able to see for themselves at first hand the kind of misfortune into which one hurls oneself by it, will pity her.

A week ago a lecture in the banquet room of the Jewish Town Hall by Dr. Theilhaber on the decline of the German Jews. It is unavoidable, for (1) if the Jews collect in the cities, the Jewish communities in the country disappear. The pursuit of profit devours them. Marriages are made only with regard to the bride's settlement. Two-child system. (2) Mixed marriages. (3) Conversion.

Amusing scene when Prof. Ehrenfels,[41] who grows more and more handsome and who—with his bald head sharply outlined against the light in a curve that is puffed out at the top, his hands pressed together, with his full voice, which he modulates like a musical instrument, and a confident smile at the meeting—declares himself in favor of mixed races.

February 5. Monday. Weary even of reading *Dichtung und Wahrheit.* I am hard on the outside, cold on the inside. Today, when I came to Dr. F., although we approached each other slowly and deliberately, it was as though we had collided like balls that drive one another back and, themselves out of control, get lost. I asked him whether he was tired. He was not tired, why did I ask? I am tired, I replied, and sat down.

To lift yourself out of such a mood, even if you have to

do it by strength of will, should be easy. I force myself out of my chair, circle the table in long strides, exercise my head and neck, make my eyes sparkle, tighten the muscles around them. Defy my own feelings, welcome Löwy enthusiastically supposing he comes to see me, amiably tolerate my sister in the room while I write, swallow all that is said at Max's, whatever pain and trouble it may cost me, in long draughts. Yet even if I manage fairly well in some of this, one obvious slip, and slips cannot be avoided, will stop the whole process, the easy and the difficult alike, and I will have to turn backward in the circle. So the best resource is to meet everything as calmly as possible, to make yourself an inert mass, and, if you feel that you are carried away, not to let yourself be lured into taking a single unnecessary step, to stare at others with the eyes of an animal, to feel no compunction, to yield to the non-conscious that you believe far away while it is precisely what is burning you, with your own hand to throttle down whatever ghostly life remains in you, that is, to enlarge the final peace of the graveyard and let nothing survive save that. A characteristic movement in such a condition is to run your little finger along your eyebrows.[42]

Short spell of faintness yesterday in the Café City with Löwy. How I bent down over a newspaper to hide it.

Goethe's beautiful silhouette. Simultaneous impression of repugnance when looking at this perfect human body, since to surpass this degree of perfection is unimaginable and yet it looks only as though it had been put together by accident. The erect posture, the dangling arms, the slender throat, the bend in the knees.

My impatience and grief because of my exhaustion are nourished especially on the prospect of the future that is thus prepared for me and which is never out of my sight. What evenings, walks, despair in bed and on the sofa (February 7) are still before me, worse than those I have already endured!

Yesterday in the factory. The girls, in their unbearably dirty and untidy clothes, their hair disheveled as though they had just got up, the expressions on their faces fixed by the incessant noise of the transmission belts and by the individual machines, automatic ones, of course, but unpredictably breaking down, they aren't people, you don't greet them, you don't apologize when you bump into them, if you call them over to do something, they do it but return to their machine at once, with a nod of the head you show them what to do, they stand there in petticoats, they are at the mercy of the pettiest power and haven't enough calm understanding to recognize this power and placate it by a glance, a bow. But when six o'clock comes and they call it out to one another, when they untie the kerchiefs from around their throats and their hair, dust themselves with a brush that passes around and is constantly called for by the impatient, when they pull their skirts on over their heads and clean their hands as well as they can—then at last they are women again, despite pallor and bad teeth they can smile, shake their stiff bodies, you can no longer bump into them, stare at them or overlook them, you move back against the greasy crates to make room for them, hold your hat in your hand when they say good evening, and do not know how to behave when one of them holds your winter coat for you to put on.

February 8. Goethe: My delight in creating was infinite.

I have become more nervous, weaker, and have lost a large part of the calm on which I prided myself years ago. Today, when I received the card from Baum in which he writes that he cannot give the talk at the evening for the Eastern Jews after all, and when I was therefore compelled to think that I should have to take it over, I was over-powered by uncontrollable twitchings the pulsing of my arteries sprang along my body like little flames; if I sat down, my knees trembled under the table and I had to press my hands together. I shall, of course, give a good lecture, that is certain, besides, the restlessness itself, heightened to an extreme on that evening, will pull me together in such a way that there will not be room for restlessness and the talk will come straight out of me as though out of a gun barrel. But it is possible that I shall collapse after it, in any event I shall not be able to get over it for a long time. So little physical strength! Even these few words are written under the influence of weakness.

Yesterday evening with Löwy at Baum's. My liveliness. Recently Löwy translated a bad Hebrew story, "The Eye," at Baum's.

February 13. I am beginning to write the lecture for Löwy's performance. It is on Sunday, the 18th. I shall not have much time to prepare and am really striking up a kind of recitative here as though in an opera. The reason is only that an incessant excitement has been oppressing me for days and that, somewhat hesitant in the face of the actual beginning of the lecture, I want to write down a few words only for myself; in that way, given a little momentum, I shall be able to stand up before the audience. Cold and heat alternate in me with the successive words of the sentence, I dream melodic rises and falls, I read sentences of Goethe's as though my whole body were running down the stresses.

February 25. Hold fast to the diary from today on! Write regularly! Don't surrender! Even if no salvation should come, I want to be worthy of it at every moment. I spent this evening at the family table in complete indifference, my right hand on the arm of the chair in which my sister sat playing cards, my left hand weak in my lap. From time to time I tried to realize my unhappiness, I barely succeeded.

I have written nothing for so long because of having arranged an evening for Löwy in the banquet room of the Jewish Town Hall on February 18th, at which I delivered a little introductory lecture on Yiddish. For two weeks I worried for fear that I could not produce the lecture. On the evening before the lecture I suddenly succeeded.

Preparations for the lecture: Conferences with the Bar Kokhba Society, getting up the program, tickets, hall, numbering the seats, key to the piano (Toynbee Hall), setting up the stage, pianist, costumes, selling tickets, newspaper notices, censorship by the police and the religious community.

Places in which I was and people with whom I spoke or to whom I wrote. In general: With Max, with Schmerler, who visited me, with Baum, who at first assumed the responsibility for the lecture but then refused it, whose mind I changed again in the course of an evening devoted to that purpose and who the next day again notified me of his refusal by special delivery, with Dr. Hugo Hermann and Leo Hermann in the Café Arco, often with Robert Weltsch at his home; about selling tickets with Dr. Bl. (in vain), Dr.

H., Dr. Fl., visit to Miss T., lecture at Afike Jehuda (by Rabb. Ehrentreu on Jeremiah and his time, during the social part of the evening that followed, a short, abortive talk about Löwy), at the teacher W.'s place (then in the Café, then for a walk, from twelve to one he stood in front of my door as large as life and would not let me go in). About the hall, at Dr. Karl B.'s, twice at L.'s house on Heuwagsplatz, several times at Otto Pick's, in the bank; about the key to the piano for the Toynbee lecture, with Mr. R. and the teacher St., then to the latter's home to get the key and to return it; about the stage, with the custodian and the porter of the town hall; about payment, in the town hall office (twice); about the sale, with Mrs. Fr. at the exposition, "The Set Table." Wrote to Miss T., to one Otto Kl. (in vain), for the *Tagblatt* (in vain), to Löwy ("I won't be able to give the talk, save me!").

Excitements: About the lecture, one night twisted up in bed, hot and sleepless, hatred of Dr. B., fear of Weltsch (he will not be able to sell anything), Afike Jehuda, the notices are not published in the papers the way in which they were expected to be, distraction in the office, the stage does not come, not enough tickets are sold, the color of the tickets upsets me, the lecture has to be interrupted because the pianist forgot his music at home in Košíř, a great deal of indifference toward Löwy, almost disgust.

Benefits: Joy in Löwy and confidence in him, proud, unearthly consciousness during my lecture (coolness in the presence of the audience, only the lack of practice kept me from using enthusiastic gestures freely), strong voice, effortless memory, recognition, but above all the power with which I loudly, decisively, determinedly, faultlessly, irresistibly, with clear eyes, almost casually, put down the impudence of the three town hall porters and gave them, instead of the twelve kronen they demanded, only six kronen, and even these with a grand air. In all this are revealed powers to which I would gladly entrust myself if they would remain. (My parents were not there.)

Also: Academy of the Herder Association on the Sophien Island. Bie shoves his hand in his trouser pocket at the beginning of the lecture. This face, satisfied despite all disappointment, of people who work as they please. Hofmannsthal reads with a false ring in his voice. A close-knit figure, beginning with the ears pressed close to his head. Wiesenthal. The beautiful parts of the dance, for example, when in sinking to the ground the natural heaviness of the body is revealed.

Impression of Toynbee Hall.

Zionist meeting. Blumenfeld. Secretary of the World Zionist Organization.

A new stabilizing force has recently appeared in my deliberations about myself which I can recognize now for the first time and only now, since during the last week I have been literally disintegrating because of sadness and uselessness.

Changing emotions among the young people in the Café Arco.

February 26. Better consciousness of myself. The beating of my heart more as I would wish it. The hissing of the gaslight above me.

I opened the front door to see whether the weather would tempt me to take a walk. The blue sky could not be denied, but large gray clouds through which the blue shimmered, with flap-shaped, curved edges, hovered low, one could see them against the nearby wooded hills. Nevertheless the street was full of people out for a walk. Baby carriages were guided by the firm hands of mothers. Here and there in the crowd a vehicle came to a stop until the people made way for the prancing horses. Meanwhile the driver, quietly holding the quivering reins, looked ahead, missed no details, examined everything several times and at the right moment set the carriage in motion. Children were able to run about, little room as there was. Girls in light clothes with hats as emphatically colored as postage stamps walked arm in arm with young men and a song, suppressed in their throats, revealed itself in their dancing pace. Families stayed close together, and even if sometimes they were shaken out into a single file, there were still arms stretched back, hands waving, pet names called, to join together those who had strayed. Men who had no part in this tried to shut themselves off even more by sticking their hands in their pockets. That was petty nonsense. First I stood in the doorway, then I leaned against the doorpost in order to look on more comfortably. Clothes brushed against me, once I seized a ribbon that ornamented the back of a girl's skirt and let her draw it out of my hand as she walked away; once, when I stroked the shoulder of a girl, just to flatter her, the passer-by behind her struck me over the fingers. But I pulled him behind the bolted half of the door, I reproached him with raised hands, with looks out of the corners of my eyes, a step toward him, a step away from him, he was happy when I let go of him with a shove. From then on, naturally, I often called people to me, a crook of my finger was enough, or a quick, unhesitating glance.

How sleepily and without effort I wrote this useless, unfinished thing.

Today I am writing to Löwy. I am copying down the letters to him here because I hope to do something with them:
Dear friend—
February 27. I have no time to write letters in duplicate.

Yesterday evening, at ten o'clock, I was walking at my sad pace down the Zeltnergasse. Near the Hess hat store a young man stops three steps in front of me, so forces me to stop too, removes his hat and then runs at me. In my first fright I step back, think at first that someone wants to know how to get to the station, but why in this way?—then think, since he approaches me confidentially and looks up into my face because I am taller: Perhaps he wants money, or something worse. My confused attention and his confused speech mingle.

"You're a lawyer, aren't you? A doctor? Please, couldn't you give me some advice? I have a case here for which I need a lawyer."

Because of caution, general suspicion and fear that I might make a fool of myself, I deny that I am a lawyer, but am ready to advise him, what is it? He begins to talk, it interests me; to increase my confidence I ask him to talk while we walk, he wants to go my way, no, I would rather go with him, I have no place in particular to go.

He is a good reciter, he was not nearly as good in the past as he is now, now he can already imitate Kainz so that no one can tell the difference. People may say he only imitates him, but he puts in a lot of his own too. He is short, to be sure, but he has mimicry, memory, presence, everything, everything. During his military service out there in Milowitz, in camp, he recited, a comrade sang, they really had a very good time. It was a beautiful time. He prefers to recite Dehmel most of all, the passionate, frivolous poems, for instance, about the bride who pictures her bridal night to herself, when he recites that it makes a huge impression, especially on the girls. Well, that is really obvious. He has Dehmel very beautifully bound in red leather. (He describes it with dropping gestures of his hands.) But the binding really doesn't matter. Aside from this he likes very much to recite Rideamus. No, they don't clash with one another at all, he sees to it that there's a transition, talks between them, whatever occurs to him, makes a fool of the public. Then "Prometheus" is on his program too. There he isn't afraid of anyone, not even of Moissi, Moissi drinks, he doesn't. Finally, he likes very much to read from Swet Marten; he's a new Scandinavian writer. Very good. It's sort of epigrams and short sayings. Those about Napoleon, especially, are excellent, but so are all the others about other great men. No, he can't recite any of this yet, he hasn't learned it yet, not even read it all, but his aunt read it to him recently and he liked it so much.

So he wanted to appear in public with this program and therefore offered himself to the Women's Progress for an evening's appearance. Really, at first he wanted to present *Eine Gutsgeschichte* by Lagerlöf, and had even lent this story to the chairwoman of the Women's Progress, Mrs. Durège-Wodnanski, to look over. She said the story was beautiful, of course, but too long to be read. He saw that, it was really too long, especially as, according to the plan of the evening, his brother was supposed to play the piano too.

This brother, twenty-one years old, a very lovely boy, is a virtuoso, he was at the music college in Berlin for two years (four years ago, now). But came home quite spoiled. Not really spoiled, but the woman with whom he boarded fell in love with him. Later he said that he was often too tired to play because he had to keep riding around on this boarding-bag.

So, since the *Gutsgeschichte* wouldn't do, they agreed on the other program: Dehmel, Rideamus, "Prometheus" and Swet Marten. But now, in order to show Mrs. Durège in advance the sort of person he really was, he brought her the manuscript of an essay, "The Joy of Life," which he had written this summer. He wrote it in a summer resort, wrote it in shorthand during the day, in the evening made a clean copy, polished, crossed out, but really it wasn't much work because it came off at once. He'll lend it to me if I like, it's written in a popular style, of course, on purpose, but there are good ideas in it and it is *betamt*, as they say. (Pointed laughter with chin raised.) I may leaf through it here under the electric light. (It is an appeal to youth not to be sad, for after all there is nature, freedom, Goethe, Schiller, Shakespeare, flowers, insects, etc.) The Durège woman said she really didn't have time to read it just then, but he could lend it to her, she would return it in a few days. He suspected something even then and didn't want to leave it there, evaded, said, for instance, "Look, Mrs. Durège, why should I leave it here, it's really just ordinary, it's well written, of course, but. . . ." None of it did any good, he had to leave it there. This was on Friday.

(February 28.) Sunday morning, while washing, it occurs to him that he hadn't seen the *Tagblatt* yet. He opens it by chance just at the first page of the magazine section. The title of the first essay, "The Child as Creator," strikes him. He reads the first few lines—and begins to cry with joy. It is his essay, word for word his essay. So for the first time he is in print, he runs to his mother and tells her. What joy! The old woman, she has diabetes and is divorced from his father, who, by the way, is in the right, is so proud. One son is already a virtuoso, now the other is becoming an author!

After the first excitement he thinks the matter over. How did the essay get into the paper? Without his consent? Without the name of the author? Without his being paid a fee? This is really a breach of faith, a fraud. This Mrs. Durège is really a devil. And women have no souls, says Mohamet (often repeated). It's really easy to see how the plagiarism came about. Here was a beautiful essay, it's not easy to come across one like it. So Mrs. D. therefore went to the *Tagblatt*, sat down with one of the editors, both of them overjoyed, and now they began to rewrite it. Of course, it had to be rewritten, for in the first place the plagiarism should not be obvious at first sight and in the second place the thirty-two-page essay was too long for the paper.

In reply to my question whether he would not show me passages which correspond, because that would interest me especially and because only then could I advise him what to do, he begins to read his essay, turns to another passage, leafs through it without finding anything, and finally says that everything was copied. Here, for instance, the paper says: The soul of the child is an unwritten page, and "unwritten page" occurs in his essay too. Or the expression "surnamed" is copied too, because how else could they hit upon "surnamed." But he can't compare individual passages. Of course, everything was copied, but in a disguised way, in a different sequence, abridged and with small, foreign interpolations.

I read aloud a few of the more striking passages from the paper. Is that in the essay? No. This? No. This? No. Yes, but these are just the interpolated passages. In its spirit, the whole thing, the whole thing, is copied. But proving it, I am afraid, will be difficult. He'll prove it, all right, with the help of a clever lawyer, that's what lawyers are for, after all. (He looks forward to this proof as an entirely new task, completely separate from this affair, and is proud of his confidence that he will be able to accomplish it.)

That it is his essay, moreover, can be seen from the very fact that it was printed within two days. Usually it takes six weeks at the very least before a piece that is accepted is printed. But here speed was necessary, of course, so that he would not be able to interfere. That's why two days were enough.

Besides, the newspaper essay is called "The Child as Creator." That clearly refers to him, and besides, it is sarcasm. By "child" they really mean him, because he used to be regarded as a "child," as "dumb" (he really was so only during his military service, he served a year and a half), and they now mean to say with this title that he, a child, had accomplished something as good as this essay, that he had therefore proved himself as a creator, but at the same time remained dumb and a child in that he let himself be cheated like this. The child who is referred to in the original essay is a cousin from the country who is at present living with his mother.

But the plagiarism is proved especially convincingly by a circumstance which he hit upon only after a considerable amount of deliberation: "The Child as Creator" is on the first page of the magazine section, but on the third there is a little story by a certain "Feldstein" woman. The name is obviously a pseudonym. Now one needn't read all of this story, a glance at the first few lines is enough to show one immediately that this is an unashamed imitation of Lagerlöf. The whole story makes it even clearer. What does this mean? This means that this Feldstein, or whatever her name is, is the Durège woman's tool, that she read the *Gutsgeschichte*, brought by him to the Durège woman, at her house, that in writing this story, she made use of what she had read and that therefore both women are exploiting him, one on the first page of the magazine section, the other on the third page. Naturally anyone can read and imitate Lagerlöf on his own initiative but in this case, after all, his influence is too apparent. (He keeps waving the page back and forth.)

Monday noon, right after the bank closed, he naturally went to see Mrs. Durège. She opens her door only a crack, she is very nervous: "But, Mr. Reichmann, why have you come at noon? My husband is asleep. I can't let you in now."—"Mrs. Durège, you must let me in by all means. It's about an important matter." She sees I am in earnest and lets me come in. Her husband, of course, was definitely not at home. In the next room I see my manuscript on the table and this immediately starts me thinking. "Mrs. Durège, what have you done with my manuscript. Without my consent you gave it to the *Tagblatt*. How much did they pay you?" She trembles, she knows nothing, has no idea how it could have gotten into the paper. "*J'accuse*, Mrs. Durège," I said, half jokingly, but still in such a way that she sees what I really mean, and I keep repeating this "*J'accuse*, Mrs. Durège" all the time I am there so that she can take note of it, and when I go I even say it several times at the door. Indeed, I understand her nervousness well. If I make it public or sue her, her position would really be impossible, she would have to leave the Women's Progress, etc.

From her house I go straight to the office of the *Tagblatt* and have the editor, Löw, fetched. He comes out quite pale, naturally, is hardly able to walk. Nevertheless I do not want to begin with my business at once and I want to test him first too. So I ask him: "Mr. Löw, are you a Zionist?" (For I know he used to be a Zionist.) "No," he says. I know enough, he must be acting a part in front of me. Now I ask about the essay. Once more incoherent talk. He knows nothing, has nothing to do with the magazine section, will, if I wish, get the editor who is in charge of it. "Mr. Wittmann, come here," he calls, and is happy that he can leave. Wittmann comes, also very pale. I ask: "Are you the editor of the magazine section?" He: "Yes." I just say, "*J'accuse*," and leave.

In the bank I immediately telephone *Bohemia*. I want to give them the story for publication. But I can't get a good connection. Do you know why? The office of the *Tagblatt* is pretty close to the telephone exchange, so from the *Tagblatt* it's easy for them to control the connections as they please, to hold them up or put them through. And as a matter of fact, I keep hearing indistinct whispering voices on the telephone, obviously the editors of the *Tagblatt*. They have, of course, a good deal of interest in not letting this call go through. Then I hear (naturally very indistinctly) some of them persuading the operator not to put the call through, while others are already connected with *Bohemia* and are trying to keep them from listening to my story. "Operator," I shout into the telephone, "if you don't put this call through at once, I'll complain to the management." My colleagues all around me in the bank laugh when they hear me talking to the telephone operator so violently. Finally I get my party. "Let me talk to Editor Kisch. I have an extremely important piece of news for *Bohemia*. If you don't take it,

I'll give it to another paper at once. It's high time." But since Kisch is not there I hang up without revealing anything.

In the evening I go to the office of *Bohemia* and have the editor, Kisch, called out. I tell him the story but he doesn't want to publish it. *Bohemia*, he says, can't do anything like that, it would cause a scandal and we can't risk it because we're dependent. Hand it over to a lawyer, that would be best.

On my way from the *Bohemia* office I met you and so I am asking your advice.

"I advise you to settle the matter in a friendly way."

"Indeed, I was thinking myself that would be best. She's a woman, after all. Women have no souls, says Mohamet, with good reason. To forgive would be more humane, too, more Goethe-like."

"Certainly. And then you wouldn't have to give up the recitation evening, either, which would otherwise be lost, after all."

"But what should I do now?"

"Go to them tomorrow and say that this one time you are willing to assume it was unconscious influence."

"That's very good. That's just what I'll do."

"But because of this you needn't give up your revenge, either. Simply have the essay published somewhere else and then send it to Mrs. Durège with a nice dedication."

"That will be the best punishment. I'll have it published in the *Deutsches Abendblatt*. They'll take it; I'm not worried about that. I'll just not ask for any payment."

Then we speak about his talent as an actor, I am of the opinion that he should really have training. "Yes, you're right about that. But where? Do you perhaps know where it can be studied?" I say: "That's difficult. I really don't know." He: "That doesn't really matter. I'll ask Kisch.

He's a journalist and has a lot of connections. He'll be able to give me good advice. I'll just telephone him, spare him and myself the trip and get all the information."

"And about Mrs. Durège, you'll do what I advised you to?"

"Yes, but I forgot; what did you advise me to do?" I repeat my advice.

"Good, that's what I'll do." He turns into the Café Corso, I go home, having experienced how refreshing it is to speak with a perfect fool. I hardly laughed, but was just thoroughly awakened.

The melancholy "formerly," used only on business plaques.

March 2. Who is to confirm for me the truth or probability of this, that it is only because of my literary mission that I am uninterested in all other things and therefore heartless.

March 3. February 28th to hear Moissi. Unnatural spectacle. He sits in apparent calm, whenever possible keeps his folded hands between his knees, his eyes on the book lying before him and lets his voice pass over us with the breath of a runner.

The hall's good acoustics. Not a word is lost, nor is there the whisper of an echo, instead everything grows gradually larger, as though the voice, already occupied with something else, continued to exercise a direct aftereffect, it grows stronger after the initial impetus and swallows us up. The possibilities one sees here for one's own voice. Just as the hall works to the advantage of Moissi's voice, his voice works to the advantage of ours. Unashamed tricks and surprises at which one must look down at the floor and which one would never use oneself: singing individual verses at the very beginning, for instance, "Sleep, Miriam, my child"; [43] wandering around of the voice in the melody; rapid utterance of the May song, it seems as if only the tip of the tongue were stuck between the words; dividing the phrase "November wind" in order to push the "wind" down and then let it whistle upward. If one looks up at the ceiling of the hall, one is drawn upward by the verses.

Goethe's poems unattainable for the reciter, but one cannot for that reason find fault with this recitation, for each poem moves toward the goal. Great effect later, when in reciting the encore, Shakespeare's "Rain Song," he stood erect, was free of the text, pulled at his handkerchief and then crushed it in his hands, and his eyes sparkled. Round cheeks and yet an angular face. Soft hair, stroked over and over again with soft movements of his hand. The enthusiastic reviews that one has read are a help to him, in our opinion, only until the first hearing, then he becomes entangled in them and cannot produce a pure impression.

This sort of reciting from a chair, with the book before one, reminds one a little of ventriloquism. The artist, seemingly not participating, sits there like us, in his bowed face we see only the mouth move from time to time, and instead of reading the verses himself, he lets them be read over his head. Despite the fact that so many melodies were to be heard, that the voice seemed as controlled as a light boat in the water, the melody of the verses could really not be heard. Many words were dissolved by the voice, they were taken hold of so gently that they shot up into the air and had nothing more to do with the human voice until, out of sheer necessity, the voice spoke some sharp consonant or other, brought the word back to earth and completed it.

Later, a walk with Ottla, Miss Taussig, the Baum couple and Pick; the Elizabeth Bridge, the Quai, the Kleinseite, the Radetzky Café, the Stone Bridge, Karlsgasse. I still saw the prospect of a good mood, so that really there was not much fault to find with me.

March 5. These revolting doctors! Businesslike, determined and so ignorant of healing that, if this businesslike determination were to leave them, they would stand at sickbeds like schoolboys. I wished I had the strength to found a nature-cure society. By scratching around in my sister's ear Dr. K. turns an inflammation of the eardrum into an inflammation of the inner ear; the maid collapses while fixing the fire, with the quick diagnosis which is his custom in the case of maids, the doctor declares it to be an upset stomach and a resulting congestion of blood, the next day she takes to her bed again, has a high fever, the doctor turns her from side to side, affirms it is angina, and runs away so that the next moment will not refute him. Even dares to speak of the "vulgarly violent reaction of this girl," which is true to this extent, that he is used to people whose physical condition is worthy of his curative power and is produced by it, and he feels insulted, more than he is aware, by the strong nature of this country girl.

Yesterday at Baum's. Read *Der Dämon*. Total impression unfriendly. Good, precise mood on the way up to Baum's, died down immediately I got up there, embarrassment in the presence of the child.

Sunday: In the Continental, at the cardplayers'. *Journalisten* with Kramer first, one and a half acts. A good deal of forced merriment can be seen in Bolz, which produces, indeed, a little that is really delicate. Met Miss Taussig in front of the theater in the intermission after the second act. Ran to the checkroom, returned with cloak flying and escorted her home.

March 8. Day before yesterday was blamed because of the factory. Then for an hour on the sofa thought about jumping-out-of-the-window.

Yesterday, Harden lecture on "The Theater." Apparently entirely impromptu, I was in a fairly good mood and therefore did not find it as empty as did the others. Began well: "At this hour in which we have met together here to discuss the theater, the curtain is rising in every theater of Europe and the other continents to reveal the stage to the audience." With an electric light attached to a stand in front of him at the level of his breast so that it can be moved about, he lights up the front of his shirt as though it were on display, and during the course of the lecture he changes the lighting by moving the light. Toe dancing to make himself taller, as well as to tighten up his talent for improvisation. Trousers tight even around the groin. A short tail coat like that tacked onto a doll. Almost strained, serious face, sometimes like an old lady's, sometimes like Napoleon's. Fading color of his forehead as of a wig. Probably corseted.

Read through some old notebooks. It takes all my strength to last it out. The unhappiness one must suffer when one interrupts oneself in a task that can never succeed except all at once, and this is what has always happened to me until now; in rereading one must re-experience this unhappiness in a more concentrated way though not as strongly as before.

Today, while bathing, I thought I felt old powers, as though they had been untouched by the long interval.

March 10. Sunday. He seduced a girl in a small place in the Iser mountains where he spent a summer to restore his delicate lungs. After a brief effort to persuade her, incomprehensibly, the way lung cases sometimes act, he threw the girl—his landlord's daughter, who liked to walk with him in the evening after work—down in the grass on the river bank and took her as she lay there unconscious with fright. Later he had to carry water from the river in his cupped hands and pour it over the girl's face to restore her. "Julie, but Julie," he said countless times, bending over her. He was ready to accept complete responsibility for his offense and was only making an effort to make himself realize how serious his situation was. Without thinking about it he could not have realized it. The simple girl who lay before him, now breathing regularly again, her eyes still closed because of fear and embarrassment, could make no difficulty for him; with the tip of his toe, he, the great, strong person, could push the girl aside. She was weak and plain, could what had happened to her have any significance that would last even until tomorrow? Would not anyone who compared the two of them have to come to this conclusion? The river stretched calmly between the meadows and fields to the distant hills. There was still sunshine only on the slope of the opposite shore. The last clouds were drifting out of the clear evening sky.

Nothing, nothing. This is the way I raise up ghosts before me. I was involved, even if only superficially, only in the passage, "Later he had. . . ." mostly in the "pour." For a moment I thought I saw something real in the description of the landscape.

So deserted by myself, by everything. Noise in the next room.

March 11. Yesterday unendurable. Why doesn't everyone join in the evening meal? That would really be so beautiful.

The reciter, Reichmann, landed in the insane asylum the day after our conversation.

Today burned many old, disgusting papers.

W., Baron von Biedermann, *Gespräche mit Goethe*. The way the daughters of the Leipzig copperplate-engraver, Stock, comb his hair, 1767.

The way, in 1772, Kestner found him lying in the grass in Garbenheim and the way he "was conversing with several people who were standing around, an Epicurean philosopher (v. Goné, a great genius), a Stoic philosopher (v. Kielmansegg) and a cross between the two (Dr. König), and he really enjoyed himself."

With Seidel [Goethe's valet] in 1783: "Once he rang in the middle of the night, and when I came into his room he had rolled his iron trundle bed from the farthest end of the room up to the window and was watching the sky. 'Haven't you seen anything in the sky?' he asked me, and when I denied this, 'Then just run to the guardroom and ask the sentry whether he saw anything.' I ran there; but the sentry had seen nothing, which I reported to my master, who was still lying in the same position fixedly regarding the sky.

'Listen,' he then said to me, 'this is an important moment. Either we are having an earthquake at this very instant or we shall have one.' And now I had to sit down on his bed and he showed me what signs had led him to this conclusion." (Messina earthquake.)

A geological walk with von Trebra (September 1783) through underbrush and rocks. Goethe in front.

To Herder's wife in 1788. Among other things he said also that before he left Rome he cried like a child every day for fourteen days. The way Herder's wife watched him in order to report everything to her husband in Italy. Goethe shows great concern for Herder in the presence of his wife.

September 14, 1794, from eleven-thirty, when Schiller got dressed, until eleven o'clock, Goethe spent the time without interruption in literary consultation with Schiller, and often so.

David Veit, October 19, 1794, Jewish kind of observation, therefore so easy to understand, as though it had happened yesterday.

"In the evening in Weimar, *Der Diener zweier Herrn* was acted quite nicely, to my surprise. Goethe was also in the theater, and indeed, as always, in the section reserved for the nobility. In the middle of the play he leaves this section—which he is supposed to do very seldom—sits down, as long as he could not speak to me, behind me (so the ladies beside me said) and as soon as the act is over comes forward, bows to me with extreme courtesy and begins in a quite intimate tone ... brief remarks and replies about the play. ... Thereupon he falls silent for a moment; meanwhile I forget that he is the director of the theater and say, 'They're acting it quite nicely too.' He still keeps looking straight ahead, and so in my stupidity—but really in a frame of mind which

I cannot analyze—I say once more, 'They are acting quite nicely.' At that moment he bows to me, but really as courteously as the first time, and he is gone! Have I insulted him or not? ... You really won't believe how distressed I still am, regardless of the fact that I already have the assurance from Humboldt, who now knows him well, that he often leaves in this sudden manner, and Humboldt has undertaken to speak to him about me once again."

Another time they were speaking about Maimon: "I kept interrupting a good deal and often came to his assistance; for usually there are many words he cannot recall and he keeps making faces."

1796. Goethe recites Hermann's conversations with his mother at the pear tree in first half of September.[44] He wept. "Thus one melts over one's own coals," he said, while drying his tears.

"The wide wooden parapet of the old gentleman's box." Goethe sometimes liked to have a supply of cold food and wine ready in his box, more for the other people—residents and friends of importance—whom he not infrequently received there.

Performance of Schlegel's *Alarcos* in 1802. "In the middle of the orchestra Goethe, serious and solemn, throning in his tall armchair." The audience becomes restless, finally at one passage a roar of laughter, the whole house shakes. "But only for a moment, in a trice Goethe jumped up, with thunderous voice and threatening gestures shouted, Silence, Silence, and it worked like a charm. In an instant the tumult subsided and the unhappy *Alarcos* went on to the end with no further disturbance, but also without the slightest sign of applause."

Staël: What the French apparently take for wit in foreigners is often only ignorance of French. Goethe called an idea of Schiller's *neuve et courageuse*, that was wonderful, but it turned out that he had intended to say *hardie*.

Was lockst Du meine Brut . . . herauf in Todesglut.[45] Staël translated *air brûlant*. Goethe said he meant the glow of coals. She found that extremely *maussade* and tasteless and said that the fine sense for the seemly is lacking in German poets.

1804. Love for Heinrich Voss.—Goethe read *Luise* together with the Sunday company. "To Goethe fell the passage about the marriage, which he read with the deepest emotion. But his voice grew dejected, he wept and gave the book to his neighbor. A holy passage, he cried out with a degree of fervor which shook us all to the depths.

"We were sitting at lunch and had just consumed the last bit of food when Goethe ordered a bone 'because Voss still looks so hungry.'

"But never is he pleasanter and more lovable than in the evening in his room when he is undressed or is sitting on the sofa.

"When I came to him I found everything quite comfortable there. He had lit a fire, had undressed down to a short woolen jacket, in which the man looks really splendid."

Books: Stilling, *Goethe Yearbook*, *Briefwechsel zwischen Rahel und David Veit*.

March 12. In the trolley rapidly passing by there sat in a corner, his cheek against the window, his left arm stretched along the back of the seat, a young man with an unbuttoned overcoat billowing around him, looking down the long, empty bench. Today he had become engaged and he could think of nothing else. His being engaged made him feel comfortable and with this feeling he sometimes looked casually up at the ceiling of the car. When the conductor came to sell him his ticket, after some jingling, he easily found the right coin, with a single motion put it into the conductor's hand and seized the ticket between two fingers held open like a pair of scissors. There was no real connection between him and the trolley and it would not have been surprising if, without using the platform or steps, he had appeared on the street and gone his way on foot with the same look.

Only the billowing overcoat remains, everything else is made up.

March 16. Saturday. Again encouragement. Again I catch hold of myself, as one catches hold of a ball in its fall. Tomorrow, today, I'll begin an extensive work which, without being forced, will shape itself according to my abilities. I will not give it up as long as I can hold out at all. Rather be sleepless than live on in this way.

Cabaret Lucerna. Several young people each sing a song. Such a performance, if we are fresh and listen closely, more strongly impresses upon us the conclusions which the text offers for our own life than is possible by the performance of experienced artists. For the singer cannot increase the force of the poetry, it always retains an independent forcefulness which tyrannizes us through the singer, who doesn't even wear patent leather shoes, whose hand sometimes will not leave his knee, and, if it must, still shows its reluctance, who throws himself quickly down on the bench in order to conceal as much as possible how many small, awkward movements he had needed.

Love scene in spring, the sort one finds on picture post-cards. Devotion, a portrayal which touches and shames the public.—Fatinitza. Viennese singer. Sweet, significant laugh. Reminds me of Hansi. A face with meaningless details, mostly too sharp, held together and smoothed down by laughter. Ineffective superiority over the audience which one must grant her when she stands on the stage and laughs out into the indifferent audience.—Thea Degen's stupid dance, with flying will-o'-the-wisps, twigs, butterflies, death's head.

Four "Rocking Girls." One very pretty. The program does not give her name. She was on the audience's extreme right. How busily she threw her arms about, in what un-usually palpable, silent movement were her thin long legs and delicately playing little joints, the way she didn't keep time, but didn't let herself be frightened out of her business, what a soft smile she had in contrast to the distorted ones of the others, how almost voluptuous her face and hair were in comparison with the spareness of her body, the way she called "slowly" to the musicians, for her sisters as well as for herself. Their dancing master, a young, strikingly dressed, thin person, stood behind the musicians and waved one hand in rhythm, regarded neither by the musicians nor by the dancers and with his own eyes on the audience.

Warnebold, fiery nervousness of a powerful person. In his movements there is sometimes a joke whose strength lifts one up. How he hurries to the piano with long steps after the number is announced.

Read *Aus dem Leben eines Schlachtenmalers*. Read Flaubert aloud with satisfaction.

The necessity of speaking of dancers with exclamation points. Because in that way one imitates their motion, because one remains in the rhythm and the thought does not then interfere with the enjoyment, because then the action always comes at the end of the sentence and prolongs its effect better.

March 17. During these days read *Morgenrot* by Stössl.[46]

Max's concert Sunday. My almost unconscious listening. From now on I can no longer be bored by music. I no longer seek, as I did in vain in the past, to penetrate this impenetrable circle which immediately forms about me together with the music, I am also careful not to jump over it, which I probably could do, but instead I remain calmly in my thoughts that develop and subside in this narrowed space without it being possible for disturbing self-observations to step into their slow swarm. The beautiful "magic circle" (by Max) that seems here and there to open the breast of the singer.

Goethe, "Trost in Tränen." *Alles geben die Götter, die unendlichen,/ Ihren Lieblingen ganz:/ Alle Freuden, die unendlichen,/ Alle Schmerzen, die unendlichen, ganz.*

My incompetence in the presence of my mother, in the presence of Miss T. and in the presence of all those in the Continental at that time and later on the street.

Mam'zelle Nitouche on Monday. The good effect of a French word in a dreary German performance. Boarding-school girls in bright dresses, with their arms outstretched, run into the garden behind a fence. Barracks-yard of the dragoon regiment at night. Some officers in a barracks in the background are having a farewell celebration in a hall that is reached by going up a few steps. Mam'zelle Nitouche enters and is persuaded by love and recklessness to take part in the celebration. The sort of thing that can happen to a girl! In the morning at the convent, in the evening a substitute for an operetta singer who couldn't come, and at night in the dragoons' barracks.

Today, painfully tired, spent the afternoon on the sofa.

March 18. I was wise, if you like, because I was prepared for death at any moment, but not because I had taken care of everything that was given me to do, rather because I had done none of it and could not even hope ever to do any of it.

March 22. (The last few days I have been writing down the wrong dates.) Baum's lecture in the lecture hall. G. F., nineteen years old, getting married next week. Dark, faultless, slender face. Distended nostrils. For years she has been wearing hats and clothes styled like a hunter's. The same dark-green gleam on her face. The strands of hair running along her cheeks seem to unite with new ones growing along the cheeks, just as in general a slight down seems to cover all her face which she has bowed down into the darkness. Points of her elbows resting lightly on the arms of her chair. Then on the Wenzelsplatz a brisk bow, completed with little energy, a turn and a drawing erect of the poorly dressed, slender body. I looked at her much less often than I wanted to.

March 24. Sunday, yesterday. *Die Sternenbraut* by Christian von Ehrenfels.—Lost in watching. The sick officer in the play. The sick body in the tight uniform that made health and decisiveness a duty.

In the morning in the bright sun at Max's for half an hour.

In the next room my mother is entertaining the L. couple. They are talking about vermin and corns. (Mr. L. has six corns on each toe.) It is easy to see that there is no real progress made in conversations of this sort. It is information that will be forgotten again by both and that even now proceeds along in self-forgetfulness without any sense of responsibility. But for the very reason that such conversations are unthinkable without absent-mindedness, they reveal empty spaces which, if one insists, can be filled only by thinking, or, better yet, by dreams.

March 25. The broom sweeping the rug in the next room sounds like the train of a dress moving in jerks.

March 26. Only not to overestimate what I have written, for in that way I make what is to be written unattainable.

March 27. Monday, on the street. The boy who, with several others, threw a large ball at a servant girl walking defenselessly in front of them; just as the ball was flying at the girl's behind I grabbed him by the throat, choked him in fury, thrust him aside, and swore. Then walked on and didn't even look at the girl. One quite forgets one's earthly existence because one is so entirely full of fury and is permitted to believe that, given the opportunity, one would in the same way fill oneself with even more beautiful emotions.

March 28. From Mrs. Fanta's lecture, "Impressions of Berlin": Grillparzer once didn't want to go to a party because he knew that Hebbel, with whom he was friendly, would also be there. "He will question me again about my opinion on God, and when I won't know what to say, he will become rude."—My awkward behavior.

March 29. Delighted with the bathroom. Gradual understanding. The afternoons I spent on my hair.

April 1. For the first time in a week an almost complete failure in writing. Why? Last week too I lived through various moods and kept their influence away from my writing; but I am afraid to write about it.

April 3. This is how a day passes—in the morning, the office, in the afternoon, the factory, now in the evening, shouting to the right and left of me at home, later brought my sister home from *Hamlet*—and I haven't been able to make use of a single moment.

April 8. Saturday before Easter. Complete knowledge of oneself. To be able to seize the whole of one's abilities like a little ball. To accept the greatest decline as something familiar and so still remain elastic in it.

Desire for a deeper sleep that dissolves more. The metaphysical urge is only the urge toward death.

How affectedly I spoke today in Haas' [47] presence because he praised Max's and my travel report, so that in this way, at least, I might make myself worthy of the praise that the report does not warrant, or so that I might continue by fraud the fraudulent or lying effect of the travel report, or in the spirit of Haas' amiable lie, which I tried to make easier for him.

May 6. 11 o'clock. For the first time in a considerable while a complete failure in writing. The feeling of a tried man.

Dreamed recently:
I was riding with my father through Berlin in a trolley. The big-city quality was represented by countless striped toll bars standing upright, finished off bluntly at the ends. Aside from that everything was almost empty, but there was a great forest of these toll bars. We came to a gate, got out without any sense of getting out, stepped through the gate. On the other side of the gate a sheer wall rose up, which my father ascended almost in a dance, his legs flew out as he climbed, so easy was it for him. There was certainly also some inconsiderateness in the fact that he did not help me one bit, for I got to the top only with the utmost effort, on all fours, often sliding back again, as though the wall had become steeper under me. At the same time it was also distressing that [the wall] was covered with human excrement so that flakes of it clung to me, chiefly to my breast. I looked down at the flakes with bowed head and ran my hand over them.

When at last I reached the top, my father, who by this time was already coming out of a building, immediately fell on my neck and kissed and embraced me. He was wearing an old-fashioned, short Prince Albert, padded on the inside like a sofa, which I remembered well. "This Dr. von

Leyden! He is an excellent man," he exclaimed over and over again. But he had by no means visited him in his capacity as doctor, but rather only as a man worth knowing. I was a little afraid that I should have to go in to see him too, but this wasn't required of me. Behind me to the left I saw, sitting in a room literally surrounded by glass walls, a man who turned his back on me. It turned out that this man was the professor's secretary, that my father had in fact spoken only with him and not with the professor himself, but that somehow or other, through the secretary, he had recognized the excellences of the professor in the flesh, so that in every respect he was as much entitled to an opinion on the professor as if he had spoken to him in person.

Lessing Theater: *Die Ratten*.
Letter to Pick because I haven't written to him. Card to Max in joy over *Arnold Beer*.

May 9. Yesterday evening in the coffeehouse with Pick. How I hold fast to my novel [48] against all restlessness, like a figure on a monument that looks into the distance and holds fast to its pedestal.

Hopeless evening with the family today. My brother-in-law needs money for the factory, my father is upset because of my sister, because of the business and because of his heart, my unhappy second sister, my mother unhappy about all of them, and I with my scribblings.

May 22. Yesterday a wonderfully beautiful evening with Max. If I love myself, I love him more. Cabaret Lucerna. *Madame la mort* by Rachilde. *Dream of a Spring Morn-*

ing. The gay, fat girl in the box. The wild one with the coarse nose, her face smudged with soot, her shoulders squeezed up out of her dress (which wasn't décolleté, however) and her back twisted to and fro, her simple, blue blouse with white polka dots, her fencer's glove, which was always visible since most of the time her right hand was either resting flat, or on its fingertips, on the right thigh of her lively mother seated beside her. Her braids twisted over her ears, a not-too-clean light-blue ribbon on the back of her head, the hair in front encircles her forehead in a thin but compact tuft that projects far out in front. Her warm, wrinkled, light cloak carelessly falling in folds when she was dickering at the box office.

May 23. Yesterday, behind us, out of boredom, a man fell from his chair.—Comparison by Rachilde: Those who rejoice in the sun and demand that others rejoice are like drunkards coming from a wedding at night who force those they meet to drink the health of the unknown bride.

Letter to Weltsch, proposed that we use "Du" to one another. Yesterday a good letter to Uncle Alfred about the factory. Day before yesterday letter to Löwy.

Now, in the evening, out of boredom, washed my hands in the bathroom three times in succession.

The child with the two little braids, bare head, loose little red dress with white dots, bare legs and feet, who, with a little basket in one hand, a little box in the other, hesitatingly walked across the street near the National Theater.

How the actors in the play, *Madame la mort,* turn their backs to the audience, on the principle that the back of an amateur is, other things being equal, as beautiful as the back of a professional actor. The conscientiousness of people!

A few days ago an excellent lecture by Davis Trietsch on colonization in Palestine.

May 25. Weak tempo, little blood.

May 27. Yesterday Whitsunday, cold weather, a not very nice excursion with Max and Weltsch. In the evening, coffeehouse, Werfel gives me *Besuch aus dem Elysium.*

Part of Niklasstrasse and all of the bridge turns around to look sentimentally at a dog who, loudly barking, is chasing an ambulance. Until suddenly the dog stops, turns away and proves to be an ordinary, strange dog who meant nothing in particular by his pursuit of the vehicle.

June 1. Wrote nothing.

June 2. Wrote almost nothing.
Yesterday lecture on America by Dr. Soukup. (The Czechs in Nebraska, all officials in America are elected, everyone must belong to one of the three parties—Republican, Democratic, Socialist—Roosevelt's election meeting, with his glass he threatened a farmer who had made an objection, street speakers who carry a small box with them to serve as a platform.) Then spring festival, met Paul Kisch who talked about his dissertation, "Hebbel and the Czechs."

June 6. Thursday. Corpus Christi. Two horses in a race, how one lowers its head out of the race and shakes its mane vigorously, then raises its head and only now, apparently feeling better, resumes the race which it has never really interrupted.

I have just read in Flaubert's letters: "My novel is the cliff on which I am hanging, and I know nothing of what is going on in the world."—Like what I noted down about myself on May 9th.

Without weight, without bones, without body, walked through the streets for two hours considering what I overcame this afternoon while writing.

June 7. Bad. Wrote nothing today. Tomorrow no time.

July 6. Monday. Began a little. Am a little sleepy. Also lost among these entirely strange people.[49]

July 9. Nothing written for so long. Begin tomorrow. Otherwise I shall again get into a prolonged, irresistible dissatisfaction; I am really in it already. The nervous states are beginning. But if I can do something, then I can do it without superstitious precautions.

The invention of the devil. If we are possessed by the devil, it cannot be by one, for then we should live, at least here on earth, quietly, as with God, in unity, without contradiction, without reflection, always sure of the man behind us. His face would not frighten us, for as diabolical beings we would, if somewhat sensitive to the sight, be clever enough to prefer to sacrifice a hand in order to keep his face covered with it. If we were possessed by only a single devil, one who had a calm, untroubled view of our whole nature, and freedom to dispose of us at any moment, then that devil would also have enough power to hold us for the length of a human life high above the spirit of God in us, and even to swing us to and fro, so that we should never get to see a glimmer of it and therefore should not be troubled from that quarter. Only a crowd of devils could account for our earthly misfortunes. Why don't they exterminate one another until only a single one is left, or why don't they subordinate themselves to one great devil? Either way would be in accord with the diabolical principle of deceiving us as completely as possible. With unity lacking, of what use is the scrupulous attention all the devils pay us? It simply goes without saying that the falling of a human hair must matter more to the devil than to God, since the devil really loses that hair and God does not. But we still do not arrive at any state of well-being so long as the many devils are within us.

August 7. Long torment. Finally wrote to Max that I cannot clear up the little pieces that still remain, do not want to force myself to it and therefore will not publish the book.[50]

August 8. Completed "Confidence Trickster" more or less satisfactorily. With the last strength of a normal state of mind. Twelve o'clock, how will I be able to sleep?

August 9. The upset night. Yesterday the maid who said to the little boy on the steps, "Hold on to my skirt!"
My inspired reading aloud of *Der arme Spielmann*. The perception in this story of what is manly in Grillparzer.

The way he can risk everything and risks nothing, because there is nothing but truth in him already, a truth that even in the face of the contradictory impressions of the moment will justify itself as such when the crucial time arrives. The calm self-possession. The slow pace that neglects nothing. The immediate readiness, when it is needed, not sooner, for long in advance he sees everything that is coming.

August 10. Wrote nothing. Was in the factory and breathed gas in the engine room for two hours. The energy of the foreman and the stoker before the engine, which for some undiscoverable reason will not start. Miserable factory.

August 11. Nothing, nothing. How much time the publishing of the little book takes from me and how much harmful, ridiculous pride comes from reading old things with an eye to publication. Only that keeps me from writing. And yet in reality I have achieved nothing, the disturbance is the best proof of it. In any event, now, after the publication of the book, I will have to stay away from magazines and reviews even more than before, if I do not wish to be content with just sticking the tips of my fingers into the truth. How immovable I have become! Formerly, if I said only one word that opposed the direction of the moment, I at once flew over to the other side, now I simply look at myself and remain as I am.

August 14. Letter to Rowohlt.
Dear Mr. Rowohlt:
I am enclosing the little prose pieces you wanted to see; they will probably be enough to make up a small book. While I was putting them together toward this end, I some-

times had to choose between satisfying my sense of responsibility and an eagerness to have a book among your beautiful books. Certainly I did not in each instance make an entirely clear-cut decision. But now I should naturally be happy if the things pleased you sufficiently to print them. After all, even with the greatest skill and the greatest understanding the bad in them is not discernible at first sight. Isn't what is most universally individual in writers the fact that each conceals his bad qualities in an entirely different way?

Faithfully—

August 15. Wasted day. Spent sleeping and lying down. Feast of St. Mary on the Altstädter Ring. The man with a voice that seemed to come from a hole in the ground. Thought much of—what embarrassment before writing down names—F. B.[51] O. has just been reciting poems by Goethe. She chooses them with right feeling. "Trost in Tränen." "An Lotte." "An Werther." "An den Mond."

Again read old diaries instead of keeping away from them. I live as irrationally as is at all possible. And the publication of the thirty-one pages is to blame for everything. Even more to blame, of course, is my weakness, which permits a thing of this sort to influence me. Instead of shaking myself, I sit here and consider how I could express all this as insultingly as possible. But my horrible calm interferes with my inventiveness. I am curious as to how I shall find a way out of this state. I don't permit others to push me, nor do I know which is "the right path." So what will happen? Have I finally run aground, a great mass in shallow water? In that case, however, I should at least be able to turn my head. That's what I do, however.

August 16. Nothing, either in the office or at home. Wrote a few pages in the Weimar diary.

This evening the whimpering of my poor mother because I don't eat.

August 20. Outside my window, across the university building site partly overgrown with weeds, the little boys, both in blue blouses, one in light blue, the other, smaller one in darker blue, are each carrying a bundle of dry hay that fills their arms. They struggle up a slope with it. Charm of it all for the eyes.

This morning the empty open wagon and the large, emaciated horse pulling it. Both, making a final effort to get up a slope, stretched out to an unusual length. Seen at an angle by the spectator. The horse, front legs raised a little, his neck stretched sideward and upward. Over him the whip of the driver.

If Rowohlt would send it back and I could lock it up again as if it had all never happened, so that I should be only as unhappy as I was before.

Miss F. B. When I arrived at Brod's on August 13th, she was sitting at the table. I was not at all curious about who she was, but rather took her for granted at once. Bony, empty face that wore its emptiness openly. Bare throat. A blouse thrown on. Looked very domestic in her dress although, as it later turned out, she by no means was. (I alienate myself from her a little by inspecting her so closely. What a state I'm in now, indeed, alienated in general from the whole of everything good, and don't even believe it yet. If the literary talk at Max's doesn't distract me too much,

I'll try to write the story about Blenkelt today. It needn't be long, but I must hit it off right.) Almost broken nose. Blond, somewhat straight, unattractive hair, strong chin. As I was taking my seat I looked at her closely for the first time, by the time I was seated I already had an unshakable opinion.

August 21. Read Lenz incessantly and—such is my state —he restored me to my senses.

The picture of dissatisfaction presented by a street, where everyone is perpetually lifting his feet to escape from the place on which he stands.

August 30. All this time did nothing. The visit of my uncle from Spain. Last Saturday in the Arco Werfel recited his "Lebenslieder" and "Opfer." A monster! But I looked him in the eye and held it all evening.

It will be hard to rouse me, and yet I am restless. When I lay in bed this afternoon and someone quickly turned a key in the lock, for a moment I had locks all over my body, as though at a fancy-dress ball, and at short intervals a lock was opened or shut here and there.

Questionnaire by the magazine *Miroir*, about love in the present and the way love has changed since the days of our grandparents. An actress answered: Never did they love as well as today.

How shaken and exalted I was after hearing Werfel! How I behaved afterward at L.'s party, wild, almost, and without a fault.

This month, which, because of the absence of the boss, could have been put to exceptionally good use, I have wasted and slept away without much excuse (sending the book off to Rowohlt, abscesses, my uncle's visit). Even this afternoon I stretched out on the bed for three hours with dreamy excuses.

September 4. My uncle from Spain. The cut of his coat. The effect of his nearness. The details of his personality. His floating through the anteroom into the toilet, in the course of which he makes no reply to what is said to him. Becomes milder from day to day, if one judges not in terms of a gradual change but by the moments which stand out.

September 5. I ask him: How is one to reconcile the fact that you are generally dissatisfied, as you recently said, and that nevertheless you are at home everywhere, as can be seen time and again (and which is revealed in the rudeness always characteristic of this sort of being-at-home, I thought). He answers, as I remember it: "In individual things I am dissatisfied, this doesn't extend to the whole. I often dine in a little French pension that is very exclusive and expensive. For example, a room for a couple, with meals, costs fifty francs a day. So I sit there between the secretary of the French legation, for example, and a Spanish general of artillery. Opposite me sit a high official of the navy ministry and some count or other. I know them all well by now, sit down in my place, greeting them on all sides, because I am in a peculiar mood I say not another word until the goodbye with which I take my leave. Then I am alone on the street and really can't see what purpose this evening served. I go home and regret that I didn't marry. Naturally this mood passes away again, whether because I have thought it through to the end, whether because the thoughts have dispersed. But on occasion it comes back again."

September 8. Sunday morning. Yesterday a letter to Dr. Schiller.

Afternoon. The way my mother, together with a crowd of women, with a very loud voice, is playing with some small children nearby and drives me out of the house. Don't cry! Don't cry! etc. That's his! That's his! etc. Two big people! etc. He doesn't want to! . . . But! But! . . . How did you like Vienna, Dolphi? Was it nice there? . . . I ask you, just look at his hands!

September 11. The evening of the day before yesterday with Utitz.

A dream: I found myself on a jetty of square-cut stones built far out into the sea. Someone, or even several people, were with me, but my awareness of myself was so strong that I hardly knew more about them than that I was speaking to them. I can remember only the raised knees of someone sitting near me. At first I did not really know where I was, only when once I accidentally stood up did I see on my left and behind me on my right the distant, clearly outlined sea with many battleships lined up in rows and at anchor. On the right New York could be seen, we were in New York Harbor. The sky was gray, but of a constant brightness. I moved back and forth in my seat, freely exposed to the air on all sides, in order to be able to see everything. In the direction of New York my glance slanted downward a little, in the direction of the sea it slanted upward. I now noticed the water rise up near us in high waves on which was borne a great cosmopolitan traffic. I can remember only that instead of the rafts we have, there were long timbers lashed together into gigantic bundles the cut ends of which kept popping out of the water during the voyage, higher or lower, according to the height of the waves, and at the same time kept turning end over end in the water. I sat down, drew up my feet, quivered with pleasure, virtually dug myself into the ground in delight, and said: Really, this is even more interesting than the traffic on a Paris boulevard.

September 12. This evening Dr. L. at our house. Another emigrant to Palestine. Is taking his bar examination a year before the end of his clerkship and is leaving (in two weeks) for Palestine with 1,200 K. Will try to get a position with the Palestine Office. All these emigrants to Palestine (Dr. B., Dr. K.) have downcast eyes, feel blinded by their listeners, fumble around on the table with the tips of their extended fingers, their voices quiver, they smile weakly and prop up these smiles with a little irony. Dr. K. told us that his students are chauvinists, have the Maccabees forever in their mouths and want to take after them.

I become aware that I wrote so eagerly and well to Dr. Schiller only because Miss B. stopped in Breslau, and I have been thinking about sending flowers to her through Dr. Schiller, and although all this was two weeks ago, a trace of it is still in the air.

September 15. Engagement of my sister Valli.

Aus dem Grunde	From the pit
der Ermattung	of exhaustion
steigen wir	we ascend
mit neuen Kräften,	with renewed strength—

Dunkle Herren,	Dark lords,
welche warten	who wait
bis die Kinder	until the children
sich entkräften.	exhaust themselves.

Love between brother and sister—the repeating of the love between mother and father.

The hollow which the work of genius has burned into our surroundings is a good place into which to put one's little light. Therefore the inspiration that emanates from genius, the universal inspiration that doesn't only drive one to imitation.

September 18. H.'s stories yesterday in the office. The stone breaker on the highway who begged a frog from him, held it by the feet and with three bites swallowed down first the little head, then the rump and finally the feet.—The best way to kill cats, who cling stubbornly to life: Squeeze their throats in a closed door and pull their tails.—His horror of vermin. In the army one night he had an itch under his nose, he slapped it in his sleep and crushed something. But the something was a bedbug and he carried the stench of it around with him for days.

Four people ate a well-prepared roast cat, but only three knew what they were eating. After the meal the three began to meow, but the fourth refused to believe it, only when they showed him the bloody skin did he believe it, could not run out fast enough to vomit everything up again and was very sick for two weeks.

This stone breaker ate nothing but bread and whatever else in the way of fruit or living flesh that he accidentally came upon, and drank nothing but brandy. Slept in the shed of a brickyard. Once H. met him at twilight in the fields. "Stand still," the man said, "or . . ." For the sport of it, H. stopped. "Give me your cigarette," the man went on. H. gave it to him. "Give me another one!"— "So you want another one?" H. asked him, held his gnarled stick in his left hand in case of trouble and struck him in the face with his right so that he dropped the cigarette. The man ran away at once, cowardly and weak, the way such brandy drinkers are.

Yesterday at B.'s with Dr. L. Song about Reb Dovidl, Reb Dovidl of Vassilko is going to Talne today. In a city between Vassilko and Talne they sing it indifferently, in Vassilko weepingly, in Talne happily.

September 19. Comptroller P. tells about the trip which he took in the company of a schoolmate at the age of thirteen with seventy kreuzers in his pocket. How one evening they came to an inn where a huge drinking bout was going on in honor of the mayor who had returned from his military service. More than fifty empty beer bottles were standing on the floor. The whole place was full of pipe smoke. The stench of the beer dregs. The two little boys against the wall. The drunken mayor who, remembering his military service, wants to maintain discipline everywhere, comes up to them and threatens to have them sent home under arrest as deserters, what he takes them for in spite of all their explanations. The boys tremble, show their Gymnasium identity cards, decline "mensa"; a half-drunk teacher looks on without helping them. Without being given any definite decision about their fate they are compelled to join in the drinking, are very pleased to get for nothing so much good beer which, with their limited means, they would never have dared to allow themselves. They drink themselves full and then, late at night, after the last guests have departed, go to sleep on thinly spread straw in this room which had not been aired, and sleep like lords. But at four o'clock a gigantic maid with a broom arrives, says she has no time, and would have swept them out into the morning mist if they had not themselves run away. When the room was cleaned up a little, two large coffee-pots, filled to the brim, were placed on the table for them. But when they stirred their coffee with their spoons, something large, dark, round kept coming to the surface from time to time. They thought it would be explained in time and drank with appetite until, in view of the half-emptied pots and the dark object, they became really worried and asked the maid's advice. Then it turned out that the black object was old, congealed goose blood which had been left in the pots from yesterday's feast and onto which the coffee had simply been poured in the stupor of the morning after. At once the boys ran out and vomited everything to the last little drop. Later they were called before the parson who, after a short examination in religion, established that they were honest boys, had the cook serve them some soup and then sent them on their way with his spiritual blessing. As pupils in a clerical Gymnasium they had this soup and this blessing given to them in almost every parsonage they came to.

September 20. Letters to Löwy and Miss Taussig yesterday, to Miss B. and Max today.

September 23.[52] This story, *The Judgment*, I wrote at one sitting during the night of the 22nd-23rd, from ten o'clock at night to six o'clock in the morning. I was hardly able to pull my legs out from under the desk, they had got so stiff from sitting. The fearful strain and joy, how the story developed before me, as if I were advancing over water. Several times during this night I heaved my own weight on my back. How everything can be said, how for everything, for the strangest fancies, there waits a great fire in which they perish and rise up again. How it turned blue outside the window. A wagon rolled by. Two men walked across the bridge. At two I looked at the clock for the last time. As the maid walked through the anteroom for the first time I wrote the last sentence. Turning out the light and the light of day. The slight pains around my heart. The weariness that disappeared in the middle of the night. The trembling entrance into my sisters' room. Reading aloud. Before that, stretching in the presence of the maid and saying, "I've been writing until now." The appearance of the undisturbed bed, as though it had just been brought in. The conviction verified that with my novel-writing I am in the shameful lowlands of writing. Only *in this way* can writing be done, only with such coherence, with such a complete opening out of the body and the soul. Morning in bed. The always clear eyes. Many emotions carried along in the writing, joy, for example, that I shall have something beautiful for Max's *Arkadia*, thoughts about Freud, of course; in one passage, of *Arnold Beer;* in another, of Wassermann; in one, of Werfel's giantess; of course, also of my "The Urban World."

I, only I, am the spectator in the orchestra.

Gustav Blenkelt was a simple man with regular habits. He didn't like any unnecessary display and had a definite opinion about people who went in for such display. Although he was a bachelor, he felt he had an absolute right to say a few deciding words in the marital affairs of his acquaintances and anyone who would even have questioned such a right would have fared badly with him. He used to speak his mind freely and did not in any way seek to detain those listeners whom his opinions happened not to suit. As there are everywhere, there were people who admired him, people who honored him, people who put up with him, and, finally, those who wanted to have nothing to do with him. Indeed, every person, even the emptiest, is, if one will only look carefully, the center of a tight circle that forms about him here and there, how could it be otherwise in the case of Gustav Blenkelt, at bottom an exceptionally social person?

In his thirty-fifth year, the last year of his life, he spent an unusual amount of time with a young couple named Strong. It is certain that for Mr. Strong, who had opened a furniture store with his wife's money, the acquaintance with Blenkelt had numerous advantages, since the largest part of the latter's acquaintances consisted of young, marriageable people who sooner or later had to think of providing new furniture for themselves and who, out of old habit, were usually accustomed not to neglect Blenkelt's advice in this matter, either. "I keep them on a tight rein," Blenkelt used to say.

September 24. My sister said: The house (in the story) is very like ours. I said: How? In that case, then, Father would have to be living in the toilet.

September 25. By force kept myself from writing. Tossed in bed. The congestion of blood in my head and the useless drifting by of things. What harmfulness!—Yesterday read at Baum's, to the Baum family, my sisters, Marta, Dr. Block's wife and her two sons (one of them a one-year-volunteer in the army). Toward the end my hand was moving uncontrollably about and actually before my face. There were tears in my eyes. The indubitability of the story was confirmed.—This evening tore myself away from my writing. Movies in the National Theater. Miss O., whom a clergyman once pursued. She came home soaked in cold sweat. Danzig. Life of Körner. The horses. The white horse. The smoke of powder. "Lützows wilde Jagd." [53]

February 11. While I read the proofs of *The Judgment*, I'll write down all the relationships which have become clear to me in the story as far as I now remember them. This is necessary because the story came out of me like a real birth, covered with filth and slime, and only I have the hand that can reach to the body itself and the strength of desire to do so:

The friend is the link between father and son, he is their strongest common bond. Sitting alone at his window, Georg rummages voluptuously in this consciousness of what they have in common, believes he has his father within him, and would be at peace with everything if it were not for a fleeting, sad thoughtfulness. In the course of the story the father, with the strengthened position that the other, lesser things they share in common give him—love, devotion to the mother, loyalty to her memory, the clientele that he (the father) had been the first to acquire for the business—uses the common bond of the friend to set himself up as Georg's antagonist. Georg is left with nothing; the bride, who lives in the story only in relation to the friend, that is, to what father and son have in common, is easily driven away by the father since no marriage has yet taken place, and so she cannot penetrate the circle of blood relationship that is drawn around father and son. What they have in common is built up entirely around the father, Georg can feel it only as something foreign, something that has become independent, that he has never given enough protection, that is exposed to Russian revolutions, and only because he himself has lost everything except his awareness of the father does the judgment, which closes off his father from him completely, have so strong an effect on him.

Georg has the same number of letters as Franz. In Bendemann, "mann" is a strengthening of "Bende" to provide for all the as yet unforeseen possibilities in the story. But Bende has exactly the same number of letters as Kafka, and the vowel *e* occurs in the same places as does the vowel *a* in Kafka.

Frieda has as many letters as F. and the same initial, Brandenfeld has the same initial as B., and in the word "Feld" a certain connection in meaning, as well. Perhaps even the thought of Berlin was not without influence and the recollection of the Mark Brandenburg perhaps had some influence.

February 12. In describing the friend I kept thinking of Steuer. Now when I happened to meet him about three months after I had written the story, he told me that he had become engaged about three months ago.

After I read the story at Weltsch's yesterday, old Mr. Weltsch went out and, when he returned after a short time, praised especially the graphic descriptions in the story. With his arm extended he said, "I see this father before me," all the time looking directly at the empty chair in which he had been sitting while I was reading.

My sister said, "It is our house." I was astonished at how mistaken she was in the setting and said, "In that case, then, Father would have to be living in the toilet."

February 28. Ernst Liman arrived in Constantinople on a business trip one rainy fall morning and, as was his custom—this was the tenth time he was making this trip—without paying attention to anything else, drove through the otherwise empty streets to the hotel at which he always stopped and which he found suited him. It was almost cool, the drizzling rain blew into the carriage and, annoyed by the bad weather which had been pursuing him all through his business trip this year, he put up the carriage window and leaned back in a corner to sleep away the fifteen minutes or so of the drive that was before him. But since the driver took him straight through the business district, he could get no rest, and the shouts of the street vendors, the rolling of the heavy wagons, as well as other noises, meaningless on the surface, such as a crowd clapping its hands, disturbed his usually sound sleep.

At the end of his drive an unpleasant surprise awaited him. During the last great fire in Stambul, about which Liman had probably read during his trip, the Hotel Kingston, at which it was his habit to stop, had been burned almost to the ground, but the driver, who of course knew this, had nevertheless carried out his passenger's instructions with complete indifference, and without a word had brought him to the site of the hotel which had burned down. Now he calmly got down from the box and would even have unloaded Liman's luggage if the latter had not seized him by the shoulder and shaken him, whereupon the driver then let go of the luggage, to be sure, but as slowly and sleepily as if not Liman but his own change of mind had diverted him from it.

Part of the ground floor of the hotel was still intact and had been made fairly habitable by being boarded over at the top and sides. A notice in Turkish and French indicated that the hotel would be rebuilt in a short time as a more beautiful and more modern structure. Yet the only sign of this was the work of three day laborers, who with shovels and rakes were heaping up the rubble at one side and loading it into a small handbarrow.

As it turned out, part of the hotel staff, unemployed because of the fire, was living in these ruins. A gentleman in a black frock coat and a bright red tie at once came running out when Liman's carriage stopped, told Liman, who sulkily listened to him, the story of the fire, meanwhile twisting the ends of his long, thin beard around his finger and interrupting this only to point out to Liman where the fire started, how it spread and how finally everything collapsed. Liman, who had hardly raised his eyes from the ground throughout this whole story and had not let go the handle of the carriage door, was just about to call out to the driver the name of another hotel to which he could drive him when the man in the frock coat, with arms raised, implored him not to go to any other hotel, but to remain loyal to this hotel, where, after all, he had always received satisfaction. Despite the fact that this was only meaningless talk and no one could remember Liman, just as Liman recognized hardly a single one of the male and female employees he saw in the door and windows, he still asked, as a man to whom his habits were dear, how, then, at the moment, he was to remain loyal to the burned down hotel. Now he learned—and involuntarily had to smile at the idea—that beautiful rooms in private homes were available for former guests of this hotel, but only for them, Liman need but say the word and he would be taken to one at once, it was quite near, there would be no time lost and the rate—they wished to oblige and the room was of course only a substitute—was unusually low, even though the food, Viennese cooking, was, if possible, even better and the service even more attentive than in the former Hotel Kingston, which had really been inadequate in some respects.

"Thank you," said Liman, and got into the carriage. "I shall be in Constantinople only five days, I really can't set myself up in a private home for this short space of time, no, I'm going to a hotel. Next year, however, when I return and your hotel has been rebuilt, I'll certainly stop only with you. Excuse me!" And Liman tried to close the carriage door, the handle of which the representative of the hotel was now holding. "Sir," the latter said pleadingly, and looked up at Liman.

"Let go!" shouted Liman, shook the door and directed the driver: "To the Hotel Royal." But whether it was because the driver did not understand him, whether it was because he was waiting for the door to be closed, in any event he sat on his box like a statue. In no case, however, did the representative of the hotel let go of the door, he even beckoned eagerly to a colleague to rouse himself and come to his aid. There was some girl he particularly hoped could do something, and he kept calling, "Fini! Hey, Fini! Where's Fini?" The people at the windows and the door had turned toward the inside of the house, they shouted in confusion, one saw them running past the windows, everyone was looking for Fini.

The man who was keeping Liman from driving off and

whom obviously only hunger gave the courage to behave like this, could have been easily pushed away from the door. He realized this and did not dare even to look at Liman; but Liman had already had too many unfortunate experiences on his travels not to know how important it is in a foreign country to avoid doing anything that attracts attention, no matter how very much in the right one might be. He therefore quietly got out of the carriage again, for the time being paid no attention to the man who was holding the door in a convulsive grip, went up to the driver, repeated his instructions, expressly added that he was to drive away from here as fast as he could, then walked up to the man at the door of the carriage, took hold of his hand with an apparently ordinary grip, but secretly squeezed the knuckles so hard that the man almost jumped and was forced to remove his hand from the door handle, shrieking "Fini!" which was at once a command and an outburst of pain.

"Here she comes! Here she comes!" shouts now came from all the windows, and a laughing girl, her hands still held to her hair which had just been dressed, her head half bowed, came running out of the house toward the carriage. "Quick! Into the carriage! It's pouring," she cried, grasping Liman by the shoulders and holding her face very close to his. "I am Fini," she then said softly, and let her hands move caressingly along his shoulders.

They really don't mean so badly by me, Liman said to himself, smiling at the girl, too bad that I'm no longer a young fellow and don't permit myself risky adventures.

"There must be some mistake, Miss," he said, and turned toward his carriage; "I neither asked them to call you nor do I intend to drive off with you." From inside the carriage he added, "Don't trouble yourself any further."

But Fini had already set one foot on the step and said, her arms crossed over her breast, "Now why won't you let me recommend a place for you to stay?"

Tired of the annoyances to which he had already been subjected, Liman leaned out to her and said, "Please don't delay me any longer with useless questions! I am going to a hotel and that's all. Take your foot off the step, otherwise you may be hurt. Go ahead, driver!"

"Stop!" the girl shouted, however, and now in earnest tried to swing herself into the carriage. Liman, shaking his head, stood up and blocked all of the door with his stout body. The girl tried to push him away, using her head and knees in the attempt, the carriage began to rock on its wretched springs, Liman had no real grip.

"And why won't you take me with you? And why won't you take me with you?" the girl kept repeating.

Certainly Liman would have been able to push away the girl without exerting any special force, even though she was strong, if the man in the frock coat, who had remained silent until now as though he had been relieved by Fini, had not now, when he saw Fini waver, hurried over with a bound, supported Fini from behind and tried to push the girl into the carriage by exerting all his strength against Liman's still restrained efforts at defense. Sensing that he was holding back, she actually forced her way into the carriage, pulled at the door which at the same time was slammed shut from the outside, said, as though to herself, "Well, now," first hastily straightened her blouse and then, more deliberately, her hair. "This is unheard of," said Liman, who had fallen back into his seat, to the girl who was sitting opposite him.

May 2. It has become very necessary to keep a diary

again. The uncertainty of my thoughts, F., the ruin in the office, the physical impossibility of writing and the inner need for it.

Valli walks out through our door behind my brother-in-law who tomorrow will leave for Czortkov for maneuvers. Remarkable, how much is implied in this following-after of a recognition of marriage as an institution which one has become thoroughly used to.

The story of the gardener's daughter who interrupted my work the day before yesterday. I, who want to cure my neurasthenia through my work, am obliged to hear that the young lady's brother, his name was Jan and he was the actual gardener and presumed successor of old Dvorsky, already even the owner of the flower garden, had poisoned himself because of melancholia two months ago at the age of twenty-eight. During the summer he felt relatively well despite his solitary nature, since at least he had to have contact with the customers, but during the winter he was entirely withdrawn. His sweetheart was a clerk—*uřednice*—a girl as melancholy as he. They often went to the cemetery together.

The gigantic Menasse at the Yiddish performance. Something magical that seized hold of me at his movements in harmony with the music. I have forgotten what.

My stupid laughter today when I told my mother that I am going to Berlin [54] at Whitsuntide. "Why are you laughing?" said my mother (among several other remarks, one of which was, "Look before you leap," all of which, however, I warded off with remarks like, "It's nothing," etc.). "Because of embarrassment," I said, and was happy for once to have said something true in this matter.

Yesterday met B.[55] Her calmness, contentedness, clarity and lack of embarrassment, even though in the last two years she has become an old woman, her plumpness—even at that time a burden to her—that will soon have reached the extreme of sterile fatness, her walk has become a sort of rolling or shuffle with the belly thrust, or rather carried, to the fore, and on her chin—at a quick glance only on her chin—hairs now curling out of what used to be down.

May 3. The terrible uncertainty of my inner existence.

How I unbutton my vest to show Mr. B. my rash. How I beckon him into another room.

The leper and his wife. The way her behind—she is lying in bed on her belly—keeps rising up with all its ulcers again and again although a guest is present. The way her husband keeps shouting at her to keep covered.

The husband has been struck from behind by a stake—no one knows where it came from—knocked down and pierced. Lying on the ground with his head raised and his arms stretched out, he laments. Later he is able to stand up unsteadily for a moment. He can talk about nothing except how he was struck, and points to the approximate direction from which in his opinion the stake came. This talk, always the same, is by now tiresome to the wife, particularly since the man is always pointing in another direction.

May 4. Always the image of a pork butcher's broad knife that quickly and with mechanical regularity chops into me from the side and cuts off very thin slices which fly off almost like shavings because of the speed of the action.

Early one morning, the streets were still empty up and down their length and breadth, a man, he was in his bare feet and wore only a nightshirt and trousers, opened the door of a large tenement on the main street. He seized the two sections of the door and took a deep breath. "Misery, oh, damned misery," he said and looked, apparently calmly, first along the street and then at some houses.

Despair from this direction too. Nowhere a welcome.

1. Digestion. 2. Neurasthenia. 3. Rash. 4. Inner insecurity.

May 24. Walk with Pick.[56] In high spirits because I consider "The Stoker" so good. This evening I read it to my parents, there is no better critic than I when I read to my father, who listens with the most extreme reluctance. Many shallow passages followed by unfathomable depths.

June 5. The inner advantages that mediocre literary works derive from the fact that their authors are still alive and present behind them. The real sense of growing old.

Löwy, story about crossing the frontier.

June 21. The anxiety I suffer from all sides. The examination by the doctor, the way he presses forward against me, I virtually empty myself out and he makes his empty speeches into me, despised and unrefuted.

The tremendous world I have in my head. But how free myself and free it without being torn to pieces. And a thousand times rather be torn to pieces than retain it in me or bury it. That, indeed, is why I am here, that is quite clear to me.

On a cold spring morning about five o'clock a tall man in a cloak that reached to his feet knocked with his fist against the door of a small hut which stood in a bare, hilly region. The moon was still white and bright in the sky. After each blow of his fist he listened, within the hut there was silence.

July 1. The wish for an unthinking, reckless solitude. To be face to face only with myself. Perhaps I shall have it in Riva.

Day before yesterday with Weiss,[57] author of *Die Galeere*. Jewish physician, Jew of the kind that is closest to the type of the Western European Jew and to whom one therefore immediately feels close. The tremendous advantage of Christians who always have and enjoy such feelings of closeness in general intercourse, for instance a Christian Czech among Christian Czechs.

The honeymoon couple that came out of the Hotel de Saxe. In the afternoon. Dropping the card in the mailbox. Wrinkled clothing, lazy pace, dreary, tepid afternoon. Faces scarcely individualized at first sight.

The picture of the celebration of the Romanov tercentenary in Yaroslavl on the Volga. The Czar, the annoyed princesses standing in the sun, only one—delicate, elderly, indolent, leaning on her parasol—is looking straight ahead. The heir to the throne on the arm of the huge, bareheaded Cossack. In another picture, men who had long since passed by are saluting in the distance.

The millionaire in the motion picture "Slaves of Gold." Mustn't forget him. The calmness, the slow movement, conscious of its goal, a faster step when necessary, a shrug of the shoulder. Rich, spoiled, lulled to sleep, but how he springs up like a servant and searches the room into which he was locked in the forest tavern.

July 2. Wept over the report of the trial of twenty-three-year old Marie Abraham who, because of poverty and hunger, strangled her not quite nine-months-old child, Barbara, with a man's tie that she used as a garter. Very routine story.

The fire with which, in the bathroom, I described to my sister a funny motion picture. Why can I never do that in the presence of strangers?

I would never have married a girl with whom I had lived in the same city for a year.

July 3. The broadening and heightening of existence through marriage. Sermon text. But I almost sense it.

When I say something it immediately and finally loses its importance, when I write it down it loses it too, but sometimes gains a new one.

A band of little golden beads around a tanned throat.

July 19. Out of a house there stepped four armed men. Each held a halberd upright before him. Now and then one of them looked to the rear to see whether he was coming on whose account they were standing here. It was early in the morning, the street was entirely empty.

So what do you want? Come!—We do not want to. Leave us!—

All the inner effort just for this! That is why the music from the coffeehouse rings so in one's ear. The stone's throw about which Elsa B. spoke becomes visible.

A woman is sitting at the distaff. A man pushes the door open with a sword which is sheathed in its scabbard (he is holding it loosely in his hand).
MAN: He was here!
WOMAN: Who? What do you want?
MAN: The horse thief. He is hiding here. Don't lie!
(He brandishes the sword.)
WOMAN *(raising the distaff to protect herself)*: No one was here. Let me alone!

July 20. Down on the river lay several boats, fishermen had cast their lines, it was a dreary day. Some youths, their legs crossed, were leaning against the railing of the dock.

When they rose to toast her departure, lifting up their champagne glasses, the dawn had already broken. Her parents and several wedding guests escorted her to the carriage.

July 21. Don't despair, not even over the fact that you

A Manuscript Page of the *Diaries*

(SEE PAGE 12)

don't despair. Just when everything seems over with, new forces come marching up, and precisely that means that you are alive. And if they don't, then everything is over with here, once and for all.

I cannot sleep. Only dreams, no sleep. Today, in my dream, I invented a new kind of vehicle for a park slope. You take a branch, it needn't be very strong, prop it up on the ground at a slight angle, hold one end in your hand, sit down on it sidesaddle, then the whole branch naturally rushes down the slope, since you are sitting on the bough you are carried along at full speed, rocking comfortably on the elastic wood. It is also possible to use the branch to ride up again. The chief advantage, aside from the simplicity of the whole device, lies in the fact that the branch, thin and flexible as it is, can be lowered or raised as necessary and gets through anywhere, even where a person by himself would get through only with difficulty.

To be pulled in through the ground-floor window of a house by a rope tied around one's neck and to be yanked up, bloody and ragged, through all the ceilings, furniture, walls and attics, without consideration, as if by a person who is paying no attention, until the empty noose, dropping the last fragments of me when it breaks through the roof tiles, is seen on the roof.

Special methods of thinking. Permeated with emotion. Everything feels itself to be a thought, even the vaguest feelings. (Dostoevsky)

This block and tackle of the inner being. A small lever is somewhere secretly released, one is hardly aware of it at first, and at once the whole apparatus is in motion. Subject to an incomprehensible power, as the watch seems subject to time, it creaks here and there, and all the chains clank down their prescribed path one after the other.

Summary of all the arguments for and against my marriage:

1. Inability to endure life alone, which does not imply inability to live, quite the contrary, it is even improbable that I know how to live with anyone, but I am incapable, alone, of bearing the assault of my own life, the demands of my own person, the attacks of time and old age, the vague pressure of the desire to write, sleeplessness, the nearness of insanity—I cannot bear all this alone. I naturally add a "perhaps" to this. The connection with F. will give my existence more strength to resist.

2. Everything immediately gives me pause. Every joke in the comic paper, what I remember about Flaubert and Grillparzer, the sight of the nightshirts on my parents' beds, laid out for the night, Max's marriage. Yesterday my sister said, "All the married people (that we know) are happy, I don't understand it," this remark too gave me pause, I became afraid again.

3. I must be alone a great deal. What I accomplished was only the result of being alone.

4. I hate everything that does not relate to literature, conversations bore me (even if they relate to literature), to visit people bores me, the sorrows and joys of my relatives bore me to my soul. Conversations take the importance, the seriousness, the truth out of everything I think.

5. The fear of the connection, of passing into the other. Then I'll never be alone again.

6. In the past, especially, the person I am in the company

of my sisters has been entirely different from the person I am in the company of other people. Fearless, powerful, surprising, moved as I otherwise am only when I write. If through the intermediation of my wife I could be like that in the presence of everyone! But then would it not be at the expense of my writing? Not that, not that!

7. Alone, I could perhaps some day really give up my job. Married, it will never be possible.

In our class, the fifth class of the Amalia Gymnasium, there was a boy named Friedrich Guss whom we all hated very much. If we came into the classroom early and saw him sitting in his place near the stove we could hardly understand how he could have pulled himself together to come to school again. But I'm not telling it right. We didn't hate only him, we hated everyone. We were a terrible confederacy. Once, when the District School Inspector was present at a lesson—it was a geography lesson and the professor, his eyes turned to the blackboard or the window like all our professors, was describing the Morea Peninsula——

It was the first day of school, evening was already approaching. The professors of the Obergymnasium were still sitting in the staff room, studying the lists of pupils, preparing new roll books, talking about their vacation trips.

Miserable creature that I am!

Just whip the horse properly! Dig the spurs into him slowly, then pull them out with a jerk, but now let them bite into the flesh with all your strength.

What an extremity!

Were we crazy? We ran through the park at night swinging branches.

I sailed in a boat into a small, natural bay.

While I was at the Gymnasium, now and then I used to visit a certain Josef Mack, a friend of my dead father. When, after graduation from the Gymnasium, I——

While he was at the Gymnasium Hugo Seifert now and then used to pay a visit to a certain Josef Kiemann, an old bachelor who had been a friend of Hugo's dead father. The visits suddenly ceased when Hugo, who received the offer of a job abroad which he had to accept at once, left his home town for several years. When he returned he intended to visit the old man, but he found no opportunity, perhaps such a visit would not have suited his changed views, and although he often went through the street where Kiemann lived and several times even saw him leaning out of the window and was probably noticed by him too, he neglected to pay the visit.

Nothing, nothing, nothing. Weakness, self-destruction, tip of a flame of hell piercing the floor.

July 23. With Felix in Rostock. The bursting sexuality of the women. Their natural impurity. The flirtation, senseless for me, with little Lena. The sight of a stout woman hunched up in a basket chair, one foot curiously pushed backward, who was sewing something and talking to an old woman, probably an old spinster, whose teeth appeared unusually large on one side of her mouth. The full-bloodedness and wisdom of the pregnant woman. Her behind almost faceted by evenly divided planes. The life on the small terrace. How I coldly took the little girl on my lap, not at all unhappy about the coolness.

How childishly a tinker, seen through the open door of his shop, sits at his work and keeps striking with his hammer.

Roskoff, "History of the Devil": Among the present-day Caribs, "he who works at night" is regarded as the creator of the world.

August 13. Perhaps everything is now ended and the letter I wrote yesterday was the last one. That would certainly be the best. What I shall suffer, what she will suffer—that cannot be compared with the common suffering that would result. I shall gradually pull myself together, she will marry, that is the only way out among the living. We cannot beat a path into the rock for the two of us, it is enough that we wept and tortured ourselves for a year. She will realize this from my last letters. If not, then I will certainly marry her, for I am too weak to resist her opinion about our common fortune and am unable not to carry out, so far as I can, something she considers possible.

Yesterday evening on the Belvedere under the stars.

August 14. The opposite has happened. There were three letters. The last letter I could not resist. I love her as far as I am capable of it, but the love lies buried to the point of suffocation under fear and self-reproaches.

Conclusion for my case from *The Judgment*. I am indirectly in her debt for the story. But Georg goes to pieces because of his fiancée.

Coitus as punishment for the happiness of being together. Live as ascetically as possible, more ascetically than a bachelor, that is the only possible way for me to endure marriage. But she?

And despite all this, if we, I and F., had equal rights, if we had the same prospects and possibilities, I would not marry. But this blind alley into which I have slowly pushed her life makes it an unavoidable duty for me, although its consequences are by no means unpredictable. Some secret law of human relationship is at work here.

I had great difficulty writing the letter to her parents, especially because a first draft, written under particularly unfavorable circumstances, for a long time resisted every change. Today, nevertheless, I have just about succeeded, at least there is no untruth in it, and after all it is still something that parents can read and understand.

August 15. Agonies in bed toward morning. Saw only solution in jumping out of the window. My mother came to my bedside and asked whether I had sent off the letter and whether it was my original text. I said it was the original text, but made even sharper. She said she does not understand me. I answered, she most certainly does not understand me, and by no means only in this matter. Later she asked me if I were going to write to Uncle Alfred, he deserved it. I asked why he deserved it. He has telegraphed, he has written, he has your welfare so much at heart. "These are simply formalities," I said, "he is a complete stranger to me, he misunderstands me entirely, he does not know what I want and need, I have nothing in common with him."

"So no one understands you," my mother said, "I suppose I am a stranger to you too, and your father as well. So we all want only what is bad for you."

"Certainly, you are all strangers to me, we are related only by blood, but that never shows itself. Of course you don't want what is bad for me."

Through this and several other observations of myself I have come to believe that there are possibilities in my ever-increasing inner decisiveness and conviction which may enable me to pass the test of marriage in spite of everything, and even to steer it in a direction favorable to my development. Of course, to a certain extent this is a belief that I grasp at when I am already on the window sill.

I'll shut myself off from everyone to the point of insensibility. Make an enemy of everyone, speak to no one.

The man with the dark, stern eyes who was carrying the pile of old coats on his shoulder.

LEOPOLD S. (*a tall, strong man, clumsy, jerky movements, loosely hanging, wrinkled, checked clothes, enters hurriedly through the door on the right into the large room, claps his hands and shouts*): Felice! Felice! (*Without pausing an instant for a reply to his shout he hurries to the middle door which he opens, again shouting*): Felice!

FELICE S. (*enters through the door at the left, stops at the door, a forty-year-old woman in a kitchen apron*): Here I am, Leo. How nervous you have become recently! What is it you want?

LEOPOLD (*turns with a jerk, then stops and bites his lips*):
Well, then, come over here! (*He walks over to the
sofa.*)

FELICE (*does not move*): Quick! What do you want? I
really have to go back to the kitchen.

LEOPOLD (*from the sofa*): Forget the kitchen! Come here!
I want to tell you something important. It will make up
for it. All right, come on!

FELICE (*walks toward him slowly, raising the shoulder
straps of her apron*): Well, what is it that's so important? If you're making a fool of me I'll be angry,
seriously. (*Stops in front of him.*)

LEOPOLD: Well, sit down, then.

FELICE: And suppose I don't want to?

LEOPOLD: Then I can't tell it to you. I must have you close
to me.

FELICE: All right, now I am sitting.

August 21. Today I got Kierkegaard's *Buch des Rich-
ters*.[58] As I suspected, his case, despite essential differences,
is very similar to mine, at least he is on the same side of the
world. He bears me out like a friend. I drafted the following letter to her father, which, if I have the strength, I will
send off tomorrow.

"You hesitate to answer my request, that is quite understandable, every father would do the same in the case of
any suitor. Hence your hesitation is not the reason for this
letter, at most it increases my hope for a calm and correct
judgment of it. I am writing this letter because I fear that
your hesitation or your considerations are caused by more
general reflections, rather than by that single passage in my
first letter which indeed makes them necessary and which

might have given me away. That is the passage concerning the unbearableness of my job.

"You will perhaps pass over what I say, but you shouldn't, you should rather inquire into it very carefully, in which case I should carefully and briefly have to answer you as follows. My job is unbearable to me because it conflicts with my only desire and my only calling, which is literature. Since I am nothing but literature and can and want to be nothing else, my job will never take possession of me, it may, however, shatter me completely, and this is by no means a remote possibility. Nervous states of the worst sort control me without pause, and this year of worry and torment about my and your daughter's future has revealed to the full my inability to resist. You might ask why I do not give up this job and—I have no money— do not try to support myself by literary work. To this I can make only the miserable reply that I don't have the strength for it, and that, as far as I can see, I shall instead be destroyed by this job, and destroyed quickly.

"And now compare me to your daughter, this healthy, gay, natural, strong girl. As often as I have repeated it to her in perhaps five hundred letters, and as often as she has calmed me with a 'no' that to be sure has no very convincing basis—it nevertheless remains true that she must be unhappy with me, so far as I can see. I am, not only because of my external circumstances but even much more because of my essential nature, a reserved, silent, unsocial, dissatisfied person, but without being able to call this my misfortune, for it is only the reflection of my goal. Conclusions can at least be drawn from the sort of life I lead at home. Well, I live in my family, among the best and most lovable people, more strange than a stranger. I have not spoken an average of twenty words a day to my mother these last years, hardly ever said more than hello to my father. I do not speak at all to my married sisters and my brothers-in-law, and not because I have anything against them. The reason for it is simply this, that I have not the slightest thing to talk to them about. Everything that is not literature bores me and I hate it, for it disturbs me or delays me, if only because I think it does. I lack all aptitude for family life except, at best, as an observer. I have no family feeling and visitors make me almost feel as though I were maliciously being attacked.

"A marriage could not change me, just as my job cannot change me."

August 30. Where am I to find salvation? How many untruths I no longer even knew about will be brought to the surface. If they are going to pervade our marriage as they pervaded the goodbye, then I have certainly done the right thing. In me, by myself, without human relationship, there are no visible lies. The limited circle is pure.[59]

October 14. The little street began with the wall of a graveyard on the one side and a low house with a balcony on the other. In the house lived the pensioned official, Friedrich Munch, and his sister, Elizabeth.

A herd of horses broke out of the enclosure.

Two friends went for a morning ride.

"Devils, save me from this benightedness!" shouted an old merchant who had wearily lain down on the sofa in the evening and now, in the night, got up with difficulty only by calling upon all his strength. There was a hollow knock at the door. "Come in, come in, everything that is outside!" he shouted.

October 15. Perhaps I have caught hold of myself again, perhaps I secretly took the shorter way again, and now I, who already despair in loneliness, have pulled myself up again. But the headaches, the sleeplessness! Well, it is worth the struggle, or rather, I have no choice.

The stay in Riva was very important to me. For the first time I understood a Christian girl and lived almost entirely within the sphere of her influence. I am incapable of writing down the important things that I need to remember. This weakness of mine makes my dull head clear and empty only in order to preserve itself, but only insofar as the confusion lets itself be crowded off to the periphery. But I almost prefer this condition to the merely dull and indefinite pressure the uncertain release from which first would require a hammer to crush me.

Unsuccessful attempt to write to E. Weiss. And yesterday, in bed, the letter was boiling in my head.

To sit in the corner of a trolley, your coat wrapped around you.

Prof. G. on the trip from Riva. His German-Bohemian nose reminding one of death, swollen, flushed, pimpled cheeks set on the bloodless leanness of his face, the blond, full beard around it. Possessed by a voracious appetite and thirst. The gulping down of the hot soup, the biting into and at the same time the licking of the unskinned heel of salami, the solemn gulps of the beer grown warm, the sweat breaking out around his nose. A loathsomeness that cannot be savored to the full even by the greediest staring and sniffing.

The house was already locked up. There was light in two windows on the second floor, and in one window on the fourth floor as well. A carriage stopped before the house. A young man stepped to the lighted window on the fourth floor, opened it and looked down into the street. In the moonlight.

It was already late in the evening. The student had lost all desire to continue working. Nor was it at all necessary, he had really made great progress the last few weeks, he could probably relax a little and reduce the amount of work he did at night. He closed his books and notebooks, arranged everything on his little table and was about to undress and go to sleep. By accident, however, he looked toward the window, and when he saw the bright full moon it occurred to him that he might still take a short walk in the beautiful fall night and somewhere or other, perhaps, refresh himself with a cup of black coffee. He turned out the lamp, took his hat and opened the door to the kitchen. Usually it did not matter to him at all that he always had to go through the kitchen, this inconvenience also considerably reduced the rent of his room, but now and then, when there was an unusual amount of noise in the kitchen, or when, as today, he wanted to go out late in the evening, it was annoying.

In despair. Today, in the half-sleep during the afternoon: In the end the pain will really burst my head. And at the temples. What I saw when I pictured this to myself was really a gunshot wound, but around the hole the jagged edges were bent straight back, as in the case of a tin can violently torn open.

Don't forget Kropotkin! [60]

October 20. The unimaginable sadness in the morning. In the evening read Jacobsohn's *Der Fall Jacobsohn*. This strength to live, to make decisions, joyfully to set one's foot in the right place. He sits in himself the way a practiced rower sits in his boat and would sit in any boat. I wanted to write to him.

Instead of which I went for a walk, erased all the emotion I had absorbed in a conversation with Haas, whom I had run into, women excited me, I am now reading *The Metamorphosis* at home and find it bad. Perhaps I am really lost, the sadness of this morning will return again, I shall not be able to resist it for long, it deprives me of all hope. I don't even have the desire to keep a diary, perhaps because there is already too much lacking in it, perhaps because I should perpetually have to describe incomplete—by all appearances *necessarily* incomplete—actions, perhaps because writing itself adds to my sadness.

I would gladly write fairy tales (why do I hate the word so?) that could please W. and that she might sometimes keep under the table at meals, read between courses and blush fearfully when she noticed that the sanatorium doctor has been standing behind her for a little while now and watching her. Her excitement sometimes—or really all of the time—when she hears stories.

I notice that I am afraid of the almost physical strain of the effort to remember, afraid of the pain beneath which the floor of the thoughtless vacuum of the mind slowly opens up, or even merely heaves up a little in preparation. All things resist being written down. If I knew that her commandment not to mention her were at work here (I have kept it faithfully, almost without effort), then I should be satisfied, but it is nothing but inability. Besides, what am I to think of the fact that this evening, for a long while, I was pondering what the acquaintance with W. had cost me in pleasures with the Russian woman, who at night perhaps (this is by no means impossible) might have let me into her room, which was diagonally across from mine. While my evening's intercourse with W. was carried on in a language of knocks whose meaning we never definitely agreed upon. I knocked on the ceiling of my room below hers, received her answer, leaned out of the window, greeted her, once let myself be blessed by her, once snatched at a ribbon she let down, sat on the window sill for hours, heard every one of her steps above, mistakenly regarded every chance knock to be the sign of an understanding, heard her coughing, her singing before she fell asleep.

October 21. Lost day. Visit to the Ringhoffer factory, Ehrenfels' seminar, at Weltsch's, dinner, walk, now here at ten o'clock. I keep thinking of the black beetle,[61] but will not write.

In the small harbor of a fishing village a bark was being fitted out for a voyage. A young man in wide sailor pants was supervising the work. Two old sailors were carrying sacks and chests to a gangplank where a tall man, his legs spread wide, took everything and handed it over into hands that stretched toward him from the dark interior of the bark. On the large, square-hewn stones enclosing a corner of the dock, half reclining, sat five men, they blew the smoke of their pipes in all directions. From time to time the man in the wide sailor pants went up to them, made a little speech and slapped them on the knees. Usually a wine jug was brought out from behind a stone in whose shade it was kept, and a glass of opaque red wine passed from man to man.

October 22. Too late. The sweetness of sorrow and of love. To be smiled at by her in the boat. That was most beautiful of all. Always only the desire to die and the not-yet-yielding; this alone is love.

Yesterday's observation. The most appropriate situation for me: To listen to a conversation between two people who are discussing a matter that concerns them closely while I have only a very remote interest in it which is in addition completely selfless.

October 26. The family sat at dinner. Through the un-curtained windows one could look out into the tropic night.

"Who am I, then?" I rebuked myself. I got up from the sofa upon which I had been lying with my knees drawn up, and sat erect. The door, which led straight from the stair-way into my room, opened and a young man with a bowed head and searching eyes entered. He walked, as far as this was possible in the narrow room, in a curve around the sofa and stopped in the darkness of the corner near the window. I wanted to see what kind of apparition this was, went over and grasped the man by the arm. He was a living person. He looked up—a little shorter than I—at me with a smile, the very carelessness with which he nodded and said "Just try me" should have convinced me. Despite that, I seized him in front by the vest and in back by the jacket and shook him. His beautiful, strong, gold watch chain attracted my attention, I grabbed it and pulled down on it so that the buttonhole to which it was fastened tore. He put up with this, simply looked down at the damage, tried in vain to keep the vest button in the torn buttonhole. "What are you doing?" he said finally, and showed me the vest. "Just be quiet!" I said threateningly.

I began to run around the room, from a walk I passed into a trot, from a trot into a gallop, every time I passed the man I raised my fist to him. He did not even look at me but worked on his vest. I felt very free, even my breathing was extraordinary, my breast felt that only my clothes prevented it from heaving gigantically.

For many months Wilhelm Menz, a bookkeeper, had been intending to accost a girl whom he used regularly to meet on the way to the office in the morning on a very long street, sometimes at one point, sometimes at another. He had already become reconciled to the fact that this would remain an intention—he was not very bold in the presence of women and besides, the morning was not a propitious time to speak to a girl who was in a hurry—when it happened that one evening, about Christmas time, he saw the girl walking right in front of him. "Miss," he said. She turned, recognized the man whom she always encountered in the morning, without stopping let her eye rest on him for a moment, and since Menz said nothing further, turned away again. They were in a brightly lit street in the midst of a great crowd of people and Menz was able, without attracting attention, to step up quite close to her. In this moment of decision Menz could think of nothing to say, but he was resolved to remain a stranger to the girl no longer, for he definitely intended to carry farther something begun so seriously, and so he made bold enough to tug at the bottom of the girl's jacket. The girl suffered it as though nothing had happened.

November 6. Whence the sudden confidence? If it would only remain! If I could go in and out of every door in this way, a passably erect person. Only I don't know whether I want that.

We didn't want to tell our parents anything about it, but every evening after nine o'clock we met, I and two cousins, near the cemetery fence at a place where a little rise in the ground provided a good view.

The iron fence of the cemetery leaves a large, grass-grown place free on the left.

November 17. Dream: On a rising way, beginning at the left when seen from below, there lay, about at the middle of the slope and mostly in the road, a pile of rubbish or solidly packed clay that had crumbled lower and lower on the right while on the left it stood up as tall as the palings of a fence. I walked on the right where the way was almost clear and saw a man on a tricycle coming toward me from below and apparently riding straight at the obstacle. He was a man who seemed to have no eyes, at least his eyes looked like holes that had been effaced. The tricycle was rickety and went along in an uncertain and shaky fashion, but nevertheless without a sound, with almost exaggerated quietness and ease. I seized the man at the last moment, held him as though he were the handle bars of his vehicle and guided the latter into the gap through which I had come. Then he fell toward me, I was as large as a giant now and yet had an awkward hold on him, besides, the vehicle, as though out of control, began to move backward, even if slowly, and pulled me after it. We went past an open van on which a number of people were standing crowded together, all dressed in dark clothes, among them a boy scout wearing a light-gray hat with the brim turned up. I expected this boy, whom I had already recognized at some distance, to help me, but he turned away and squeezed himself in among the people. Then, behind this open van—the tricycle kept rolling on and I, bent low, with legs astraddle, had to follow —there came toward me someone who brought me help, but whom I cannot remember. I only know that he was a trustworthy person who is now concealing himself as though behind a black cloth curtain and whose conceal-ment I should respect.

November 18. I will write again, but how many doubts have I meanwhile had about my writing. At bottom I am an incapable, ignorant person who, if he had not been com-pelled—without any effort on his own part and scarcely aware of the compulsion—to go to school, would be fit only to crouch in a kennel, to leap out when food is offered him and to leap back when he has swallowed it.

Two dogs in a yard into which the sun shone hotly ran toward each other from opposite directions.

Worried and slaved over the beginning of a letter to Miss Bl.

November 19. The reading of the diary moves me. Is it because I no longer have the slightest confidence now? Everything appears to me to be an artificial construction of the mind. Every remark by someone else, every chance look throws everything in me over on the other side, even what has been forgotten, even what is entirely insignificant. I am more uncertain than I ever was, I feel only the power of life. And I am senselessly empty. I am really like a lost sheep in the night and in the mountains, or like a sheep which is running after this sheep. To be so lost and not have the strength to regret it.

I intentionally walk through the streets where there are whores. Walking past them excites me, the remote but nevertheless existent possibility of going with one. Is that grossness? But I know no better, and doing this seems basically innocent to me and causes me almost no regret. I want only the stout, older ones, with outmoded clothes that have, however, a certain luxuriousness because of various adornments. One woman probably knows me by now. I met her this afternoon, she was not yet in her working clothes, her hair was still flat against her head, she was wearing no hat, a work blouse like a cook's, and was carrying a bundle of some sort, perhaps to the laundress. No one would have found anything exciting in her, only I. We looked at each other fleetingly. Now, in the evening, it had meanwhile grown cold, I saw her, wearing a tight-fitting, yellowish-brown coat, on the other side of the narrow street that branches off from Zeltnerstrasse, where she has her beat. I looked back at her twice, she caught the glance too, but then I really ran away from her.

This uncertainty is surely the result of thinking about F.

November 20. Was at the movies. "Lolotte." The good minister. The little bicycle. The reconciliation of the parents. Was tremendously entertained. Before it, a sad film, "The Accident on the Dock," after it, the gay "Alone at Last." Am entirely empty and insensible, the passing trolley has more living feeling.

November 21. Dream: The French cabinet, four men, is sitting around a table. A conference is taking place. I remember the man sitting on the long right side of the table, with his face flattened out in profile, yellowish colored skin, his very straight nose jutting far forward (jutting so far forward because of the flatness of his face) and an oily, black, heavy mustache arching over his mouth.

Miserable observation which again is certainly the result of something artificially constructed whose lower end is swinging in emptiness somewhere: When I picked up the inkwell from the desk to carry it into the living room I felt a sort of firmness in me, just as, for instance, the corner of a tall building appears in the mist and at once disappears again. I did not feel lost, something waited in me that was independent of people, even of F. What would happen if I were to run away, as one sometimes runs through the fields?

These predictions, this imitating of models, this fear of something definite, is ridiculous. These are constructions that even in the imagination, where they are alone sovereign, only approach the living surface but then are always suddenly driven under. Who has the magic hand to thrust into the machinery without its being torn to pieces and scattered by a thousand knives?

I am on the hunt for constructions. I come into a room and find them whitely merging in a corner.

November 24. Evening before last at Max's. He is becoming more and more a stranger, he has often been one to me, now I am becoming one to him too. Yesterday evening simply went to bed.

A dream toward morning: I am sitting in the garden of a sanatorium at a long table, at the very head, and in the dream I actually see my back. It is a gloomy day, I must have gone on a trip and am in an automobile that arrived a short time ago, driving up in a curve to the front of the platform. They are just about to bring in the food when I see one of the waitresses, a young, delicate girl wearing a dress the color of autumn leaves, approaching with a very light or unsteady step through the pillared hall that served as the porch of the sanatorium, and going down into the garden. I don't yet know what she wants but nevertheless point questioningly at myself to learn whether she wants me. And in fact she brings me a letter. I think, this can't be the letter I'm expecting, it is a very thin letter and a strange, thin, unsure handwriting. But I open it and a great number of thin sheets covered with writing come out, all of them in the strange handwriting. I begin to read, leaf through the pages and recognize that it must be a very important letter and apparently from F.'s youngest sister. I eagerly begin to read, then my neighbor on the right, I don't know whether man or woman, probably a child, looks down over my arm at the letter. I scream, "No!" The round table of nervous people begins to tremble. I have probably caused a disaster. I attempt to apologize with a few hasty words in order to be able to go on with the reading. I bend over my letter again, only to wake up without resistance, as if awakened by my own scream. With complete awareness I force myself to fall asleep again, the scene reappears, in fact I quickly read two or three more misty lines of the letter, nothing of which I remember, and lose the dream in further sleep.

The old merchant, a huge man, his knees giving way beneath him, mounted the stairs to his room, not holding the banister but rather pressing against it with his hand. He was about to take his keys out of his trouser pocket, as he always did, in front of the door to the room, a latticed glass door, when he noticed in a dark corner a young man who now bowed.

"Who are you? What do you want?" asked the merchant, still groaning from the exertion of the climb.

"Are you the merchant Messner?" the young man asked.

"Yes," said the merchant.

"Then I have some information for you. Who I am is really beside the point here, for I myself have no part at all in the matter, am only delivering the message. Nevertheless I will introduce myself, my name is Kette and I am a student."

"So," said Messner, considering this for a moment. "Well, and the message?" he then said.

"We can discuss that better in your room," said the student. "It is something that can't be disposed of on the stairs."

"I didn't know that I was to receive any such message," said Messner, and looked out of the corner of his eye at the floor.

"That may be," said the student.

"Besides," said Messner, "it is past eleven o'clock now, no one will overhear us here."

"No," the student replied, "it is impossible for me to say it here."

"And I," said Messner, "do not receive guests at night," and he stuck the key into the lock so violently that the other keys in the bunch continued to jingle for a while.

"Now look, I've been waiting here since eight o'clock, three hours," said the student.

"That only proves that the message is important to you. But I don't want to receive any messages. Every message that I am spared is a gain, I am not curious, only go, go." He took the student by his thin overcoat and pushed him away a little. Then he opened the door part way and tremendous heat flowed from the room into the cold hall. "Besides, is it a business message?" he asked further, when he was already standing in the open doorway.

"That too I cannot say here," said the student.

"Then I wish you good night," said Messner, went into his room, locked the door with the key, turned on the light of the electric bed lamp, filled a small glass at a little wall cabinet in which were several bottles of liquor, emptied it with a smack of his lips and began to undress. Leaning back against the high pillows, he was on the point of beginning to read a newspaper when it seemed to him that someone was knocking softly on the door. He laid the newspaper back on the bed cover, crossed his arms and listened. And in fact the knock was repeated, very softly and as though down very low on the door. "A really impertinent puppy," laughed Messner. When the knocking stopped, he again picked up the newspaper. But now the knocking came more strongly, there was a real banging on the door. The knocking came the way children at play scatter their knocks over the whole door, now down low, dull against the wood, now up high, clear against the glass. "I shall have to get up," Messner thought, shaking his head. "I can't telephone the housekeeper because the instrument is over there in the anteroom and I should have to wake the land-lady to get to it. There's nothing else I can do except to throw the boy down the stairs myself." He pulled a felt cap over his head, threw back the cover, pulled himself to the edge of the bed with his weight on his hands, slowly put his feet on the floor and pulled on high, quilted slippers. "Well now," he thought, and, chewing his upper lip, stared at the door; "now it is quiet again. But I must have peace once and for all," he then said to himself, pulled a stick with a horn knob out of a stand, held it by the middle and went to the door.

"Is anyone still out there?" he asked through the closed door.

"Yes," came the answer. "Please open the door for me."

"I'll open it," said Messner, opened the door and stepped out holding the stick.

"Don't hit me," said the student threateningly, and took a step backward.

"Then go!" said Messner, and pointed his index finger in the direction of the stairs.

"But I can't," said the student, and ran up to Messner so surprisingly——

November 27. I must stop without actually being shaken off. Nor do I feel any danger that I might get lost, still, I feel helpless and an outsider. The firmness, however, which the most insignificant writing brings about in me is beyond doubt and wonderful. The comprehensive view I had of everything on my walk yesterday!

The child of the housekeeper who opened the gate. Bun-

dled up in a woman's old shawl, pale, numb, fleshy little
face. At night is carried to the gate like that by the housekeeper.

The housekeeper's poodle that sits downstairs on a step
and listens when I begin tramping down from the fourth
floor, looks at me when I pass by. Pleasant feeling of in-
timacy, since he is not frightened by me and includes me
in the familiar house and its noise.

Picture: Baptism of the cabin boys when crossing the
equator. The sailors lounging around. The ship, clambered
over in every direction and at every level, everywhere pro-
vides them with places to sit. The tall sailors hanging on the
ship's ladders, one foot in front of the other, pressing their
powerful, round shoulders against the side of the ship and
looking down on the play.

A small room. ELSA *and* GERTRUD *are sitting at the window
with their needlework. It is beginning to get dark.*
E: Someone is ringing. (*Both listen.*)
G: Was there really a ring? I didn't hear anything, I keep
    hearing less all the time.
E: It was just very low. (*Goes into the anteroom to open
    the door. A few words are exchanged. Then the voice.*)
E: Please step in here. Be careful not to stumble. Please
    walk ahead, there's only my sister in the room.

Recently the cattle dealer Morsin told us the following
story. He was still excited when he told it, despite the fact
that the matter is several months old now:
"I very often have business in the city, on the average it
certainly comes to ten days a month. Since I must usually

spend the night there too, and have always tried, whenever it is at all possible, to avoid stopping at a hotel, I rented a private room that simply——"

December 4. Viewed from the outside it is terrible for a young but mature person to die, or worse, to kill himself. Hopelessly to depart in a complete confusion that would make sense only within a further development, or with the sole hope that in the great account this appearance in life will be considered as not having taken place. Such would be my plight now. To die would mean nothing else than to surrender a nothing to the nothing, but that would be impossible to conceive, for how could a person, even only as a nothing, consciously surrender himself to the nothing, and not merely to an empty nothing but rather to a roaring nothing whose nothingness consists only in its incomprehensibility.

A group of men, masters and servants. Roughhewn faces shining with living colors. The master sits down and the servant brings him food on a tray. Between the two there is no greater difference, no difference of another category than, for instance, that between a man who as a result of countless circumstances is an Englishman and lives in London, and another who is a Laplander and at the very same instant is sailing on the sea, alone in his boat during a storm. Certainly the servant can—and this only under certain conditions—become a master, but this question, no matter how it may be answered, does not change anything here, for this is a matter that concerns the present evaluation of a present situation.

The unity of mankind, now and then doubted, even if

only emotionally, by everyone, even by the most approachable and adaptable person, on the other hand also reveals itself to everyone, or seems to reveal itself, in the complete harmony, discernible time and again, between the development of mankind as a whole and of the individual man. Even in the most secret emotions of the individual.

The fear of folly. To see folly in every emotion that strives straight ahead and makes one forget everything else. What, then, is non-folly? Non-folly is to stand like a beggar before the threshold, to one side of the entrance, to rot and collapse. But P. and O. are really disgusting fools. There must be follies greater than those who perpetrate them. What is disgusting, perhaps, is this puffing-themselves-up of the little fools in their great folly. But did not Christ appear in the same light to the Pharisees?

Wonderful, entirely self-contradictory idea that someone who died at 3 A.M., for instance, immediately thereafter, about dawn, enters into a higher life. What incompatibility there is between the visibly human and everything else! How out of one mystery there always comes a greater one! In the first moment the breath leaves the human calculator. Really one should be afraid to step out of one's house.

December 5. How furious I am with my mother! I need only begin to talk to her and I am irritated, almost scream.

O. is really suffering and I do not believe that she is suffering, that she is capable of suffering, do not believe it in the face of my knowing better, do not believe it in order not to have to stand by her, which I could not do, for she irritates me too.

Externally I see only little details of F., at least sometimes, so few they may be counted. By these her picture is made clear, pure, original, distinct and lofty, all at once.

December 8. Artificial constructions in Weiss's novel. The strength to abolish them, the duty to do so. I almost deny experience. I want peace, step by step or running, but not calculated leaps by grasshoppers.

December 9. Weiss's *Galeere*. Weakening of the effect when the end of the story begins. The world is conquered and we have watched it with open eyes. We can therefore quietly turn away and live on.

Hatred of active introspection. Explanations of one's soul, such as: Yesterday I was so, and for this reason; today I am so, and for this reason. It is not true, not for this reason and not for that reason, and therefore also not so and so. To put up with oneself calmly, without being precipitate, to live as one must, not to chase one's tail like a dog.

I fell asleep in the underbrush. A noise awakened me. I found in my hands a book in which I had previously been reading. I threw it away and sprang up. It was shortly after midday; in front of the hill on which I stood there lay spread out a great lowland with villages and ponds and uniformly shaped, tall, reed-like hedges between them. I put my hands on my hips, examined everything with my eyes, and at the same time listened to the noise.

December 10. Discoveries have forced themselves on people.

The laughing, boyish, sly, revealing face of the chief inspector, a face that I have never before seen him wear and noticed only today at the moment when I was reading him a report by the director and happened to glance up from it. At the same time he also stuck his right hand into his trouser pocket with a shrug of his shoulder as though he were another person.

It is never possible to take note of and evaluate all the circumstances that influence the mood of the moment, are even at work within it, and finally are at work in the evaluation, hence it is false to say that I felt resolute yesterday, that I am in despair today. Such differentiations only prove that one desires to influence oneself, and, as far removed from oneself as possible, hidden behind prejudices and fantasies, temporarily to create an artificial life, as sometimes someone in the corner of a tavern, sufficiently concealed behind a small glass of whiskey, entirely alone with himself, entertains himself with nothing but false, unprovable imaginings and dreams.

Toward midnight a young man in a tight, pale-gray, checked overcoat sprinkled with snow came down the stairs into the little music hall. He paid his admission at the cashier's desk behind which a dozing young lady started up and looked straight at him with large, black eyes, and then he stopped for a moment to survey the hall lying three steps below him.

Almost every evening I go to the railroad station, today, because it was raining, I walked up and down the hall there for half an hour. The boy who kept eating candy from the slot machine. His reaching into his pocket, out of which he pulls a pile of change, the careless dropping of a coin into the slot, reading the labels while he eats, the dropping of some pieces which he picks up from the dirty floor and sticks right into his mouth. The man, calmly chewing, who is speaking confidentially at the window with a woman, a relative.

December 11. In Toynbee Hall read the beginning of *Michael Kohlhaas*. Complete and utter fiasco. Badly chosen, badly presented, finally swam senselessly around in the text. Model audience. Very small boys in the front row. One of them tries to overcome his innocent boredom by carefully throwing his cap on the floor and then carefully picking it up, and then again, over and over. Since he is too small to accomplish this from his seat, he has to keep sliding off the chair a little. Read wildly and badly and carelessly and unintelligibly. And in the afternoon I was already trembling with eagerness to read, could hardly keep my mouth shut.

No push is really needed, only a withdrawal of the last force placed at my disposal, and I fall into a despair that rips me to pieces. Today, when I imagined that I would certainly be calm during the lecture, I asked myself what sort of calm this would be, on what it would be based, and I could only say that it would merely be a calm for its own sake, an incomprehensible grace, nothing else.

December 12. And in the morning I got up relatively quite fresh.

Yesterday, on my way home, the little boy bundled in gray who was running along beside a group of boys, hitting himself on the thigh, catching hold of another boy with his other hand and shouting—rather absentmindedly, which I must not forget—*"Dnes to bylo docela hezky"* [Very nicely done today].[62]

The freshness with which, after a somewhat altered division of the day, I walked along the street about six o'clock today. Ridiculous observation, when will I get rid of this habit.

I looked closely at myself in the mirror awhile ago—though only by artificial light and with the light coming from behind me, so that actually only the down at the edges of my ears was illuminated—and my face, even after fairly close examination, appeared to me better than I know it to be. A clear, well-shaped, almost beautifully outlined face. The black of the hair, the brows and the eye sockets stand livingly forth from the rest of the passive mass. The glance is by no means haggard, there is no trace of that, but neither is it childish, rather unbelievably energetic, but perhaps only because it was observing me, since I was just then observing myself and wanted to frighten myself.

December 12. Yesterday did not fall asleep for a long time. F. B. Finally decided—and with that I fell uncertainly asleep—to ask Weiss to go to her office with a letter, and to write nothing else in this letter other than that I must have news from her or about her and have therefore sent Weiss there so that he might write me about her. Meanwhile Weiss is sitting beside her desk, waits until she has finished reading the letter, bows, and—since he has no further instructions and it is highly unlikely that he will receive an answer—leaves.

Discussion evening at the officials' club. I presided. Funny, what sources of self-respect one can draw upon. My introductory sentence: "I must begin the discussion this evening with a regret that it is taking place." For I was not advised in time and therefore not prepared.

December 14. Lecture by Beermann. Nothing, but presented with a self-satisfaction that is here and there contagious. Girlish face with a goiter. Before almost every sentence the same contraction of muscles in his face as in sneezing. A verse from the Christmas Fair in his newspaper column today.

> Sir, buy it for your little lad
> So he'll laugh and not be sad.

Quoted Shaw: "I am a sedentary, fainthearted civilian."

Wrote a letter to F. in the office.

The fright this morning on the way to the office when I met the girl from the seminar who resembles F., for the moment did not know who it was and simply saw that she resembled F., was not F., but had some sort of further relationship to F. beyond that, namely this, that in the seminar, at the sight of her, I thought of F. a great deal.

Now read in Dostoevsky the passage that reminds me so of my "being unhappy."

When I put my left hand inside my trousers while I was reading and felt the lukewarm upper part of my thigh.

December 15. Letters to Dr. Weiss and Uncle Alfred. No telegram came.

Read *Wir Jungen von 1870–71*. Again read with suppressed sobs of the victories and scenes of enthusiasm. To be a father and speak calmly to one's son. For this, however, one shouldn't have a little toy hammer in place of a heart.

"Have you written to your uncle yet?" my mother asked me, as I had maliciously been expecting for some time. She had long been watching me with concern, for various reasons did not dare in the first place to ask me, and in the second place to ask me in front of my father, and at last, in her concern when she saw that I was about to leave, asked me nevertheless. When I passed behind her chair she looked up from her cards, turned her face to me with a long-vanished, tender motion somehow revived for the moment, and asked me, looking up only furtively, smiling shyly and already humbled in the asking of the question, before any answer had been received.

December 16. "The thundering scream of the seraphim's delight."

I sat in the rocking chair at Weltsch's, we spoke of the disorder of our lives, he always with a certain confidence ("One must want the impossible"), I without it, eying my fingers with the feeling that I was the representative of my inner emptiness, an emptiness that replaces everything else and is not even very great.

December 17. Letter to W. commissioning him "to overflow and yet be only a pot on the cold hearth."

Lecture by Bergmann, "Moses and the Present." Pure

impression.—In any event I have nothing to do with it. The truly terrible paths between freedom and slavery cross each other with no guide to the way ahead and accompanied by an immediate obliterating of those paths already traversed. There are a countless number of such paths, or only one, it cannot be determined, for there is no vantage ground from which to observe. There am I. I cannot leave. I have nothing to complain about. I do not suffer excessively, for I do not suffer consistently, it does not pile up, at least I do not feel it for the time being, and the degree of my suffering is far less than the suffering that is perhaps my due.

The silhouette of a man who, his arms half raised at different levels, confronts the thick mist in order to enter it.

The good, strong way in which Judaism separates things. There is room there for a person. One sees oneself better, one judges oneself better.

December 18. I am going to sleep, I am tired. Perhaps it has already been decided there. Many dreams about it.

December 19. Letter from F. Beautiful morning, warmth in my blood.

December 20. No letter.

The effect of a peaceful face, calm speech, especially when exercised by a strange person one hasn't seen through yet. The voice of God out of a human mouth.

An old man walked through the streets in the mist one

winter evening. It was icy cold. The streets were empty. No one passed near him, only now and then he saw in the distance, half concealed by the mist, a tall policeman or a woman in furs or shawls. Nothing troubled him, he merely intended to visit a friend at whose house he had not been for a long time and who had just now sent a servant girl to ask him to come.

It was long past midnight when there came a soft knock on the door of the room of the merchant Messner. It wasn't necessary to wake him, he fell asleep only toward morning, and until that time he used to lie awake in bed on his belly, his face pressed into the pillow, his arms extended and his hands clasped over his head. He had heard the knocking immediately. "Who is it?" he asked. An indistinct murmur, softer than the knocking, replied. "The door is open," he said, and turned on the electric light. A small, delicate woman in a large gray shawl entered.

1 A member of the Russian Ballet during its guest appearance at the German theater in Prague.

2 This remark is connected with the entry of December 16, 1910, concerning Gerhart Hauptmann's comedy, *Jungfern vom Bischofsberg.*

3 Kafka was twenty-eight years old at the time.

4 The story "Unhappiness," from *Meditation,* follows here, without title. This particular draft breaks off several lines before the end. Only a title, "The Little Dweller in the Ruins," follows on a fresh page; this, apparently, is related to the preceding fragments of Kafka's critique of his education. The fragments that now follow form a mosaic difficult to arrange, since many things are repeated several times. The tale begins over and over again with the same words, and ripples of it are still to be seen in 1911.

The whole has many points of contact with several chapters of "Description of a Struggle," cf. especially that part of it called "Conversation with the Supplicant." See also the sketch, "Unmasking a Confidence Trickster," from *Meditation.*

5 The poet Paul Claudel, who at that time was the French consul in Prague. Kafka never met him.

6 Paul Wiegler, the translator of *Moralités légendaires* by Jules Laforgue. The reading of this translation (and later of the original as well) was an important experience for Kafka and the Editor.

7 Kafka was survived by three sisters. All three sisters, including Kafka's favorite, Ottla, and the larger part of their families, were killed by the Nazis.

8 Oscar Baum, the blind author of *Das Volk des harten Schlafes,* one of the closest friends of Kafka and the Editor.

9 The paragraph ending at this point was crossed out by Kafka.

10 A reminiscence of the journey to Paris during the previous year (1910).

11 The title (*Wie erlangt man Erkenntnisse der höheren Welten*) of a book by Dr. Rudolf Steiner.

12 Another fragment of the story begun on p. 22.

13 The diary of the Lugano-Erlenbach-Paris journey follows at this point in the manuscript. It will be published, together with the other travel journals, at the end of the second volume of the *Diaries*.

14 This entry is connected with the plan that Kafka and the Editor developed, during the Lugano-Erlenbach-Paris trip, to write together the novel, "Richard and Samuel," one chapter of which has been preserved under the title, "Die erste lange Eisenbahnfahrt."

15 Longen is the biographer of Jaroslav Hašek, author of *The Good Soldier Schweik*.

16 The prayer that opens the service on the Day of Atonement.

17 A Yiddish theater troupe from Eastern Europe. The troupe performed in a small café. Another troupe had performed in the same café in 1910.

18 "The Apostate." It is probably not unjustified to see in the two figures described here, who act as a sort of chorus, the first sketch of the two "assistants" in *The Castle*.

19 A Czech folk dance.

20 *Mezuzah* ("doorpost"), a small roll of parchment inscribed with certain biblical verses (Deut. 6:4–9; 11:13–20) and encased in a small wood or metal box. It hangs on the doorpost of the home of every orthodox Jew.

21 Preliminary work on the novel, "Richard and Samuel." R. is the woman who appears in the first chapter as Dora Lippert.

22 The Czech word *pavlač* means "balcony" and has passed into the German of Prague and Vienna. It refers to the characteristic open balcony running the entire length of an upper story on the side of a house facing the court.

23 Kafka was actually twenty-eight years old at the time.

24 Otto Brod, the writer and brother of the Editor. The three of us took a trip together to Riva and Brescia in 1909. Otto Brod, his wife and child were murdered by the Nazis in 1944.

25 The Editor's future wife.

26 A novel by Wilhelm Schäfer. Kafka had a great deal of respect for this writer. He later went over to the Nazis.

27 One of Kafka's sisters.

28 A rough translation of the Yiddish would be: "crazy hothead."

29 "Enough for *parnusse*," enough to live on.

30 "The Aeroplanes at Brescia." See Max Brod, *Franz Kafka, a Biography*, Appendix II.

31 This entry appeared later, with a few changes and omissions, in *Meditation*, under the title, "Bachelor's Ill Luck." The version Kafka published has been translated by Willa and Edwin Muir and will appear in a forthcoming volume of Kafka's early sketches and stories. The translation appearing here is by the Muirs, except in those places where the German text of the published version and the version in the *Diaries* differ.

32 Written at the time Kafka was studying for his bar examination.

33 Emil Utitz, later a professor of philosophy, a fellow student of Kafka's at the Gymnasium.

34 The family of Egon Erwin Kisch, author of *Der rasende Reporter*. His brother, Paul Kisch, studied Germanics.

35 A toy through the aperture of which one perceived the successive positions of a figure affixed to a revolving wheel. It thus created the illusion of motion.

36 An uneducated person. Kafka acquired this and similar expressions from his conversations with the actor Löwy.

37 Felix Weltsch, the philosopher and author of *Gnade und Freiheit*.

38 Properly, *mohel*—"circumciser."

39 A novel by Emil Strauss, whom Kafka estimated highly.

40 This entry, slightly changed, appeared under the title of "The Sudden Walk," in *Meditation*. The translation is based on one made by the Muirs (see *n* 31 above).

41 Christian von Ehrenfels, the philosopher and originator of the *Gestalt* theory in psychology.

42 Cf. this entry with "Resolutions," in *Meditation*. The translation is based on one made by the Muirs (see *n* 31 above).

43 "Schlaflied für Mirjam," by Richard Beer-Hofmann.

44 In *Hermann und Dorothea*.

45 From Goethe's "Der Fischer."

46 The distinguished Viennese novelist Otto Stössl, of whom Kafka had a very high opinion.

47 Willi Haas, the editor of *Die Literarische Welt*. At the time Kafka wrote this, Haas was editing *Die Herderblätter* in Prague, in which he published the first chapter of "Richard and Samuel," and also some of Werfel's early work.

48 Kafka was then working on the novel, *Amerika*, the title of which at that time was "Der Verschollene."

49 Written during the vacation trip to Weimar and the Harz Mountains (June 28 to July 29, 1912).

50 Kafka's first published work, *Meditation*, which I had urged him very strongly to finish—or, rather, to put together out of his prose pieces that for the most part were already finished. In the middle of August he finally gave me the finished manuscript, which I sent off to the Rowohlt Publishers (Kurt Wolff). The book was published early in 1913.

51 Two days earlier Kafka had met Miss F. B. of Berlin, later his fiancée.

52 This entry is preceded by the complete draft of *The Judgment*.

53 This entry is followed by the final version, untitled, of "The Stoker," chapter one of *Amerika*.

54 On a visit to F. B.

55 Kafka's governess in his childhood.

56 The writer and critic Otto Pick, later editor of the *Prager Presse*.

57 The very talented novelist and dramatist Ernst Weiss, who later was quite close to Kafka. His first novel, *Die Galeere*, was published in 1913. He fled to France in 1933 and took his own life when the Nazis occupied Paris.

58 An anthology of Kierkegaard's writings.

59 Kafka's trip to the Hartungen Sanatorium in Riva took place between this and the following entry.

60 Kropotkin's memoirs were among Kafka's favorite books, as were the memoirs of Alexander Herzen.

61 Of *The Metamorphosis*. In the next entry is probably to be

found the germ of "The Hunter Gracchus" (in the book *The Great Wall of China*), the scene of which is Riva.

62 This remark which the boy addressed to Kafka was in commendation of the unhappy reading of Kleist's *Michael Kohlhaas* that Kafka mentions in the entry of December 11, 1913. Kafka told this anecdote with so much humor that among his friends the boy's remark became proverbial. Kafka said that the boy even added, quite precociously: "Very good!" Whenever someone, haughtily, patronizingly and with the air of a connoisseur, praised something he was entirely ignorant of, we liked to quote this "very good" and everyone immediately knew what was meant.

Actually, the quite unimportant incident of the reading was a much less melancholy affair than Kafka's account would indicate. Kafka, needless to say, read wonderfully; I was present at the reading and remember it quite well. It was only that he had chosen a selection that was much too long, and in the end was obliged to shorten it as he read. In addition, there was the quite incongruous contrast between this great literature and the uninterested and inferior audience, the majority of whom came to benefit affairs of this kind only for the sake of the free cup of tea that they received.

1883 Born July 3 in Prague

1903 Graduates from the German Gymnasium

1906 Doctorate in Jurisprudence from Karl-Ferdinand University in Prague

1907–08 Temporary employment in the "Assicurazioni Generali," an Italian insurance company

1908 Appointed to post with government-sponsored "Arbeiter-Unfall-Versicherungs-Anstalt für das Königreich Böhmen in Prag"

1909 Publication of "Conversation with the Supplicant" and "Conversation with the Drunken Man," two dialogues from "Description of a Struggle," in the literary periodical *Hyperion* Publication of "The Aeroplanes at Brescia" in the Prague newspaper *Bohemia*

1910 Publication in *Bohemia* of several short pieces later included in *Meditation*

1911 Trip to Switzerland, Italy and Paris Meets Yiddish theater troupe in Prague

1912 Publication in the literary periodical, *Herderblätter*, of "Die erste lange Eisenbahnfahrt," first chapter of "Richard and Samuel"

Begins *Amerika*
Trip to Weimar and the Harz Mountains
Writes *The Judgment*
Completes "The Stoker," chapter one of *Amerika*

1913 Publication of *Meditation*
Publication of *The Judgment* in the literary year-
book *Arkadia*
Trip to Riva

The Diaries of Franz Kafka will appear in their entirety in two volumes, of which this present volume is the first. The second, and final, volume is in preparation; it will contain a postscript by Max Brod describing the manuscript of the *Diaries* and the manner in which it has been edited.

It was not possible to identify all the authors and artists mentioned in the text. In such cases their names are not listed here.

* Listed only when mentioned in the text as an author.

Phèdre, by Jean Racine: 30

Pick, Otto (1887–), Jewish journalist from Prague: 234, 247, 261, 287, *n* 56

Pines, Meyer Isser (1881–), Jewish literary historian from Russia: 223, 224

"Podriatechik, Der," by Nahum Meir Schaikewitz: 225

Prager Presse, German-language newspaper edited by Otto Pick: *n* 56

Prager Tagblatt, Prague German-language newspaper: 178, 234, 239, 240, 242, 243

Rabinowitz, Solomon, see Sholom Aleichem

Rachilde, pseud. for Marguerite Vallette (1862–1935), French novelist and playwright: 261, 262, 263

Racine, Jean (1639–1699): 30

Ratten, Die, by Gerhart Hauptmann: 261

Reiseschatten, by Justinus Kerner: 34

"Resolutions," by Franz Kafka: *n* 42 (230)

"Richard and Samuel," by Max Brod and Franz Kafka: 123, 151, 156, 163, 169, 170, 210, *n* 14 (66), *n* 21 (91), *n* 47

Richepin, Jean (1849–1926), French poet, novelist and dramatist: 146, 148, 149

Richter, Moses (1873–1939), Yiddish playwright: 176, 223

Rideamus, pseud. for Fritz Oliver (1874–), German satirical poet: 238, 239

Rosenfeld, Morris (1862–1917), Yiddish poet: 101, 108, 109, 222, 226

Roskoff, Gustav (1814–1889), German author of *Geschichte des Teufels:* 295

Rowohlt, Ernst, German publisher: 266, 268, 270, *n* 50 (266)

Rückert, Friedrich (1788–1866), German poet: 165

Rundschau, see *Neue Rundschau, Die*

Schadow, Johann Gottfried (1764–1850), German sculptor: 42

Schäfer, Wilhelm (1868–), German novelist: 124, 125, 168, 173, 174, 178, *n* 26 (124)

Scharkansky, A. M., Polish Jewish poet and playwright: 106, 112, 217

Schaubühne, literary weekly edited by S. Jacobsohn, published 1905–1918 in Berlin, then absorbed in *Die Weltbühne:* 117

Schechite, by Jacob Gordin: 161

Schicksals Spiele und Ernst, Des, by Oskar Baum: 221

Schiller, Friedrich (1759–1805): 42, 73, 145, 169, 177, 239, 251, 253

Schlegel, Friedrich (1772–1824), German romantic poet and critic: 252

Schmidtbonn, Wilhelm (1876–), German writer: 223